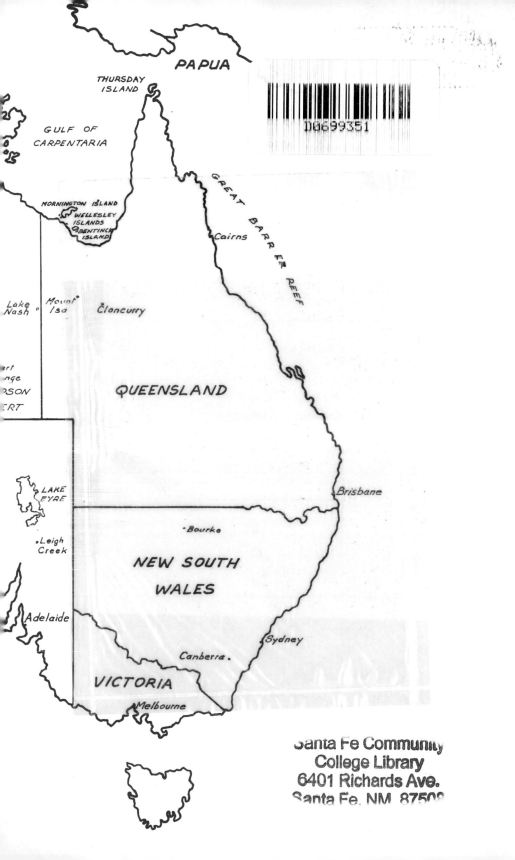

PAPUA

THURSDAY
ISLAND

GULF OF
CARPENTARIA

MORNINGTON ISLAND
WELLESLEY
ISLANDS
BENTINCK
ISLAND

GREAT BARRER REEF

Cairns

Lake
Nash

Mount
Isa

Cloncurry

art
nge
PSON
RT

QUEENSLAND

LAKE
EYRE

Brisbane

Bourke

Leigh
Creek

NEW SOUTH

WALES

Adelaide

Sydney

Canberra.

VICTORIA

Melbourne

MEDICINE IS THE LAW

Medicine Is the Law

STUDIES IN PSYCHIATRIC ANTHROPOLOGY

OF AUSTRALIAN TRIBAL SOCIETIES

JOHN CAWTE

Foreword by William P. Lebra

THE UNIVERSITY PRESS OF HAWAII
Honolulu

The author wishes to make the following acknowledgments for permission to use material previously printed elsewhere. Chapter 1 in *Oceania* 34 (1964):170–190. Chapter 3 in *The Medical Journal of Australia* 2(1964): 977–983. Chapter 4 in *Oceania* 36(1966):264–282. Chapter 8 in *The British Journal of Medical Psychology* 39(1966):245–253. Chapters 10 and 11 in *The British Journal of Psychiatry* 111(1965):1069–1077, 1079–1085. Chapter 13 in *Psychiatry: Journal for the Study of Interpersonal Processes* 30(1967):149–161, by special permission of the William Alanson White Psychiatric Foundation, Inc., holders of the copyright. The Envoi is taken from "Multidisciplinary Teamwork in Ethnopsychiatry Research," published in *Proceedings of V World Congress of Psychiatry* (Amsterdam: Excerpta Medica, 1973).

Contents

Foreword

ALTHOUGH TRANSCULTURAL PSYCHIATRY and psychological anthropology (formerly, culture and personality) are of recent coinage, the mutual influencing of anthropology and psychiatry extends back over at least several decades. The psychiatrist, for his part, was obviously interested in the role of cultural factors in mental disorders; whereas, the anthropologist was concerned with the influence of culture on human behavior (normative behavior, some would say). Formerly, there was a more or less strict division of labor; the anthropologist worked in the field producing the data, and the psychiatrist tended to theorize on "primitive" man, which in those days meant anything non-Western. This division of labor did not serve either group too well; some anthropologists became imitations of poor psychiatrists, and fell into the trap of rather generously applying the language of pathology to the description of cultural behavior. The psychiatrists, for their part, tended to be castigated as armchair theorists about behavior and culture. This worked to the detriment of both disciplines. Fortunately, in recent years this dichotomization of work effort has broken down, sending anthropologists into psychiatric clinics and into mental hospitals in their own culture and, happily, putting psychiatrists into field situations where formerly only anthropologists had dared to tread. The work of John Cawte represents a part of these new welcome developments in transcultural psychiatry.

For more than a decade now, Dr. Cawte and his associates, with the cooperation of universities, hospitals, missions, and the government, have traveled to various parts of Australia studying the mental health problems of the Aborigines and providing advice for improvement. The status of the Australian Aborigines has been one of steady decline, since the time of the first landings of white men at Botany Bay, paralleling that of the New World Aborigines and the Africans carried there as slaves. With the postwar population growth and improvement in communications and mobility, little of the Australian continent now remains beyond the influence of European Australia. As a consequence, the last of the isolated and once autonomous tribes are vanishing, to become instead ethnic minorities. The destruction of the tribes and the "integration" of Aborigines into the larger Australian society has placed them at the bottom of the heap, so to speak, as Dr. Cawte so tellingly describes. Moreover, a concomitant of their passage into the larger society with its access to improved nutrition and medical services has been the engendering of a population explosion, one of the most rapid in recorded history. What remains is not a rapidly disappearing laboratory for the anthropologist or the social scientist, but a burgeoning social problem for the nation.

Dr. Cawte writes with a knowledge that can only derive from intimacy, respect, and fondness for his informants. The fact that he is a competent psychiatrist adds to the depth of his insight. Though some anthropologists or other social scientists may take issue here and there with some of his points, they are refreshing to this anthropologist. Indeed, he has discerned and recorded insights that have been passed over by many of us, because of our lack of clinical experience and training. He has talked with Aboriginal medical practitioners as coworkers; his interviews with the victims of sorcery offer new understanding; and certainly *malgri* will take its place among the culture-bound syndromes with *latah*, *koro*, *amok*, *imu*, and others. It is my belief that Dr. Cawte, in this volume, makes not only a welcome contribution to anthropology but also a contribution toward improving the well-being of his countrymen.

WILLIAM P. LEBRA
Social Science Research Institute
University of Hawaii

Acknowledgments

THE DATA REPORTED in this book were gathered in the course of a series of expeditions, extending over some ten years, to remote communities. The Institute of Aboriginal Studies, Canberra, provided funds for the expeditions to central Australia, Arnhem Land, and the gulf country of Queensland. The expedition to Western Australia was supported in part by the Wenner-Gren Foundation and by the University of Adelaide. The University of New South Wales and Prince Henry Hospital, Sydney, granted me leave of absence on these occasions. I am deeply appreciative of the support of these institutions, as I am to my host mission and settlement communities,

I wish to acknowledge the assistance provided by the Social Science Research Institute (NIMH Grant MH 09243) and the East-West Center at the University of Hawaii in the form of an invitation to utilize their facilities in the preparation of this book. In particular, the generous support of the then director of the Social Science Research Institute, Dr. William Lebra, and the efficiency of Ms. Freda Hellinger in the publications department, are greatly appreciated. Dr. Leslie Kiloh and Dr. Virginia Huffer, who kindly read the manuscript, helped me say what I wanted to say.

Some of the material in this book was previously printed and the kind permission to reprint or quote is gratefully acknowledged to: *Oceania; The Medical Journal of Australia; The British Journal of Medical Psychology; The British Journal of Psychiatry; Psychiatry: Journal for the Study of Interpersonal Processes,* by special permission of the William Alanson White Psychiatric Foundation,

Inc., holders of the copyright; and Excerpta Medica. Full bibliographic citations are presented on the copyright page.

Return of thanks to some of the many people who have assisted these studies in remote communities is in order.

During visits to the Walbiri tribe at Yuendumu in the Northern Territory I enjoyed the company of Murray J. Barrett M.D.S., F.A.C.D., and his collaborators of the Department of Dental Science, University of Adelaide. Mr. Barrett was primarily engaged in a study of craniofacial morphology but found time to make his invaluable film records of traditional life. The Reverend and Mrs. T. J. Fleming were warmly hospitable and informative. Details of Walbiri culture are presented in chapters 3, 8, 9, and 10. In the investigation of subincision described in chapter 8, the interviewing was carried out jointly by the author in company with Murray Barrett and Nari Djagamara, assistant teacher at the Yuendumu Settlement School. We are particularly indebted to the Walbiri men who took part in the intimate discussions quoted in part in this chapter. The willingness to confide of these men, whom the author counts as friends and kinsmen in the Walbiri manner, stemmed from the conviction that something of their old and secret way was being saved.

At Kalumburu, in the Kimberley region of Western Australia, I had the cooperation of the Spanish Benedictine mission, led by the Reverend Fathers Seraphim Sanz and Rosendo Sosa. In particular I enjoyed the warmth and hospitality of the Spanish nuns. This expedition was led and organized by Professor A. A. Abbie, of the Department of Anatomy, University of Adelaide. It was Professor Abbie's encouragement that first led me to apply the methods of psychiatry to the study of Aborigines in the field, one result of which is the present work. Professor Abbie's breadth of outlook is well shown in his book *The Original Australians* (1969), widely regarded as the best introductory text on Aborigines for the general reader.

At Lake Nash, on the Georgina River in the east of the Northern Territory, hospitality was appreciated from the manager of this huge cattle station, Mr. Arthur Jones, and his wife. My chief guide and general informant at Lake Nash was Wagon Willy (tribal name not known) who was the surviving authority on the local

Yowera culture. In the medical part of this study, the assistance of Mr. Les Penhall and Mr. Creed Lovegrove of the Aboriginal Welfare Branch of the Northern Territory Administration at Alice Springs is appreciatively acknowledged.

Mornington Island, in the Gulf of Carpentaria, joins the list of islands in which intensive epidemiological studies have been carried out. These studies are presented in *Cruel, Poor and Brutal Nations* (Cawte 1972). The island population was propitious for these studies, but equally valuable was the assistance afforded by the Reverend Douglas Belcher, M.B.E., chief missionary of the Presbyterian diocese of Carpentaria. In the study of the victim of sorcery in chapter 6, many of the sorcery artifacts were revealed by Mr. Kenny Roughsey (totemic name: Rough Sea), eldest brother of this exceptional Aboriginal family.

While my expeditions to the Yolngu of northeast Arnhem Land do not furnish the topic for any of the chapters in this work, they do provide some of the illustrations and examples used in the discussion. I am much obliged to the help of the Methodist mission at Elcho Island, and in particular to Mr. Burramarra and his Yolngu kinsmen.

My indebtedness to my many Aboriginal friends, patients, and informants is profound. May they enjoy their birthright at last, with the proper backing of medicine and justice from their new society.

Introduction

SOME OF THE THEORETICAL PRINCIPLES underlying a rather atheoretical book should be stated at the outset. The first is that there are no seignorial rights to the raw material of anthropology. No one group owns it; it should be worked upon, in the field, by all scientific disciplines. Anthropology has the right to expect, for example, that the twin perspectives of psychiatry—psychiatric anthropology and transcultural psychiatry—be employed *in the field*, and not in the armchair, in order to evaluate primary data. This is the objective of this book. It attempts to apply a combination of psychiatric anthropology and transcultural psychiatry to the field study of primitives,[1] the Australian Aborigines.[2] The first half of the book is chiefly concerned with psychiatric anthropology: it examines aspects of the traditional life, selected according to the interests and areas of competence of modern psychiatry. The second half is concerned with transcultural psychiatry: it addresses itself to acculturation problems and to their alleviation by sociomedical means.

Medicine, in return, has a right to expect more invigoration from anthropological methods and techniques. This book, insofar as it depicts ethnographically Aborigines as *naturels* or *naturvölker* in a world before Western contact, deals with the forms of medicine, law, and religion developed by a hunting-gathering people. But

[1] The term is offered with some hesitation because of some misleading connotations. It is used at the outset here because it is less cumbersome than the alternatives prehistoric, preliterate, preagricultural, pretechnological, and so forth.

[2] By convention, where the generic term *aborigine* is used to refer to the first Australians, it is capitalized: thus, *Aborigine, Aborigines* (noun forms) and *Aboriginal* (adjective).

people such as these are not to be viewed as curiosities of a dying culture, embalmed as it were for some museum basement display. They have living relevance to modern medical science, insofar as they are motivated by those pan-human regularities of human behavior: sickness and suffering. Modern medical science needs to know how man, without much aid from technology, reduced his suffering. Furthermore, in studying contemporary Aborigines as they struggle to evolve new social institutions to cope with catastrophic upsets caused by Western influence, medical science is concerned with another matter vital to its own development: rapid social change. The study of pretechnological man, at first sight of interest mainly to antiquarians, offers insights which medicine, in its modern rush into technology, cannot afford to neglect.

The first half of this book is a physician's view of primitive medicine and justice as social institutions. The second half is affectionately devoted to individuals whose deviations from the normal were big enough to bring them to the attention of the modern institutions of medicine and the law. As a physician and psychiatrist, I confess I feel on securer ground in the second half of the book. But the ethnographic material in the first half is essential to the whole, and it is valuable primary data in its own right. This material is derived from informants' statements to me and from my own field observations, and often from both of these sources together. Since I, in common with all observers, form a part of the system being observed, and since I am a physician, my material is bound to be medically slanted. I have not in this book drawn upon other fieldworkers' descriptions recorded in the literature, except to direct attention to some widely accepted beliefs that appear to be open to question insofar as my findings are concerned. In relying upon my own observations rather than the literature, my misgiving is not whether they provide an informative setting for the case material which is at the core of my work, but whether they provide an epidemiologically valid one. The main problem is one of sampling. Generalizations about regularities in human behavior in a given society may have little scientific value if they are based upon data from a small number of informants. I am reassured about my generalizations, however, because I am concerned with small communities, in which one can use a high proportion of informants in the total population. If one is fortunate enough to have six or ten informants in a community of less than a thousand, it improves the prospects that generalizations are reliable. I have in the main been careful to use a high proportion of informants in any community. Where appropriate, the whole communities were surveyed, or at least sampled.

Although the book deals with primitive medicine, the law, and religion, it is not an armchair dissertation of the social institutions evolved by man to manage suffering. The substantive data are clinical observations of living Aboriginal men and women showing these processes at work, and the purpose is specific: to record case material while it is still available. The reader is of course free to modify the interpretations I have placed on the case material. The main task that I have set myself in this book is to present a collection of histories of illness from a preagricultural class of mankind, utilizing the methods of modern medicine and psychiatry in doing so. However much or little I may have succeeded in this task, there is extreme urgency about the attempt. As the twentieth century nears its close, the imprint of the West, and of the East, has left little that was primitive the way it was before. Few moderns would question the scientific importance of compiling various kinds of collections of primitive cosmology before it disappears. Few clinicians and psychiatrists are finding the time and opportunity to carry out the clinical studies that would complement the work of anthropologists.

On a dozen expeditions to remote Aboriginal communities, and in city clinics, I have kept two sets of notebooks. One is the record of personal histories, with an emphasis on individual and group behavior. The other is the parallel record of observations under the general heading of cultural description. Material from my two notebooks are combined in this book in order to provide a case-illustrated representation of medicine and law, and sometimes of religion, in a primitive society. Temporally, the record spans the traditional life and the alien culture contact. I assure the reader that although these cases are "clinical" in the sense that they are observations of a medical practitioner, he is not going to find them "dry." The special feature of the clinical approach to anthropological material is that it conveys a deep and intimate sense of personal suffering, and coping, within a culture.

Some explanation is needed of how I, as a clinician, became involved. I was conditioned to think about the difficulties of Aborigines by a childhood spent in a remote country town having a rather rootless population of Aboriginal fringe-dwellers. My direct responsibilities toward Aborigines did not begin until 1951 when I became the superintendent of a hospital for acute psychiatric disorders. This was in Adelaide, South Australia, and the hospital received Aboriginal patients from the distant regions of South Australia and Northern Territory. The difficulties and frustrations of understanding and of managing this group of patients in this setting can readily be imagined. But they were trivial in comparison with the difficulties and frustrations of the patients themselves.

It was not until 1963, after my appointment to the medical faculty of the University of New South Wales, that I had the opportunity to travel regularly to black communities in remote regions of Australia. In these communities one could evaluate, classify, and enumerate adaptational problems not in a hospital but in the community context that made them intelligible. One could study traditional medicine, and the obstacles to the delivery of modern medicine. One came to know many traditional practitioners "professionally," and to appreciate many others for their personal qualities.

At first, these visits were cautiously made in the company of physical anthropologists engaged in anthropometric and dental research. Later, I began to visit the field with my own teams of biological, behavioral, and social scientists. An example of the methodology that evolved in these ventures is published as *Cruel, Poor and Brutal Nations* (Cawte 1972). The present book contains chiefly my own observations, for which I alone must accept responsibility. They are made independently of university research in anthropology; in fact my university, while outstanding in applied science, has no department of anthropology. Although I hold a Ph.D. degree for studies in anthropology, my orientation is primarily that of an M.D. interested in the behavioral sciences as well as medicine.

There is, however, a theoretical framework for these studies that is indebted to well-worked fields of anthropology. I am basically interested in the two sides of the culture-and-mental-health coin: how individual behavior is determined by the social and physical environment, and in turn how the disturbed behavior of an individual may have an adverse retroflexive effect upon the group in which he lives. The latter viewpoint, less commonly considered, is perhaps the more distinctively psychiatric one. This theoretical framework involves us in a consideration of the social institutions of medicine, the law, and religion. And since these institutions will form units of our discourse—they have been used in the title of this book—it is important at the outset to make some dissection of them.

Universal categories such as medicine and the law seem to have only a limited currency in anthropology at present. How much universality exists for these categories? Kluckhohn's scholarly review (1962) of the "universal categories of culture" indicates the limits within which cultural variation is constrained by pan-human regularities in biology, psychology, and social interaction. Despite these pan-human regularities, the institutions of medicine, the law, and religion, as understood in a modern society, do not closely correspond with these categories in a primitive society. Indeed, the lack of correspondence between ancient and modern social institutions, as encountered by people undergoing alien contact, is a constant source of difficulties for them. But since I depend on these categories of medicine and the law I should define what is intended by them. Incompleteness of correspondence cross-culturally is not a reason for dispensing with them.

By the definition adopted here, medicine is the science and art concerned with the alleviation, cure, and prevention of suffering, with the preservation of health, and with the correction of environmental conditions conducive to sickness. In primitive society, medicine is also concerned with magical power over natural objects, exercised through rites, spells, and charms. Modern physicians like to think themselves emancipated from magic, though this is wishful thinking. They admit some responsibility, through the branch of psychiatry, for the control of emotional and behavioral disturbances.

The law as it is used here is concerned with the rules of conduct enforced by a controlling authority, and with the sanctions and injunctions that a community recognizes as binding upon its members. In addition to human law, I am concerned in this book with divine law: the commandments of the religious system or the will of a divinity as revealed in myth or in traditional practice. Another observer of the same material might justifiably have emphasized the categories of religion and magic. But with the broad definitions of medicine and the law adopted here, it is expedient to include religion and magic together with them. They are supporting institutions in the general scheme for the relief of suffering, the safeguarding of security, and the resolution of disputes.

While on the subject of preliminary definitions, it is important before beginning a transcultural psychiatric study to devote a few paragraphs to the criteria used for psychiatric diagnosis and for mental illness. I have preferred in most parts of this book the concept of *adaptive and adjustive responses. Adaptive* refers to behaviors and bodily states that result in survival, for the individual or group; *adjustive* (or defensive) refers to responses that relieve the inner tensions stimulating the individual. Adaptive and adjustive responses are not necessarily the same, as a consideration of the act of suicide shows.

The use of the concept of adaptive and adjustive responses conveniently helps get around clinical terms such as schizophrenia and endogenous depression, which, however meaningful to medical readers, evoke mystification or mistrust in others. Though I have not been so radical as to discard this particular medical heritage, my criteria of mental disorder tend rather to be maladaptation and maladjustment, evidenced by the individual's social inefficiency or personal discomfort. These are respectable indices of mental disorder, used in modern medical research (Frank 1961), and they more readily relate the individual to his life situation than does the "medical model." The medical model comes into its own in epidemiological enquiries, such as have been made on some of the field expeditions to be reported in this book.

There is a good deal of misunderstanding of how the medical model is—or should be—used in making a psychiatric diagnosis. In psychiatric anthropology, as in psychiatry generally, a clinical diagnosis should never be made on the basis of a single complaint or statement, involving, say, a hallucination or a delusion. Diagnosis is reached only after considering the presenting clinical picture of the individual, in conjunction with his history and past personality, with the opinions and reactions of his peers, and with the course, trajectory, and outcome of the condition. It should be made in this painstaking and time-honored manner, and not by an obviously invalid and arbitrary medical model such as that criticized by Szasz (1964), in which a psychiatrist attaches a depreciatory medical label to some objectionable behavior, and so functions as the inquisitor of a society requiring a witch hunt for unacceptable behaviors. Such miscarriages happen, and when they do it is bad psychiatry, no more to be condoned than bad medicine, bad engineering, or bad anthropology.

In the present work, whenever a definition of a "case" is needed for epidemiological purposes, the guideline suggested by the World Health Organization (1960) is followed: the individual's reaction has to resemble some established psychiatric entity, and it has also to be severe enough to cause loss of working or social capacity, or both.

"Adaptive and adjustive responses" is a concept more suited than is the medical model to the all-important question of cultural change. The classical functionalist approach in anthropology, exemplified by the works of Malinowski and Radcliffe-Brown, is more appropriate for a steady, synchronic level of a society. When the time variable is present, as it is in my studies, we become concerned with the collapse of old forms and the construction of new. In a setting of social turbulence, we become more sharply aware of the wide range of individual responses. Adaptation and adjustment provide highly relevant concepts for use with primitive people undergoing alien contact and cultural change.

Summarizing the preliminary definitions, my subject is the adaptation and adjustment of primitive people, and of the social institutions serving them, commonly called medicine and the law. The time perspective is diachronic; the occasion is alien contact. My combination of ethnographic descriptions and clinical histories, though uncommonly employed, is not original; it represents a methodology long since recommended by Kluckhohn (1939), described by him as *extensive* excursions supplemented by *intensive* penetrations.

Australian Aborigines are important for the behavioral and social sciences in that they provide a chance to study prehistoric, preliterate, preagricultural, pretechnological man. Their traditional society fits the world's image generally of a Stone Age life-style; they have even been described as primeval rather than merely primitive. After millennia of isolation, they operate what is considered to be one of the most ancient surviving social systems. Valuable as this opportunity may be, its heuristic value may reside more in the fact that Aborigines represent not one culture, but a diversity of hunting-gathering cultures. A comparative study of the medico-legal machinery of desert and coastal Aborigines, for example, provides the basis for a determination of what may be constants, or consistently recurring features, of primitive societies and what may be variables, the regional features. The question of habitat proves to be a matter of neglected significance in primitive medicine, where the constants have been emphasized at the expense of variables in surveys of ethnographic literature, by Clements (1932), Hallowell (1935), Rogers (1944), and Whiting and Child (1953).

Some anthropologists have asserted that all that there is left to study is acculturation—for example that it is no longer possible in Australia to make a systematic study of traditional processes such as sorcery or culture-bound syndromes. Such statements have a modicum of truth, but also suggest a research fatigue, due to restricted methods. If new techniques are introduced into fieldwork, it is still possible to invigorate and extend the "classical" observations. A subject matter like this, that has not disappeared but is rapidly disappearing, calls for an innovative and pluralistic attack. A decade, of diminishing returns, remains before time runs out for most of the disciplines, other than the archaeological. Not a few Aboriginal doctors remain in remote Australia. Some are anxious and grateful to talk, even to demonstrate. The adaptive and adjustive machinery of a primitive society is conveniently approached through contact with these officials. But insofar as the "clever man's" business combines functions that modern society now differentiates, the approach should be eclectic, carried out by a team representing several disciplines. My approach has not been as eclectic as it might have been, but it has been deliberately diversified, as the chapters of this book will show.

It is true however that an important aspect of primitive medico-legal machinery is its response to culture contact. In any society that is accessible to study, the observer and his culture form part of the system being studied; it would be an artificial exercise to present an account of medicine and the law in primitive society that failed to be concerned with its reaction to alien contact. Inevitably this presentation will be a culture history of a people responding to contact and undergoing substantial social disorganization because of it. Since alien contact is not to be ignored, it should be evaluated. In this book I have tried to evaluate psychological adjustment to cultural change by measuring psychiatric morbidity. As in all epidemiological studies, the practical purpose is to furnish a sociomedical document with implications for the health of the subjects.

A further word about the interrelationship of medicine and the law is in order, to explain the title and chief thrust of this book. Medicine and the law are conceived as spanning a large part of man's relationship with other men and with nature. Societies that function effectively, rather than merely survive, are preoccupied with these relationships: with the care (medicine) and control (law) of their members. The combination of medical and legal perspectives is a logical approach to primitive cosmology; in any case, I find it is a matter of necessity, because in primitive society medicine and the law tend to be fused. I doubt if one can study medicine separately, or the law separately; one studies a blend, a category different from the familiar modern ones.

The synthesis of medicine and the law in Aboriginal society is evident from the extent of the common ground shared by the procedures for preserving health and the procedures for controlling social behavior. Is this synthesis a peculiarity of the Australian Aborigine, or a universal aspect of primitive society? Primitive systems of medicine and justice are not the same in different cultures; but certain patterns do emerge among different cultures, overlaid by the variables of regional situations. Thus Turner (1964) has observed a medico-legal synthesis in tribal Rhodesia similar to that which I have observed in Australia. The Ndembu, described by

Turner, believe that persistent or severe sickness is caused by the punitive action of ancestral spirits, for negligence in religion, for ritual interdictions, or "because kin are not living well together." Medical ritual has a redressive function in these interpersonal or factional disputes; the Ndembu doctor sees his task less as curing the individual patient than as remedying the ills of a corporate group. Illness is for him a mark of undue deviation from the behavioral norm.

Aboriginal Australian societies that I shall describe, for example in the central desert, take advantage of the polarization that disease creates in society: the power of doctors and the dependency of patients. This domination-submission reciprocity is exploited by native doctors as an inducement toward social conformity. The native doctor says, in effect: conform lest you become ill. He may take a similar advantage of misfortune, utilizing its occurrence or threatened occurrence to persuade dissident parties toward compromised courses of action, so that kin live better together. In the native doctor's philosophy, *medicine is the law*, and the law is medicine, and the amalgam is perfused and strengthened by the authority of tradition, religion, and the arts such as music, the dance, and painting.

Physicians and lawyers in advanced societies are usually struck by this synthesis when they are first made aware of it. They are surprised to find that their respective professions arise from a common source in prehistoric societies, because today these streams are so sharply differentiated that physicians and lawyers scarcely move in the same circles or talk the same language. The formation of medico-legal societies testifies to the need felt by members of these great societal professions to integrate more closely. They feel that *care* and *control* of members of society should not be divorced. Some may find it tantalizing that primitive man achieves a synthesis of medicine and justice that escapes the technocrats of today; others may accept this dissociation as the price of specialization and "progress."

An early step toward specialization in primitive society is the emergence of native doctors. In the first half of this book, these officials are the central figures and chief informants. They are the counterparts neither of modern physicians and psychiatrists, nor of modern attorneys and counsels. Aboriginal English has a word for them: clever men or clever fellows. Elkin (1945) called them Aboriginal men of high degree. In countries other than Australia they are commonly called shamans (especially in northern America and Asia) and medicine men. Although not specialized in the sense that they earn their livelihood from their vocation, their role in society is nevertheless to represent medical and legal belief and authority. Since they are aligned against members who deviate, they cannot represent distressed individuals in quite the way that modern physicians and lawyers may be hired to befriend their clients and defend their interests. If they are to maintain their positions, native doctors predominantly represent the power-holding cadre, tradition, or perhaps gerontocracy, depending on the structure of the corporate group.

The reaction to modern society provides some measure of the correspondence between primitive medicine and law and modern. The reason that Australian Aborigines were so severely affected by intruding nineteenth-century British culture is not merely that the bearers of British culture were ruthlessly aggressive. There was a cause on the other side: Aboriginal social institutions did not pave the way for change, in the manner that the bartering practice of the New Guinea highlanders prepared them for today's *bisnis*. The Aboriginal medical system is so different, in purpose and design, that it is virtually inapplicable in the alien contact. The same may be said of a legal system that is not based, as is British justice, on the laws of real property. There are not the social institutions, not the specialists, in a hunting-gathering society to achieve even an approximate correspondence with an industrial society. This is the essential catastrophe of the culture contact: there is no ready means of picking up the new culture and using it.

The epidemiological studies of the later chapters return the theme, full circle, to the essential application: the adaptive and adjustive reactions of an aboriginal people confronted by an invading alien culture. At the conclusion of the book the altitude of the observation is raised from local samples of tribal groups, lineages, and individuals to a panoramic view. The Aboriginal people are seen in the variety of social identities and acculturation levels that they have now assumed, united chiefly by common experience of cultural exclusion, low economy, overcrowded living, and poor health. These themes Australian Aborigines share with many disadvantaged ethnic minorities elsewhere in the world, such as North American Indians. It is my thesis that only the vigorous and integrated application of modern medicine and justice can now redeem them from this limbo. The liability of medicine and the law in primitive society has shifted to medicine and the law of the modern state. But it is a liability that these institutions are slow to recognize, acknowledge, or accept. They will not grasp the magnitude of the problem until they attempt to solve it.

CHAPTER ONE

Cross-cultural Rapport

WORKING WITH PRELITERATE PEOPLE, where the observer looks across his own cultural boundary into another's, unclear communication is a barrier. Confusions of cultural understanding, of language, of trust, and of expectation compound the encumbrances to communication often already present by virtue of the individual's adjustive posture. Not infrequently, a frank psychiatric condition is present. For those concerned with adaptation and adjustment of people in an emerging country, obstructed communication is a paramount issue.

Those involved in this work need expert guidance. Physicians and lawyers who are also Aborigines will eventually graduate from the universities, but contemporary problems can hardly await this. In any case the personal qualities necessary for this achievement may not incline nor fit the individual concerned for rapport with his original group. The learned professions in general cannot become sufficiently familiar with the life-style and language of any small Aboriginal group; these are the acquisitions of the resident: especially nurse, teacher, trade instructor, missionary, and occasionally anthropologist. The impasse between the troubled individual and the medical and legal professions invites underdiagnosis, misdiagnosis, underrepresentation, and neglect. There is a gulf between what is known and what is practiced, what is offered and what is delivered.

PSYCHIATRIC BARRIERS TO COMMUNICATION

When an Aboriginal patient is admitted to a hospital, and there is more time for interview and observation, the communication that

develops clinically is usually inadequate for the patient's full benefit. It is a problem that has filled me with a sense of professional
frustration and personal regret. The obstacles to achieving rapport
with the troubled individual can be better indicated by case histories than by discussion.[1] Three histories, selected from my hospital casebook, illustrate these problems and also exemplify the psychological reactions of the socially disruptive kind that in the present
era are sent to a hospital, or to jail.

"The Birth of the Blues"—A Puerperal Agitated Depression

A thirty-seven-year-old full-blood mission-educated Aboriginal
woman, from one of the broken tribes near Lake Eyre, in the north
of South Australia, left a suicide note at the Leigh Creek police
station. In it she claimed she had caused her own mother's death
two months previously because she had been an adulteress. She had
six children and was expecting a seventh in a few weeks. The township doctor took the suicide risk seriously and sent her to the city
of Adelaide for psychiatric care. Suicide and suicide threat is so
uncommon in outback Aborigines as to create surprise and to leave
no doubt of mental disorder.

In hospital, she continued to be agitated. She felt she was having
a nervous breakdown and said that hard times were the cause. She
had been afraid since Mother's Day when she noticed blood in the
toilet and thought that one of her children had harmed her. She
said she meant to kill herself: she would be happier and better off
dead. She went on to reveal a maze of interpersonal intrigues and
other contingencies occurring in her family and on the settlement
where she lived. The situation there was that her husband was not
working, and there was no money to feed and clothe the children
and send them to school. In addition, she had been upset by the
gossip of her husband's sisters that she had committed adultery
with an Aborigine named Harry, who was working and who, they
said, had given her money. She told the doctor that she wanted to
cut Harry's throat and then her own because of what he did to her
mother who had died two months before. Asked what Harry had

---

[1] The case histories presented here were originally reported in J. E. Cawte,
"Australian Aborigines in Mental Hospitals, pt. 2: Patterns of Transitional Psychosis," *Oceania* 36(4): 272–282.

to do with her mother's death, she answered "blackfellow's way."

Her statements were a mixture of ideas and beliefs from her two cultures and it was hard to disentangle them. Her relationship with the hospital and its medicine was acutely ambivalent. She asked that blood that had been sucked from her arm for clinical pathology purposes be placed in a human bone; only blackfellow's medicine could help her. She blamed the tranquillizing tablets for her illness and asked to be handed over to a blackfellow doctor in Port Augusta.

A letter was sent to her doctor in Leigh Creek asking for further information. In a helpful reply, he outlined the nature of the domestic trouble: the patient did the work while the husband loafed, or did an occasional bit of fencing. She wanted to take her children and leave him to live with another Aborigine, Harry, who could supply her with money. But the trouble that this would bring was emphasized to her at the mission; it was explained that by leaving her husband for Harry, she would be an adulteress according to the Ten Commandments.

Her husband took a different view of his wife's condition. He told the township doctor that because of some bone-pointing,[2] his wife could not come face-to-face with any Aborigine, including himself, that all she could do was fall to the ground and cry, and that there were ghosts of Aborigines traveling with her, talking to her. He reported also that lightning had struck a goanna and its tail had pointed toward her stomach, and suggested that in consequence of this omen both she and the baby she was carrying were going to die.

As the date of delivery approached she became more disturbed, moaning and wailing. She took no interest in helping the nurses prepare the layette. She complained that her clothes were ragged—as they were. She was prompt to blame others in the ward; for example, she said that she had found the white patients laughing at her, despite their assurance that they were laughing about something else. She complained of sore throats, headaches, and other discomforts.

In this agitated condition she came into labor and delivered a healthy boy. The baby was kept with her so she could breast-feed

[2] In the central tribes, bone-pointing by means of a human ulna or kangaroo fibula is a form of sorcery by projective magic. See chapter 3.

him, but he could be given to her only under supervision, since she would try to feed him when he was fast asleep or would disturb him in other ways. Her agitation mounted: she lay awake most of the night, talking to herself and crying and calling out apparently in answer to her auditory hallucinations. She said the nurses called her a fishing spider and accused her of loafing in hospital for free rest and food. In one of her spectacular outbursts she bit the ample bosom of the nurse in charge of the ward, inflicting toothmarks on the nurse's nipple through the apron of the uniform.

Happily for the records, this patient was literate and scrawled letters to relatives and officials. Some of these were saved. Though disorganized and fragmentary, they provide an indication of the conflicting points of reference. Contrasting with Aboriginal themes of sorcery and sacrilege are themes from the white culture, the both combining to form a background to the complaints and illustrating what may be regarded as a value polymorphism (Wittkower 1969)—the coexistence within the same individual of values that are antagonistic. In view of their disorganizing effect, one might go further and, to adapt the term of Bateson (1956), regard them as a cultural double bind. Some of the recurring ideas from the letters, phrased in her own words, are extrapolated here.

> I got married in church and not with a firestick, so I don't think I'll ever see my darling little family again, because I went against our law. No one gave me a firestick because I wasn't wanted to marry this man.
> I don't care now if I die, because I misunderstood the blackfellow ways and got myself into trouble.
> They got my blood in a human bone. I found this out in a dream, so there's going to be a war on. My life is kept at Port Augusta in a human bone.
> My hair was singed and burned at Leigh Creek by some blackfellows to make me mad; I found it by my navel and afterwards I can't hold anything secret.
> Blackfellow caught me with a whirlwind and made me go mad, and I was told not to give my mother's name because people might think I am infectious.
> When Harry couldn't get me in the first place with the whirlwind, he got my mother; so that's what broke me down on Mother's Day and that's how I know I'll never get over my sickness.
> I was boned in the head when I was small. I still can see the danger

ahead. . . . my mother treated me real bad and so I got married to this man to get out of trouble but his sisters got very nasty.

My mother left the mission because they called her her father's name. This is a place called Black Gully where no women are allowed to walk. The boys took its name in vain so everybody's going to serve trouble.

At first she had hallucinated. The voices were "my peoples" and mostly came to her in the night, especially as she was going to sleep; they were "these people that's dead and gone" and they told her what was going to happen, before anybody else knew; they were spirit ancestors. With further stay in the hospital, and no further exposure to her double culture, her regression to old Aboriginal themes diminished and her security—in the Western culture—gradually became reestablished. After three months her hallucinations faded. When she reached the stage where she was working well in the hospital, looking after subnormal children with a motherly interest, she was allowed to return to the mission, with a supply of tranquillizing tablets.

"The Wary Walkabout"—A Paranoid Panic and Flight

A full-blood male Aborigine aged about forty living at a mission near the west coast of South Australia became fearful and panicky. He accused everyone there, including the Lutheran pastor, of being against him and of plotting to murder him. He thought that they were trying to poison or shoot him, and he formed the conviction that his wife was already dead, despite the fact that she was present, alive, and well. Taking a .22 caliber rifle he then fled from the mission into the bush. On the first night he traveled thirty miles. The tracking party did not catch up with him until a week later. The arrival of the party, armed with rifles, served to confirm his persecutory ideas; there was an exchange of rifle fire, in which nobody was hit, before he was taken into custody.

Brought by police to the nearest town, 120 miles away, he insisted to the examining doctor that his wife definitely had been killed the Friday previous, and that he had been at her funeral. The missionaries escorting him equally insisted that his wife was alive and reassured him once more that nobody was trying to poison or kill him. Since he would not be convinced, the doctor decided that he was paranoid and in need of psychiatric treatment obtainable only in the city, five hundred miles away. In his letter to the psychiatric center the doctor, a member of the aerial medical service, wrote of his regret at his difficulty in assessing cases of this sort, where language, intellect, and native lore became barriers to understanding. It was not unusual for natives to take to the bush when in a state of fear, but the reasons for their doing so were largely conjectural.

In the city hospital the patient was calm and cooperative, but persisted with his ideas about the tenuousness of his life at the mission. Speaking in Aboriginal English, he said he had gone bush to save his life. He had planned to walk to another mission on the River Murray, Berri way, where his son lived, so he could tell him about his mother's murder and get his help. Nothing he said at this time suggested that he attributed his persecution to sorcery, sacrilege, or other Aboriginal assumptions; he believed the natives and staff of the mission were simply out to kill him for no known reason. He denied alcoholism or recent drinking—the possibility of delirium tremens had been raised in the hospital because he said a group of men armed with rifles were out to get him while he was in the bush. However, it seemed probable that this was not a hallucination, but a misinterpretation of the intentions of the tracking party.

The pertinent cultural background of this psychosis was pieced together from the patient himself, from the Aboriginal Welfare Department, and from a knowledge of the circumstances of the mission. The patient was described there as being unoccupied and shiftless. His main occupation was given as opal gouger, and he was apparently neither a successful nor a persistent one. Alcoholism was not corroborated. After an early childhood of tribally oriented life in the spinifex plains country, he had been brought up at a mission originally established at a soak (water hole) in a semidesert area near the border of South and Western Australia. The soak formerly had been a ceremonial meeting ground, and the region had resources enough for the subsistence of nomads who conserved the food and water. Kangaroos, scrub turkeys, lizards, and snakes were plentiful. But the recent concentration of Aborigines, missionaries, and domestic animals had denuded the area of timber, vegetation, and fauna. With the loss of hunting and foraging interests, the people were subject to idleness and to dependency on the mission for handouts of rations. The mission had been continued for many years with extreme difficulty, amidst creeping red sandhills, until it was finally removed to a new location.

During the patient's formal education, received at the mission, there had been a systematic destruction of the cultural past, features of which have been described for this area by Berndt and Berndt (1951) These authors state that it was the policy of the mission to extinguish as rapidly as possible traces of Aboriginal customs, laws, ritual, and ceremonial, replacing them with the Western legal code and the moral code of the mission, which was fundamentalist with a heavy emphasis on the conflict between good and evil. The rite of circumcision, for example, which normally preceded fuller participation in tribal government and domestic life, was condemned and prohibited. The mission opposed it both as an ordeal and as an occasion for pagan ceremony. Uncircumcised men were thus married in defiance of tribal law, and resulting disturbances were quelled by mission authority with police support. Ceremonies in general were classed as sins, along with fighting and spearing.

Partly because of the patient's limited English and partly because of the secretive nature of his illness, it was difficult for me to enter his confidence. Rapport and trust were meager, intervention largely unhelpful. Most of the time in hospital he sat morosely in corners. With encouragement he took part in group meetings, and once spoke with animation when asked to describe hunting; he demonstrated spearing kangaroos and rabbits, using a throwing stick. The hospital staff could not finally decide whether his mood should be interpreted as one of fear and mistrust associated with delusional ideas or as nostalgia associated with loneliness and bewilderment in the hospital environment. He said he did not want to return home and enquiries revealed that he could not expect a welcome or supervision if he did. The mission was naturally reluctant to take a man who has been disturbed and dangerous, and the social worker from the Aboriginal Welfare Department urged caution, writing that "the tribes dread mental sickness and will never accept these people again"—probably a misconception, but originating from an influential source.

During continued observation, the patient's initial improvement was not sustained. Into the same ward had been admitted another Aborigine, from an area one thousand miles to the north, who had no language in common with our patient. This man had much less culture-contact experience and was virtually tribally oriented; nevertheless, he was able to mix better in the ward. His presence seemed to revive fears in our patient, who recoiled from him. The significance of this development was fully appreciated by the staff only in retrospect. It was observed that the patient suffered hallucinations—he said he heard the voices of his daughter and of the new Aborigine patient in the ward.

Twice he absconded during his hospital stay, but was returned by the police each time before he had gotten clear of the suburbs on his way north. Awaiting his opportunity, he finally escaped one night by pulling out a window, and this time he succeeded in eluding the police and traversing the suburbs. He did not return to his mission nor did he go to his son; he has not been heard of since. It is presumed he continued his "wary walkabout." It is possible that he succeeded in finding a safe territory, but more likely that he has not survived his psychosis. A fatal outcome is thought to be a not uncommon denouement to the "wary walkabout."

· "The Hapless Wanderer"—With a Prison Psychosis

An itinerant part-Aborigine of eighteen was sentenced by the police court at Katherine in the Northern Territory to six months in prison for supplying liquor to a "native ward," that is, a person under the protection of the Aboriginal Welfare Board, and not permitted by law to drink liquor. While serving his sentence in Fannie Bay Gaol, Darwin, he became excited, talked aloud to himself, and behaved strangely. He was transferred to Darwin hospital but during observation there became more disturbed. He was aggressive toward the staff, and when alone inflicted injuries upon himself. Given tranquillizing medication, his condition deteriorated and he developed ideas that the staff was persecuting him. He repeatedly struck his head against the wall. A course of electric convulsive therapy was given but he became worse, so that injections of tranquillizer drugs were needed to quieten his noisy outbursts. Darwin had then no psychiatric service. It was thought wise to remove him to Adelaide for further psychiatric care, rather than return him to Darwin jail to complete his sentence while in such a disturbed frame of mind.

In Adelaide, at first interview, he answered the doctor's questions disinterestedly, punctuating them with a monotonous refrain, "Do you think I can get back in a week's time? I've got horses to break in . . . I want to get back to my job. There's nothing wrong with me." He admitted that he had sold liquor to natives for a big profit and exhibited no self-recriminations about doing so. He admitted that he talked to himself: "I always talk aloud to myself when I'm working with horses. It's a habit. I might laugh or smile when I think about something funny." Questioning failed to confirm the existence of hallucinations.

A letter from his sister shed light on the patient's progressive retreat from authority and institutions and his adoption of vagrancy as a way of life. He was the sixth of eight children in a New South Wales outback part-Aboriginal family. He was removed from the family at an early age and reared in orphanages in country towns. At the age of fifteen, a job was found for him as a bellboy in a Sydney hotel, but he longed to go to Queensland to be a drover, or to do something that permitted him to live outdoors and to ride horses. He ran away one night but the police traced him to a town in Queensland, intercepting him as he got off the train. He convinced them that he did not want to return, and a job was found for him on a sheep station. But a sheep station was unacceptable; again he ran away, and his sister had no further news for two years. A photograph of him as the "Champion Calf Rider of the North" was seen in a country magazine. By chance, another sister saw him in Cloncurry in west Queensland; he was on his way to Normanton and the Gulf of Carpentaria. She expressed her thought that he was not looking after himself very well, but he said he was doing all right as a roving station hand and was rough-riding at the shows up that way. The next news that the family received concerned his admission to hospital in Adelaide, arising out of the trouble in Darwin.

The restraints imposed by hospital life made him very anxious. He adapted poorly to requirements of routine, fretting at the various restrictions. He paced restlessly up and down, talking to himself or to his reflection in the mirror. Sometimes he shouted out loud, but when questioned would deny that he had done so. He could not say why he bashed his own head on the wall in Darwin hospital, except that he must have been "barmy" to do it. He claimed he had been put in hospital as an attempt to drive him insane. To the patients, he boasted he was the man "they" couldn't send mad. He said that "they" had given him needles in Darwin to send him mad, and then embroidered this by saying that some Aborigines had stung him with a stingray tail to send him mad. He boasted of his police reputation in the Northern Territory as a supplier of liquor to Aborigines and also as a horse-stealer—an offense for which he had never been charged. A letter to his sister in New South Wales showed similar compensations for his obvious inadequacies; he wrote her that he was a popular singer and guitar player.

In view of his upbringing and schooling in a New South Wales country town, it was thought that the Wechsler scale was probably applicable culturally. There appeared clinically to be an intellectual subnormality, "subcultural" in nature. The assessment by the Wechsler scale showed a verbal I.Q. of 90 and a performance I.Q. of 74, a full-scale I.Q. of 82. The clinical psychologist thought that with more concentration and less vacillation, the patient could probably have performed better on the performance subtests than he in fact did. His optimum I.Q. was thought to be probably at the lower end of the normal range.

Large amounts of tranquillizing medication were needed to dull his rather disorganized protests. Gradually the patient's restlessness subsided and he accepted hospital routine and authority without violent reactions. Meanwhile his sister in the New South Wales country town had written expressing her concern. His jail sentence having elapsed while he was in hospital, he was referred to her care, but with no real expectation that he would stay with her.

The labels used for the selected patterns are deliberately colloquial, intended to dramatize some themes of Aboriginal adaptational difficulties. "The Birth of the Blues," "The Wary Walkabout," and "The Hapless Wanderer" are examples of themes and conflicts that are not exclusive to psychotic Aborigines, any more than the familiar conflicts of Western patients are exclusive to people who become patients. Without doubt, these conflicts trouble Aborigines who never come to medical notice because they never force that denouement by violent and spectacular social disruptions. The majority of Aborigines handle these cultural conflicts more successfully—or more quietly—protected by the good fortune of their constitution, training or social network.

It is not proposed here to give a detailed analysis of these case histories. They speak for themselves, and anthropologist readers will grasp some nuances better than physician readers. For example, the first patient's lament, "My mother left the mission because they called her her father's name," refers to the breakup of the matrilineal family organization characteristic of tribes of this region. Some commentary is in order, however, on the significance of the psychodynamics depicted.

"The Birth of the Blues" in this context is a term calculated to draw the attention of health workers to the observation that the "Blues," or intrapunitiveness, from being a comparative rarity in the traditional culture, emerges more prominently in the transitional culture. With it comes suicide and attempted suicide, events supposedly uncharacteristic of tribal life before the "Blues" was born. Various hypotheses have been advanced for similar findings in other emerging peoples (Stainbrook 1954). Our patient illustrates several of these hypotheses. The breakup of the extended family and its enforced replacement by the Western conjugal arrangement is clearly a factor in her case. The engendering of guilt feelings, from introjection and incomplete repression of moral-punitive elements of her early environment, is another. In the crisis of stress, an affect of guilt is expressed rather than of blame, which is more characteristic of the traditional culture. Finally, the loss of objects that sustain the patient's self-esteem and identity is another. It is unnecessary to ask which of these hypotheses is primary. Modern psychiatry finds simple cause-effect stereotypes inappropriate, aware that symptoms and syndromes are multiply determined.

"The Wary Walkabout" is a traditional Aboriginal expression of paranoid illness. A classical sequence observed by me was that of a Kimberley Aborigine who picked out a solitary course over a stony plateau to conceal his tracks, and lit campfires at night, which he then deserted to mislead his supposed assassins. On examination, this Kimberley man could be diagnosed as suffering from paranoid schizophrenia, in modern clinical terminology. In the wary walkabout pattern the individual acts logically upon his conviction that he is the quarry of avengers or judicial executioners, perhaps because of his breach of tribal sanctions. In most instances the conviction is delusional, a rationalization of an intrapsychic fear. A similar though less frequent pattern is known in Western patients. Due to the Aborigines' bushcraft, "escape" is apt to be consummated—and fatal. The persistence of this pattern in detribalizing Aborigines, as in our case history, shows that old ideas die hard. It reflects the tendency toward regression to the assumptive world of the earlier years. Such assumptions are not easily extinguished, even by the most rigorous Western indoctrination and suppressive measures.

"The Hapless Wanderer" refers to a type of vagrancy not uncommon in fringe-dwelling Aborigines, and is connected only remotely, if at all, with the purposeful movements around the countryside made by the traditional horde. It reflects the individual's social alienation, rather than the social integration of true nomadism. It should be recognized as a psychiatric syndrome rather than as the tendency to "walkabout," popularly supposed to be part of the Aboriginal makeup. The individual presented in our case history shows distinctly autistic and grandiose defenses. He achieves a partial adjustment through a vagabondage that conserves interpersonal distances. When this adjustment is threatened by enforced institutionalization, in prison or in hospital, full-blown psychosis erupts.

PSYCHOLINGUISTIC BARRIERS TO COMMUNICATION

Paradoxically, I have found that communication with traditionally oriented communities in which people do not speak much English is apt to be better than with fringe-dwelling groups in which everybody has basic English. The problems of rapport with the two groups are distinct. In the traditional group they are linguistic. Though language is a barrier, enough school-educated younger people can be found to act as interpreters and enough older people can be found willing to impart their knowledge. One learns to respect the conversational style: the shyness and lack of assertiveness. One learns not to be hasty nor talkative nor to adopt Western procedures of cross-examination. With ordinary courtesy and hospitality, reasonable rapport is attained and communication is rewarding. This does not necessarily apply, of course, to those who are psychiatrically disturbed, who are not communicating well even with their own people.

Some psycholinguistic problems seem especially relevant to clinical enquiries. I observed the importance of Kinesic communication, by gesture and posture. The Walbiri of central Australia, for example, have an elaborate language of hand signs and head gestures that probably evolved to serve communication between people whose foraging activities caused them to be frequently out of comfortable earshot. In infancy, the verbal exchange between the mother and the child of two or three years is very low, the mother relying on stereotyped gestures and noises.[3]

The psycholinguistic aspect of the cultural change that puzzled me particularly concerns the extent of psychological correspondence between the vernacular language and English. Do mental associations in one language resemble those in the other? In commenting on this, an abbreviated account may be given here of experiments that are reported in more detail in the journal literature (Cawte and Kiloh 1967; Veness and Hoskin 1968).

In order to gain some simple measure of the effect of language upon perception in Aborigines, Professor Kiloh and I examined pictorial representation in some bilingual Aboriginal children. Our data consist of the responses of these children to questions phrased alternatively in Walbiri vernacular and in English. Pictorial responses were chosen, because it is thought that they have some relevance to the understanding of the psychology of the subjects, and because they have the advantage of simplicity of measurement.

---

[3] Dr. Annette Hamilton of the Department of Anthropology, Sydney University, has conducted an interactional analysis, in an Arnhem Land subcommunity, of intimate proceedings between a mother and her children, with the aim of studying how children learn the rules of society. Her study supports our observation of low verbal exchange in the mother-infant pair.

Such assumptions underlie the widespread use of pictorial representation tests in the practice of clinical psychology.

The technique used was based on the "cross-cultural fruit-tree study" originated by L. L. Adler (1965) of the American Museum of Natural History, New York. Adler invited local correspondents in many parts of the world to instruct children between the ages of five and twelve years: "Draw a picture—any scene, in color—with a fruit tree in it." If the term fruit tree does not exist in a native language, Adler's instruction becomes: "A tree which bears fruit we can eat." When the drawing is completed, the child is asked: "What kind of a fruit tree is it?" and the answer is recorded on the back of the paper with the age and sex of the child.

As used by Adler, the fruit-tree study permits a comparison of children's drawings from many countries and has the object of investigating the influence of the introduced cultural environment as contrasted with that of the natural environment. Margaret Mead (1945) had previously noted the need to survey the drawings of children for standardization and cross-cultural comparison. Some years ago Bender, then chief psychiatrist of the Children's Service of Bellevue Hospital, New York, observed that the majority of children draw apple trees even when they live in areas growing mainly citrus fruits (Adler 1965).

Analyzing the results of 2,403 pictures from ten countries, Adler found that children tend to draw trees that grow in their local environment; only two countries, Congo and Netherlands Antilles, did not show this trend. However, data pooled from all countries showed that a decided majority favored apple trees. The reason for the general predilection for apple trees is conjectural. It is tempting to infer a connection with the apple's universal symbolism, exemplified by the forbidden fruit in the Adam and Eve legend. Aside from its attractive qualities as a fruit, the shape of the apple may contribute to its symbolic significance and to its predilection for the child artists in Adler's experiment. Adler concluded that the hypothesis "children from all over the world tend to draw more apple trees than any other fruit tree" can be accepted, though the hypothesis must be partially rejected with qualifications on a regional basis.

Using Adler's findings for children's fruit-tree drawings as a basis, we sought to discover whether the hypothesis must also be qualified on account of language. The children at Yuendumu are taught English at school but use Walbiri vernacular in the school-yard and at home in their camps. They are the main bilingual groups of the Walbiri people, who have had less than twenty years' close contact with European Australian society. Apart from the very occasional child who may have visited Adelaide, none of the children has had the opportunity to see an apple tree, though apples now form part of their regular diet. Orange and lemon trees grow in the settlement. The indigenous fruit trees of central Australia are of a completely different order. Thus in this experiment, the children had available for their use two languages and two sets of fruit trees.

The help of the teachers was obtained to use the classrooms. In the first part of the investigation two separate classes of children, A and B, were used. Each class consisted of about thirty children, occupying separate rooms. The classes varied in number from day to day, were equally distributed as to sex, and ranged in age from six to twelve years.

The English instruction was: "Draw a picture in which there is a tree from which you can get fruit, a fruit tree." The concept "fruit" or "fruit tree" does not exist in Walbiri language; instead, names of the individual edible products of trees are used. Thus in Walbiri the nearest equivalent of the English "fruit tree" appears to be "food tree." The Walbiri instruction was: "*Yira kalu wadija gujugangalu miyi mani*," literally, "Draw a picture with a tree where you can get food." These instructions were given by a Walbiri assistant teacher.

On the first occasion, class A received its instruction in English and class B in Walbiri. Three days later the procedure was reversed, class A being instructed in Walbiri and Class B in English. The interpretation of the drawings was made by the children to the authors in English, but in some cases the assistant teacher discussed the drawings with the children in Walbiri. No child varied his interpretation when questioned both in English and in Walbiri.

In the second part of the investigation a replication of the study was made in a third class, C, but this time no cross-over was attempted. Class C contained older children, between twelve and fifteen years. For the experiment, the class was randomly divided into two halves, each receiving their instructions in separate rooms, in English and in Walbiri respectively. The children's drawings were examined in the same way as those from classes A and B.

In the majority of cases from all classes the children included single fruit trees in their drawings, or if multiple trees were drawn, they were all of the same species. A few drew up to four species. In most of these drawings of multiple trees the trees were all either indigenous or introduced, but there were two instances in which trees of mixed origins were included. The responses were classified as "native," "introduced," and "mixed" respectively. All the drawings were scenic, the backgrounds often being appropriate to the type of fruit depicted. Introduced fruit trees were usually associated with man-modified landscapes, native trees with an undisturbed countryside.

The results demonstrated that the type of tree drawn varies with the language of instruction. It is possible that these results might be due to the contrast between the native culture and the recently introduced Western school culture. If so one might expect that the effect would not be so pronounced in older children in whom there was a greater degree of integration of the two cultures. Accordingly a third group of children aged twelve to fifteen years was tested. When instructed in English, 78 percent drew introduced trees, results very similar to those obtained with the younger children.

It can be seen therefore that when instructed in English the children tended to draw introduced fruit trees and when instructed in Walbiri they tended to draw native fruit trees. We found the difference to be very highly significant (chi square $= 15.5$; $p < 0.001$). It seems to be unaffected by the temporal sequence of the instruction, the age of the child, or the duration of contact with the contrasting cultures.

The chief art form available for Walbiri children was until recently the sand smoothed for drawing by the palm of the hand, and it formed an important instrument of education. On this "canvas" children were required to master the art of reproducing, with the fingers, patterns and spoors made by the bird and animal life of the region. The intricacies of camp arrangement and kinship relationships and avoidances were learned by making "toy" camps in the sand, with leaves for people. Children's stories were illustrated by finger drawings upon the smoothed sand. Thus a Walbiri child picturing a fruit tree in its literal form is adopting an introduced artistic convention. He is expressing himself in a new way imparted to him in school where he is provided with paper, colored pencils, and instruction in the Western artistic conventions.

Although the Walbiri child is learning to represent the world in this new way, the study shows that he is still free to express indigenous or introduced subjects, depending largely on whether he is instructed in the indigenous or the introduced tongue. The study reveals the importance of language in determining his pictorial representations. In doing so, it would appear to provide some support for the Sapir-Whorf hypothesis, that language shapes our perception of the physical world (Whorf 1956). At the least, it shapes our representation of it.

The behavioral sciences must therefore enquire to what extent human responses are regulated by the concepts that happen to be available or unavailable in a given language. This is of some moment in education, where educators are already recommending that the children of Aborigines learn to read in the vernacular and then learn to read in English. It is considered possible that in this way children may learn more quickly and efficiently, and that what they learn has more meaning for them. At present most of the Walbiri children learn basic English or, rather, less, and tend to acquire defeatist attitudes toward their studies.

The implications for psychiatry seem equally important. It is conceivable for example that the general social and personality inertia observed in behavioral studies of the Walbiri people may be related in part to the divided lingual environment. The situation is not comparable with the divergence that exists between two modern European languages, such as English and Spanish, for the Walbiri people find themselves in a situation of ambiguity, where two languages with extremely divergent symbols and associations compete for their responses. It is in this situation that the Walbiri child is learning to understand the world about him, building in his mind the model on which his mental health and social efficiency will largely depend—the "assumptive world" emphasized by J. D. Frank (1961).

SOCIOECONOMIC BARRIERS TO COMMUNICATION

The communication difficulty with fringe-dwellers in the country towns is of an entirely different order. Vernacular is largely lost in the general social disintegration; a patois of English is spoken. But because of poverty and illiteracy, the social distance from European Australians is great and many fringe-dwellers have learned "the art of not talking." This is the phrase coined by my friend and colleague Dr. R. E. Coolican, for twenty years a general practitioner in a New South Wales country town that has a fringe settlement of Aborigines.[4] I invited Dr. Coolican recently to lecture to the medical students of the University of New South Wales on the medical aspects of this community. This emotionally gripping commentary, of an experienced country physician, quoted verbatim here, needs no amplification. It highlights, as nothing else could, the difficulties that fringe Aboriginal society and European Australian society have in communicating—indeed in articulating at all.

> The greatest ecological handicap to life in the far west of New South Wales is to be born an Aborigine. This term includes all shades of dark persons who regard themselves as Aborigines or who associate with and are regarded by other Aborigines as one of their own.
>
> We have about 520 of them—200 live on the reserve, 100 have moved into the ten new houses built for them by the Aboriginal Welfare Board, another 60 live around the town, 80 live in a nearby township, and the remaining 80 live on properties in the district.
>
> These people are the problem of Australia—their care is managed by few and criticized by many. They are the descendants of nomads who walked the land and lived from it as hunters. Their way of life was an irregular one, and this irregularity still marks their way of life today: no set meal times, gorging then starving, drinking to excess followed by periods of abstinence.
>
> They were a communal society, in that all shared the hunter's spoils. Children inherited their maternal surnames. A sense of togetherness and loyalty characterized the tribe.
>
> They were hunted from the rivers and an attempt was made to ex-

---

[4] Dr. Coolican's findings have been published in a book on rural medical practice (1973).

terminate them when they interfered with progress as we pushed out into the northwest of New South Wales—120 years ago. Bounty was paid at the rate of a half-crown a scalp; hence the many "Bloody" this or that waterhole signifying the site where some hunter had shot so many Aborigines. We crossed them with some good white and some bad white blood. Finally we brought them into reserves, dressed them in our clothes, let them build shanties, provided them with foodstuffs that required cooking—unfortunately they lacked the cultural cooking background that we have, as well as the implements.

Their own food was denied them as we settled the areas around the reserves—kangaroos, emus, and game moved farther inland—and so they sank into a state of subnutrition, which is still present today in each generation. Breakfast may be cold boiled meat (pieces from the butcher), tinned corned beef if they're in the money, or bread and syrup or jam, or cereal and bread and jam.

Lunch is taken at school or the cafe—sandwiches; the main meal is stew and bread—a very thin stew—meat and two onions and two potatoes for, say, six people. Butter is rarely eaten; it doesn't keep in the hot weather. And they don't like cheese.

Occasionally they'll have a big feed of fruit or meat. Potato chips, soft drinks, and sweets will often replace a meal, and if they are drinking they don't eat at all. This continues day by day—seven days a week—fifty-two weeks a year.

Let's take a quick look at this place we put them in called "the reserve." Most western towns have them—about thirteen acres of land one mile on the down-river side of the town. Ours is a fairly good one; we have a communal pan system, hot water in the ablution block, a laundry, and one central tap where people can draw water for their houses. The water supply is pumped straight from the river. They tend to cluster in family groups all over the reserve—one family and all descendants at one end, another with descendants at the other end.

There are two stoves among the shanties that are used in the winter and two kerosene refrigerators. The latter don't work, but they are used as storehouses for food. Most cooking is done over an open fire outside. In the wintertime they use buckets filled with coals to keep warm, for they have no electricity.

We put them in these concentration camps and left them there—we needed to—they smelled, were lousy, they lied, cheated, stole, and when they got their hands on some alcohol bought from an unscrupulous publican at four dollars a flagon of wine they fought and brawled and tried to kill us.

We gave them work—their labor was cheap—bought their women with alcohol—still do—the police arrested them in droves when the town needed cleaning up for some special occasion, or the daily average dropped, but by and large we treated them well.

We tolerated them in our schools—they were indifferent students, unpunctual—irregular attendants—never went if it rained because it was too far to walk through boggy black soil. They were difficult kids, and so they grew up almost illiterate. We allowed them into the pictures and the cafes where they acquired their cooking culture, and occasionally we let a family or two live at the other end of the town.

Such was the situation until about fifteen years ago when we started to remove our barriers. Then we found that they wouldn't come out and mix with us and discovered they didn't like us—indeed a faint suspicion that they despised us.

So much for the background of our Aborigine. What is his life like compared to ours? He'll be one of eight or ten children. His mother will be thin and worn out at thirty—a fifty-fifty chance that she will have lost one child through stillbirth or in its neonatal period; she'll have a low blood folate, a hemoglobin of close to 9 gm percent—very rarely will she have a megaloblastic anemia. He will be born in the local hospital and his mother will spend seven to ten days there—establishing breast-feeding. He'll be a smaller baby than his white counterpart—5½ to 6½ pounds—and he'll be breast-fed for up to six months.

For the next three years he'll be in and out of the hospital. If he lives on the reserve he'll be an inpatient five times—twice if he's a town Aborigine. His white brother has a 0.4 percent chance of admission.

He'll have gastroenteritis twice, some form of respiratory infection including otitis media twice, and once he'll come in for treatment of staphylococcal skin infection, burns, kerosene inhalation, or some form of trauma. His gastroenteritis will often be associated with pneumonia or bronchitis—and one in ten such admissions require transfusions.

His gastroenteritis will be due to a variety of causes. Some will be due to lactose deficiency, some coeliac disease, some viral during the course of an epidemic, some will be due to Shigella flexner or salmonella dysentery, some to Giardia lhamblia infestation, some to worms—thread, round, trichiuria, or our latest acquisition, the dwarf tapeworm.

His illness will respond to therapy; he'll look a little better but his hemoglobin will continue to fall for the week after he's been sick, then flatten out and slowly rise. If he's kept in hospital for four weeks after his illness is cured, he'll change from a pallid dull-skinned infant to a healthy glowing baby.

His respiratory tract infections will include bronchopneumonia, pneumonia, and otitis media—about 20 percent have chronic perforation of their ear drums, though marked deafness is rarely a complication of this finding. His hemoglobin and general return to health will be the same as his brother with the gastroenteritis.

On the reserve he'll learn the facts of life early. Alcohol is the great leveler, and to quote the words of an old minister, "In drink they take their pleasures when the mood seizes them without regard to place or privacy."

He will continue irregular meals, living close to the edge of starvation, gorging on fruit today then none for a fortnight, lots of soft drinks, potato chips. The pictures once or twice a week.

He'll share the same room as the rest of his family, sleeping often in the one bed, sharing food and infection.

School starts at five—it used to be seven—today they attend regularly. At the primary school 40 percent of the pupils are part-Aborigines. In the main, though willing, they are slow learners, usually below average and filling the G.A. and O.A. [General Activities and Opportunity Activities] classes. This of course is due to lack of language stimulation and to parental disinterest.

In the eight to fifteen age group, 80 percent of the boys will have had police interviews; their crimes will usually be petty larceny, sex offences, or carnal knowledge. Virginity is rare after thirteen, unknown at fifteen, and pregnancy is usually experienced no later than seventeen. Prosecution is rare; 1 percent will be sent away to homes.

In the high school, attendance is not as good, and they exhibit passive resistance to learning—probably because our educational standards are geared to a way of life that is beyond them.

They have talent—for mechanical things—spend hours tinkering with old cars to get them going. Many can draw and paint well. They all have good hand-eye coordination, are quick on their feet, and dominate the first half of the football match. Lack of stamina slows them up in the second half—this is due to subnutrition.

They leave school at fifteen, and walk the streets for a year or eighteen months—they enjoy freedom. The boys will turn then to laboring work—shearing, droving, picking cotton. Eighty percent of the girls will be unemployable; the remainder will get occasional jobs at the cafes, hotels, or in domestic service before they become pregnant.

At sixteen the males start drinking. Ninety-five percent of the male Aboriginal population will have been imprisoned by the time they reach nineteen—petty larceny, carnal knowledge, street offences, for example, drunkenness and brawls, bad language, urinating in the street.

He'll learn to fight the police when they come to arrest him, and the art of "not talking." He will exhibit loyalty to his peers that lasts throughout his life. No Aborigine can ever remember who hit him with a stick and broke his head or his leg. He will have an even-money chance of acquiring gonorrhea, and the same odds if a syphilitic vector is about.

He'll drink heavily until he's twenty-four and then settle down. If he's still drinking heavily at twenty-five he'll become an Aboriginal alcoholic—frequent delirium tremens but rarely portal cirrhosis. He will not develop acute appendicitis, either, but has a one in fifteen chance of developing tuberculosis.

The adult section can be divided into three groups—20 percent are in regular employment, 25 percent are down and outs—alcoholics who live on the earnings of others, based on the old communal system. A man can come into town with a check for two hundred dollars, cash it, and by next morning he'll have a hangover and no money. One Aborigine collected $3,000, and spent it in three months. No doubt he had happy memories, but his only material acquisition was a nippergram.

The remaining 55 percent will work when it's available—usually about three months per year. This is the group that drifts down to Menindee in January for the fruit picking, returning in March, or is now at Wee Waa chipping cotton.

He'll spend his money on his mates—alcohol, taxi rides, pictures, confectionery, and food in that order. He'll gamble—Aborigines are inveterate gamblers. The 2 percent that don't, have "religion" in some form or other. Card playing and horses occupy their spare time. He will have three hospital admissions before he comes in to die in his terminal illness. So he leads his life, aging prematurely; he'll look thirty at twenty, sixty at forty-five.

Depressed, apathetic, and illiterate, acquiring his culture from the pictures, cafes, and prison cells, he will die about ten years earlier than his white counterpart, enjoying for a short time only the pension, that magic gift that will ensure a regular income and raise his status with his peers, and with the storekeeper, publican, and the doctor.

The causes of their deaths are similar to ours—perhaps a few more drownings and suicides while drunk among the adults, certainly more stillbirths and neonatal deaths than occur in the white population.

So much for the poorest of the poor. I wish I could forecast a happy ending to this story, but I can't, for it continues day by day. I hope some of you people will grace general practice and some serve in the far west of New South Wales or other outposts in Australia. If you meet this problem there are but three courses open to you—ignore it—accept it—or fight it. Whatever your choice, I wish you luck; but do remember this: sixteen percent of your practice will be concerned with the care of these people.

CHAPTER TWO

The Aboriginal Doctor

THE NATIVE DOCTOR is the key to understanding the primitive systems of medicine and the law with which we are concerned. His survival poses the question of the attitude to be adopted by modern medicine toward traditional medicine. In countries where modern and traditional coexist, modern medicine usually disparages or ignores the older medical stream. In the upsurge of literature relating social and cultural sciences to natural and medical sciences, there is a tendency to idealize the native doctor, as if to compensate for the ethnocentric attitudes of former years. Of this tendency, Lebra (1969: 13) comments: "Considerable sympathy is displayed for the folk healer and no small amount of disdain for the modern medical practitioner. To the extent that much of this is only good fun—for which of us has not witnessed at one time or another pomposity on the part of M.D.s—I would not quibble. But to overidealize the traditional at the expense of the modern and scientific is a distortion which glosses over the ignorance and frequent devastation wrought by the former."

Modern doctors in Australia have for the most part simply overlooked native doctors. In recent years, when the improved training of modern physicians in social and psychological medicine might have brought them closer together, the establishment of aerial medical services kept the two groups apart. The modern doctors in these regions tend to live in the towns, paying only flying visits to the remote communities in which the native doctors live. In this chapter, I shall try to present the native doctor as I believe modern medicine would see him, if it had the opportunity: assessing his personality, practices, and social role, without contempt for his ignorance nor admiration for his supposedly supernatural powers.

To anticipate a general conclusion, the role of the native doctor does not correspond closely with that of the modern. He is not merely a folk healer, but an agent of social order who operates in the context of sickness. In order to appreciate the social role one must understand the society. The reader may infer, from the outline of Aboriginal society which follows, that there is a basic Aboriginal way of life. This impression in this chapter is the consequence of brevity and is not completely accurate; there are, as we shall see in the following chapters, crucial regional differences.

ABORIGINAL ORIGINS

Australian Aborigines are generally considered the most primitive men on earth, relics of the Stone Age, passed over by time because of their geographical isolation from the progressive peoples of the earth. They used tools of stone hafted to wood, but were ignorant of writing, pottery, agriculture, and animal husbandry. Naked for the most part, they wandered their land in small bands foraging for food. So they appeared to the white settler of the nineteenth century. How primitive was the medicine and law they practiced?

The popular view that the Aborigine represents "Early Man" proves in some respects to be misinformed and unscientific. Though his hunting-gathering culture is certainly that of the Stone Age, R. M. and C. H. Berndt (1964) point out that there is no evidence that it is closer than modern Western culture to the original state of man in any phylogenetic or evolutionary sense. Nor is it closer in an archaeological sense, except in the matter of technology. The Aborigine should be regarded as modern man who developed in an unusual direction because of exceptional circumstances. His origins are uncertain. A. A. Abbie (1969), a leading Australian physical anthropologist and a teacher of the author, considers it logical to class Aborigines as "proto-caucasoids," closer to Caucasians generally than to any other people. He states (1969: 210) "there is every reason for believing that the ancestors of the Aborigines came from Asia but none whatever for deriving them specifically from such fossil Javanese relics as *Pithecanthropus*." He suggests that the Indian, the Indonesian, and the Australian "australoids" could have migrated from a common proto-caucasoid group in central Asia. There are resemblances. Like Caucasians, Aborigines belong chiefly to blood groups A and O. B is more characteristic of Asia. In Aborigines, B occurs only in the far north, where it has probably been imported from Indonesia and Melanesia. But unlike the Caucasian, no Aborigine has ever been found Rhesus (Rh) negative. As for outer appearances, the Aborigine is unique. The broad nose is more characteristic of Oceanic negroids or Negritoo than caucasoids. Or so it seems to one who has traveled in the Pacific.

The prehistorian Mulvaney (1966) finds a prophetic comment in the journal of the early Australian explorer Count Strzelecki (1845: 333), who observed of the Aborigines that "their origin is involved in impenetrable obscurity; and such authors as have attempted to trace their migrations, or to detect the links which connect them with any of the predominant or primitive races of mankind, have not succeeded. . . ." The connection of the australoid with southern India was advocated by T. H. Huxley in his social systematization of man in 1870. He held that the only people outside Australia who possess the chief characteristics of the Australians in a well-marked form are the hill tribes of the Deccan. Despite this, the evidence for a social connection with Southeast Asia may be stronger.

Whatever their origins, it may be concluded that the Aborigines are now a unique people, and as Abbie points out, strikingly homogeneous, as would be expected of a single group isolated from the world for ages.

When the Aborigines came to Australia, they did not walk into their new homeland. Had they walked, tigers and other predators would have walked after them over Weber's line that separates the mammals of Asia from the marsupials of Australia; and the marsupials would now be extinct. Hence they made a water crossing, for which the minimum craft would be a raft. Such crossings might not have been too difficult in the late Pleistocene era when the seas between Indonesia on the Asian side and New Guinea-Australia on the other were relatively narrow. Even in the post-Pleistocene era it was possible for a seafarer to come to Australia accidentally, blown from Indonesia by the northwest monsoons of summer. Confirmatory evidence of immigration in the Pleistocene era comes from carbon dating of samples found associated with stone tools: the earliest dates are about 25,000 years B.P. Evidence of human remains is more recent. With the melting of the polar ice caps as the Pleistocene ended, the elevation of the seas and the direction of ocean currents left little chance of a return to Asia or of trade. Adaptation to the drying subcontinent of the postglacial period became progressively formidable.

The Aborigines remained isolated until the time of the Macassar traders of the last few centuries, retaining comparatively intact their culture and physical characteristics. Europe imported progress in the form of pottery, the wheel, writing, the germinal idea, and agriculture probably some 10,000 years B.P. but these inventions did not reach Australian shores. Not only this, indigenous plants were as unsuitable for agriculture as the animals were for husbandry. They remain unsuitable today; modern technology has done nothing to develop them for human subsistence, although experiments are being conducted on the suitability of the kangaroo as a source of protein in arid climates. While Aboriginal technology necessarily remained elementary, it is not safe to assume that the same applies to such items as social organization and control, awareness of the natural environment, art, song, dance, and language. Oral literature and mythology became rich, and the totemic complex of ideas achieved an ecological relevance and a practical sustenance rarely attained by religious institutions of other primitive cultures.

ABORIGINAL MEDICINE AND LAW

As for Aboriginal medicine and law, it is again no safe assumption that they are of uniformly primitive order. We do not know, for example, whether a local hunting-gathering band had full rights to a given territory or would share it with another band having affinal ties under pressures of ecological privation. But we discern systems for managing such matters (see chapter 7). There is evidence that Aboriginal doctors were the pivotal figures in the health and adaptation of their people. They practiced medicine and law together. The culture was so conservative that they were probably practicing the same sort of medicine and law at the end of their epoch as at the beginning. The end is in sight; now they practice openly only in the remote areas of the subcontinent and their total eclipse may take no more than thirty years.

I have indicated the scientific medical value of a study of the social institutions of prehistoric man. Another reason for such studies involves what may be called reparation. For some European Australians, making up for past neglect is a real motivation. What we know of the prehistory of Australia suggests that the people were in the hands of Aboriginal doctors for some 20,000 years. Less than 200 years ago the European invasion began, and Western doctors and law-givers started to take over. In this period the decline of the Aboriginal people was catastrophic. Numbers did not merely decline, they plummeted toward extinction. A population estimated at a quarter to a half a million at the time of Captain Cook's landing in 1770 became a tattered remnant of 50,000 a few generations later. Tasmanians died out entirely. The invasion was comparable in some respects to community disasters such as flood, fire, famine, hurricane, or earthquake. The Aboriginal behavioral aftermath to alien contact will be compared, in chapter 12, to the psychological responses to gross stress. While it would be going too far for Australian physicians and magistrates to accept all responsibility for this, the awareness of what has happened to health and adjustment strikes them with special force and clarity. This awareness makes it an appropriate task to conduct research on the Australian Aborigines' decline, both physical and behavioral. By establishing a belated communication with the native doctor, it may be possible in a few communities to bring some advantage to this potentially regressive people through their elders, an influential group that tends to be neglected.

A medical motive for the study of the native doctor involves identification. Those who have had the chance of associating with these men in the bush feel its force. Respect grows through acquaintance, and once relationships are established with them there is a feeling of association and interest, arising from the common concern with health and conduct. In addition to this common ground, there is a sense of privilege that marks discussions that are not the business of the rank and file of society. Any reluctance to speak in these "professional conventions" does not come from the Aborigines' side. In the desert country of the Walbiri people, the elder doctor Tjapaltjari formed the habit of visiting us, ostensibly to impart some new bit of information about his craft. Since he spoke about as much English as we did Walbiri vernacular, it was often just social visiting. Neither side felt that the two systems were totally incompatible in spirit and intention, separated by any uncrossable gulf, whatever the differences in technology. An assumption of social authority was common to each.

Some of the recorded literary description of the native doctor is distinctly admiring or marveling in tone. Where this is so, I suspect that it arises because the historian is attentive to the native doctors' powers and procedures, rather than to the actual details of the illness or social conflict. Anything seems more marvelous when the explanation is not available. Some of the most reliable observers tend to dwell on supposedly supernatural powers, such as telepathy and divination (Elkin 1954). Interest in the medical and legal crises of primitive Australian society gained ground in the 1950s (Berndt and Berndt 1951) and was firmly established in the 1960s (Meggitt 1962; Hiatt 1965). It then became possible in judicious descriptions of the native doctor, of which the most useful from a medical point of view is that of Catherine Berndt (1964), to relate his activities more closely to the social problems affecting his group. As to the common medical crises of these beleaguered communities, frontier clinicians had first-hand acquaintance with the actual disease patterns (Packer 1961; Cook 1966), but were rarely concerned in correlating them with the efforts of the native doctor.

MEDICAL "MAGIC"

Older descriptions of the doctor are inevitably "marvelous" when they neglect the actual medical and legal problems of tribal life with which he is coping. Notwithstanding this misleading emphasis, the "magical" aspect of the native doctor is in some ways valid, and a conventional way to begin to describe him. We may therefore form in our mind a composite picture of his "marvelous" public image or official presence, although it tells little about him personally.

The native doctor's personality may be identified, in my experience, as one of three types: mystic, sociopathic, or altruistic. The mystic doctor is an introspective individual, preoccupied with dreams and the spirit world, and experiencing dissociative trances. Such a man may be considered psychotic by some observers, or subject to psychotic episodes. The sociopathic doctor is a manipulative individual whose personal interest in medicine and the law is calculated from the prospects it offers for power and profit. Such a person tends to show an aggressive zeal that earns him a reputation as a charlatan among white observers. The altruistic doctor is a shrewd, alert man who is more identified with the aims of society and the adjustment of individuals. Because of his character traits, society elects him to mediate toward these ends.

Ackerknecht (1942*a, b;* 1943) and others have emphasized the psychic experiences of the shaman, suggesting that the career as shaman protects him against his personal illness, even against psychotic breakdown. This is very much a regional or cultural phenomenon. A report coming from Korea (Kim 1970) indicates that in that country there are two types of shaman, the hereditary priestly shaman and the charismatic shaman. The charismatic shaman suffers "mu disease," a religious experience involving psychosomatic and mental symptoms that can be cured only after becoming a shaman, through experience of trance states. The term "shamanism" is coming to mean in the literature on the subject the ability to enter a state of trance so as to speak and behave like the god "possessing" the shaman. In a psychiatric study of shamanism in Taiwan, Tseng (1972) observes that a person with the ability to dissociate can be trained to utilize his talent as a shaman. Becoming a shaman fulfills the individual's psychological needs and solves his own personal problems such as feelings of insecurity and inferiority.

Catherine Berndt's study (1964), especially her case histories, suggests that the altruistic-mediating type is the common character of native doctors in Australia, rather than the mystic-shamanistic. This also is my experience. The other types certainly occur, but, as will be seen, they tend not to hold their appointments for so long. Their conflicts cannot be sublimated in the culturally integrated care of the sick.

While ecstatic states, group trance phenomena, and altered consciousness are not common, magical feats are nevertheless a striking aspect of the Aboriginal doctor. A reputation for special powers and authority seems essential to his office, setting him apart from the rank and file. The rank and file complement his power and authority by their faith in it and expectation from it. This makes possible the protective and therapeutic relationship. In order to gain his reputation, the doctor undergoes training and rituals. There is some uniformity about the training of native doctors, but, as will be seen, a regional variation is even more apparent.

Some doctors recount a journey to a sacred place where they received their wisdom and power, perhaps in the symbolic form of a doctor's charm that they now possess. Sometimes, indeed, they have a song to sing about it. A song may have some quality of magic, as the derivation of the English words "charm," "chant," "incantation" suggests. As they tell it in song, their adventure is apt to begin by levitation and by their being spirited through the sky as in a trance. Invisibility is part of the professional reputation and can be assumed at will. Special visual powers—ability to see spirits, or inside a person's body—are usually claimed. Magic surgery, with internal rearrangements in the body, that leaves no scar on the skin is frequent. Telepathy, extrasensory perception, knowledge of distant happenings, prophecy of death, all form part of the native doctor's public image and aura of power.

The Australian clever man has as many symbols of office as a Western physician, or any other physician. His symbol is commonly the rainbow serpent, a mythical being of widespread importance in Aboriginal Australia. The clever man usually claims a special relationship with the rainbow serpent and with its powers for good or ill. Elkin (1933), the student of Australian totemism, calls this "individual" or "personal" totemism, involving the relationship between the doctor and the reptile. I am hesitant to use the word totem since Levi-Strauss (1963) has asserted that it is an overinclusive concept—a false category or illusion. Levi-Strauss' opening volley "Totemism is like hysteria . . ." is especially convincing to a psychiatrist! The question "Is 'totem' taboo?" continues to be examined by modern anthropologists (Hiatt 1969; Kessler 1971). If I use the word here, it is out of respect for Elkin's contribution and for expedient conventions. The doctor has a set of emblems, from string bags to bullroarers to ironwood blades, which he uses in diagnosis or divination, and through which he makes contact with the spirits. Characteristically, he carries his own spirit familiars, or personal totems—small animals that he can pull from or rub out of his body to do his magic errands. And he possesses the power of removing, by the use of his mouth and hands, foreign objects from the sick person's body.

These are the typical feats that build the doctor's mystique, his reputation for magic. I shall not pause here to rationalize these miracles, except for one comment that, if I omitted it, would result in confusion for the student having a mental image of the healer as a histrionic shaman. It concerns the questions: How are these feats, magical claims, and conjuring compatible with his role as altruistic healer and guide of his community? Do they not suggest trance states and dissociative behaviors, as with the shaman?

The answer in part seems to be that the magical feats of the Aboriginal doctor are more honored in the breach than in the observance. A doctor with a solid reputation does not need to exploit magic, and does not do so, in the events of everyday practice. In these events, his reputation, experience, and authority suffice. He must judge when a demonstration of his magical powers is required; with luck, it may be infrequent. As to levitation, invisibility, translocation, and other feats that a Westerner refers to as magic, he has no concept of them as magic. When I have questioned the Aboriginal doctor about these feats, it is his *spirit* that was raised into the sky or crossed the plains like the wind. There is no inconsistency or impossibility about the acts of spirits in dreams; it should not surprise us that they go anywhere and do anything.

The native doctor is called upon by the people in situations which they cannot manage by themselves, or in which their course of action is doubtful. He is not called for minor ailments, for which first-aid procedures are generally known. Nor is he invariably called for the disorders of the very young or very old, which are so predictable that they are not commonly attributed to malign influence. He may not be called for the traditional traumatic hazards, from club or spear. However he is found at the hub of matters in poorly understood illnesses where a malign influence is suspected, such as sorcery or spirit intrusion. And he is involved in crises and social disturbances, which are usually accompanied by claims of sorcery. Thus he is involved in the control of antisocial behavior. He may also be involved in the control of antisocial nature—the bad weather or the failing supply of food. He is emphatically involved with the health hazards introduced by alien contact; but in this situation in which the people lack the natural immunities and therefore have a reduced fitness, his power and authority is waning. He is sabotaged not only by his loss of authority resulting from the general social disintegration, but by the two competing healing systems that now appear: the medical system from the bush nurse in her dispensary and the spiritual system from the missionary in his church.

DOCTORS OF DIFFERENT REGIONS

A sketch of some individual doctors known to me—most of whom may still be found in remote regions of Australia—will add reality to the composite "Identikit" picture just given. Here it will be just a few strokes of the brush—no portrait, but enough to dispel any impression that may have been given of uniformity and predictability about native doctors.

In Arnhem Land, where the Goyder River spills into the Arafura swamps, there is a grassy plain rich with bird and animal life. Here lives a horde of some thirty or forty Aboriginal adults and children. Their main contact with the outside world is the missionary who flies from Elcho Island every month or so in his Cessna. The leading man of the group is Djiburu, who is also the clever man, *marngitj*. (The word *marngi* means 'know'.) He received me freely when he found I was a doctor and knew something about his medicine. At my request, he sent for his doctor's bag *malaka*, and from its nest of wild kapok he drew his magic carved objects and demonstrated their use. He had great confidence in them, for preparing infusions for a sick man, or for pulling buffalo into the vicinity for food.

This Arnhem Land clever man says that he has X-ray vision that enables him to penetrate tree, cloud, or human body to determine the cause of the sickness. His power comes from healing spirit servants, called *gulun*. He relates that when a man is made a doctor, *gulun* stupefy him for five days, and while he is asleep they operate surgically, inserting a kangaroo fibula into his thigh, rubbing away the wound with water. On awakening, the man recognizes that he is now a *marngitj* because he can see through objects. He must now be a clever man and heal his people. He must employ his spirit servants, the *gulun*, to divine whether the illness is due to *raggalk* the sorcerer or to the body's possession by *mangata*, the disease spirit that lives in the swamp. His framework of belief is essentially a bipolar system of good and evil, not unlike medieval Christianity standing in opposition to Satanism. In Arnhem Land, the benevolent native doctor *marngitj* and his clever or healing spirits *gulun* stand opposed to the sorcerer *raggalk* and his henchman, the disease spirit *mangata*. Djiburu's little horde is mostly self-sufficient (though without the visits of the missionary I suspect they would regularly visit the main settlement for tobacco) and live in what seems reasonable health and harmony.

In the North Kimberley region of Western Australia near the mouth of the King Edward River is a pool called Tjindi. In this pool lives Ungur the rainbow serpent who personifies the healing power of the doctor. Ungur is the doctor's "assisting totem," in the phrase of Elkin (1933). When a boy is selected to be trained as a doctor, his induction includes rolling the scum of the pool into a pill, which is inserted into his navel. The scum is Ungur's spittle, and the pill is an egg, which hatches in the boy's belly. While it grows, the boy takes nothing hot to eat or drink for fear of disturbing it. Thenceforth the serpent is his servant and the embodiment of medical power. The stones at the bottom of Tjindi are *tjagolo*, Ungur's eggs, and only the native doctor dares dive for them. It is believed that these stones, by projection through the air, can produce sickness in a victim's body. Only the native doctor can exorcise them.

I once saw in the North Kimberley an old clever man remove a *tjagolo* from a sick man. With deliberate care, much spitting and breathing upon palms, much cracking of knuckles, he stroked toward the heart the arm veins of the patient, at the same time rolling a ball of nasal mucus and dust, which he finally produced as the offending *tjagolo*. It was an impressive performance. A sophisticated Aborigine who watched it said: "Of course you don't believe it. But you know what: That man get better. You know why: Make 'im glad, eat 'im tucker straight away. From his heart he feel glad and get better."

Going south to the Walbiri people on the western border of Northern Territory, I found that the rainbow serpent is important as a cause of disease but that the native doctor has a different assistant. This totem is a little animal called *mabanba*, living in the doctor's body and capable of being pulled out to go on diagnostic errands. *Mabanba* makes a little ticking sound around the camp that anyone may hear, but only the Walbiri doctor understands its message. One of the doctors was kind enough to draw me a picture of *mabanba*. The Walbiri doctor interprets some sickness as the result of human malevolence or sorcery. The agency of the malevolence is the *yarda* or poison stick, which is pointed at the victim during an incantation and assumed to inject its poison or itself into his body. Some suitably awe-inspiring specimens are in my collection at the University of New South Wales. Details of the Walbiri medical system are described in chapter 3.

For those looking for conceptual links, the Walbiri doctor has taken a step in diagnosis that was made in Western medicine only eighty years ago, with Breuer and Freud's *Studies on Hysteria* (1895). He recognizes that a symptom such as a paralyzed arm can have a motivational meaning for the patient, and not just a differential diagnostic meaning for the physician. Thus each Walbiri man believes he has a twin brother, who is invisible and watches over him in case he breaks some law, for example, if he commits a sacrilege or adultery. These spirit-counterparts, *millelba*, may cause their transgressing mortal brothers to fall ill. A native doctor, sensing the current of events in his people, can diagnose illness produced by *millelba*, spiritual projection of what a medico-legal mind might call conscience or a religious mind might call the soul.

THE SOCIAL FUNCTIONS OF THE DOCTOR

These beliefs and their functions will be described in more detail when we come to consider various communities in remote regions of Australia. At this stage, the point to be emphasized about them is that they represent the mainstream of knowledge and thought in these cultures. The native doctor's functions are ordained by his

society. He is the socially appointed interpreter of illness, sometimes in medical terms, sometimes in legal. He uses sickness as a
lever to induce social conformity. We will return to this point, for
it sets him apart from the healer of today. Indeed, I am not sure
that we should call healing, or therapy, his main function. True,
healing must have been a different matter in the traditional Australian disease pattern, before the recent advent of diseases such as
tuberculosis. He is as unfitted to cope with these illnesses as was
modern medicine until a few years ago.

Delaying his inevitable decline is a powerful regressive tendency
in his society. Aborigines have had a look at the European Australian way of life, and many are not sure they want it, or could
attain it if they did. They continue to respect old ways and seek
their old doctor. But he is sabotaged from within, by the changing
social character of Aborigines themselves; how can one continue to
be a faith healer when the faith of one's flock becomes fragmented?
This generation of bush Aborigines did not experience consistent
training, by rewards and punishments, in the beliefs of the world,
Aboriginal's or white man's. The Walbiri medicine man laments that
his servant *mabanba* has lost its potency, poisoned by the aspirin
from the whitefellow's sick bay. What is happening has been expressed by Matthew Arnold:

> The Sea of Faith
> Was once, too, at the full, and round earth's shore
> Lay like the folds of a bright girdle furled.
> But now I only hear
> Its melancholy, long, withdrawing roar.
>   [*Dover Beach*]

What is this faith that recedes when needed? Few physicians
consider that a patient's faith in a physician is entirely or even
mostly rational—the just reward of his merit! Physicians' symbolic
roles, still partially retained in modern society—healer, teacher,
scientist, priest—are all ambivalently regarded by their people. At
the one extreme, patients are capable of regarding physicians as
good parents, watchful shepherds, painstaking teachers, benevolent
magicians. At the other extreme, they fantasy that they are self-
interested, aloof, exploiting, hostile; so they do not take their medi-

cine or advice, or if they do, develop reactions unconsciously de-signed to thwart their physicians and make them feel guilty. Such extremists die young, or become the sickest patients. These atti-tudes are all part of the primary data of patients and comprise what Freud called transference—transference to the physician of atti-tudes that properly belong to figures in the patient's world when a child. Erikson (1950) suggests that basic trust in existence comes from the childhood experience that the breast will be provided if the child is hungry, that mother will come to the rescue if the child is hurt or frightened, that the big people are consistent and depend-able. This "original" faith tends to be repeated in later-life situa-tions unconsciously, though it may be developed into a formulated faith, or absence of faith.

Transference to the healer of trusting and expectant attitudes makes faith healing possible. This is where lay healers deceive themselves when they attribute their therapy to their theoretical systems—of Scientology, pentecostal, chiropractic, homeopathy, hypnosis. Modern physicians are equally deceived when they fail to recognize the transference aspects of their transactions with patients. The lay healer of today differs from the native doctor in his inability to use the knowledge available in the culture. Because he does not have access to the full extent of available science, he is less responsible to society. He may be responsible to a minority that finds itself in various ways at odds with society. But the Aboriginal tribal doctor is educated in his culture, its religion, and its interper-sonal nuances. Elkin (1954) calls him an Aboriginal man of high degree. At best, he holds a position of responsibility to society not inferior to that shared by the medical and legal professions of to-day, although of a different quality.

As I foreshadowed, the work of the primitive doctor is not limited to healing by faith. He is also an influencer of behavior. Jerome D. Frank (1961) compared modern psychotherapy with faith healing and with thought reform, extracting the common features such as expectation of relief by the sufferer and use of status and coercion by the influencer. Significantly, Frank entitled his book *Persuasion and Healing* rather than *Healing and Persua-sion;* the influencer, as the agent of the larger group, is primarily committed to producing a desirable behavioral change in the sub-

·ject. When a person falls sick the Australian native doctor has many diagnostic alternatives, depending not on the sickness itself, but on the social context and the doctor's obligation in it. Is it sorcery from introjection of a foreign object "sung" into the body by the incantation of an ill-wisher? Is it possession by spirits, of whom Aborigines identify a legion, or by devil animals, of which they know a whole menagerie? Is it attention by social avengers, the anonymous and invisible executors of retaliatory sanctions, appointed by the elders? Is it the man's own spirit-counterpart or soul? Let us suppose that the doctor decides that the illness is due to interference by the spirit-counterpart. The diagnosis is not made randomly or haphazardly, but from an intimate knowledge of the man's life and transgressions. In this situation there is less need for exploratory interviewing than in the Western clinic, for the doctor usually knows the story already. Spirit-counterparts are mostly concerned with infringements of religious laws. Cases I have seen include a man who was planning to make a boomerang and cut down a tree growing in some other man's territory; the spirit-counterpart sang his shoulder sore. Another man ignorantly restored, in preparation for a ceremony, a cave painting not belonging to his own subsection or "skin." He should have known better; the spirit-counterpart did not overlook it. If the infringement is not serious, the doctor may persuade the spirit-counterpart to quit the victim's body after a week or two. If it is serious, a life may be forfeit.

Examining this system from the Western point of view, we note that the threat of sickness is exploited by the doctor as an inducement to the patient and to others to conform and integrate themselves to society. Illnesses are thus closely linked with social exchanges and with laws; the doctor operates within this framework. It is open to question how specifically he appreciates these linkages; it would be safer to say that he works a system that has evolved to meet requirements of the rules that govern his people. An essential feature of such a system, if it is not to be applied in a haphazard manner that would disintegrate society rather than cement it, is that it is based on a knowledge of interpersonal events and domestic detail. In this respect at least, the native doctor must be a family doctor and a family solicitor. This comes easily to Aborigines, perhaps especially to the shrewd and manipulative people who become doctors. Aborigines are intensely interested in families, kinships, and relationships. They are preoccupied, even fascinated, by kinship arrangements so complex that people have described Aborigines as sociological geniuses.

Whatever the justice of that claim, there is little doubt of the native doctor's effectiveness in carrying out the medico-legal rules governing society. He is not specially concerned with materia medica or medicaments, though herbal infusions are used for diarrhea and constipation, nor with what Rivers (1926) calls primitive household remedies, such as incision for snakebite. These remedies are the property of the people as a whole, and the special province of the old women, who correspond with the trained nurse in Western society. The Aboriginal doctor is rather the socially appointed interpreter of sickness, privy to a system that has evolved not merely to explain the occurrence of sickness and to treat it—as with Hippocratic medicine—but to exploit it in order to conserve the cohesiveness and integrity of the people. Impelled by these objectives, his practice reveals to Western eyes individual cruelties, incongruities, and failures. His system is also affected by personal factors in his own character structure. Aborigines are as open to exploitation by unscrupulous and ambitious medical men as any other branch of humanity.

As a description of activities so subtly and effectively evolved and developed, the term "primitive" hardly seems adequate. To state the general conclusion, primitive medicine and the law is weak on disease and behavioral entities, but strong on family orientation, influencing behavior, and forestalling conflicts. Though it has little technology, it has other features that modern Western society might envy and even strive to recapture.

Before further comment is made on the nature of primitive medicine, it is important to examine the sources of information more closely, on a regional, cultural, and ecological basis.

CHAPTER THREE

The Law of the Desert

DESERT ABORIGINES developed a system of medical practice that contributes to the policing of behavior; it is part of the special law of the desert. We shall see that much of the activity of native doctors in these regions is directed at social control and law enforcement rather than at relieving the sufferer. Opportunities came for me in 1964 and 1965 to visit Yuendumu, a Walbiri settlement 180 air miles northwest of Alice Springs in central Australia. My commission, sponsored by the Australian Institute of Aboriginal Studies, was to study Aboriginal medicine in a tribal setting.

What is called a Stone Age culture from the evidence of archaeology when seen in the living flesh is a wood culture. The stone artifacts that survive the passage of time are inconspicuous, merely the tips of the tools that fashion the wooden objects that provide the basis of the material culture. Walbiri territory is in an arid zone (average annual rainfall five to ten inches) but not in a desert in the common conception of shifting sandhills devoid of vegetation. The dominant tree is the hardwood mulga (*Acacia aneura*) growing to ten feet, or as high as thirty in areas of moister soil.

The basic material for these Aborigines' implements, mulga is becoming less prevalent due to the introduction of cattle, which eat the young saplings. Of the wide variety of other trees that provide the material of the wood culture, the most conspicuous are "ghost" gums, eucalypts whose milky white trunks stand out in the normally dry water courses. The plains between the rugged hills are covered by expanses of porcupine grass, tufts locally called spinifex. This country is difficult for walking, but Aborigines develop a horny layer on the soles of their feet. The desert bird, animal, and vegetable life that provided the Walbiri hordes with food are depicted in a fine color film *So They Did Eat* (Campbell et al. 1954).

The Walbiri are one of the most important peoples of central Australia, if only because of their numbers. The country that they regard as their own extends for about two hundred miles around the central western border of the Northern Territory. Their contact with white society is comparatively recent and is for the most part centered upon four government settlements developed after World War II, at Hooker Creek, Warrabri, Yuendumu, and Papunya. Nomadic people with no previous white contact are even today arriving at some settlements, notably Pintubi people from the west coming to Papunya. The Walbiri are in a shock phase of cessation of their hunting and foraging existence. At Yuendumu they live in temporary brush shelters within camps stationed outside the settlement compound. Eventually they are to occupy simple huts, to be built in a village after the Western manner. A population recorded here at 350 in 1954 exceeded 700 in 1964 and was estimated at 1,000 in 1970. The rate of increase shows no sign of slackening.

These Aborigines are faced with serious hazards. As though the sudden enforced relinquishment of their way of life were not problem enough, they are burdened by an imbalance between population and economy. The population explosion of this decade highlights the lack of industry, especially in the arid zone—one of many factors that offset the development of a healthy social personality. It is a stumbling block for the small army of people trying to pave the way for Aborigines on settlements, missions, cattle stations or ranches, and in towns.

Since the intention of this chapter is to describe the Walbiri medico-legal system, problems of alien contact will be deferred until later chapters. Case histories of maladaptation among the Walbiri will be found in chapter 10, where the traditional classification of illness is juxtaposed with the modern. Also omitted from this chapter are detailed case histories illustrating sorcery, which are in chapter 6, and histories illustrating intrusion by spirits, in chapter 7. When discussion is restricted to the phenomena of disease as expounded by tribal informants, a predictable response from my clinical colleagues will be: "How do you know your native doctor is reliable? How do you know that what he tells you represents the accepted belief and practice of his people? In his attempts to please you, and get rewarded for it, he may be on a mere flight of fancy or feel involved in a story-telling competition." The problem of reliability of the informant is well known; books have been written without regard to it. I was determined to try to overcome the objection so far as possible by utilizing several informants independently and afterwards correlating their information. Using this procedure, matching information was more likely to represent accepted belief, unmatching information to be idiosyncratic.

THE WALBIRI DOCTORS

In order to impose this control upon the investigation, information provided by each native doctor was compared with information provided by the others. To this end, eight Walbiri doctors at Yuendumu were identified and interrogated in their usual context —in the settlement, in the camp, and out in the bush. Since English was inadequate for the purpose, several other Walbiri men were employed as interpreters.

The Walbiri doctors were seen separately. I interviewed them, leaving my assistant Dr. M. A. Kidson free to interrupt to clarify issues that seemed unclear to him. We each kept a notebook of the proceedings and recorded a considerable amount of the material on tape. The data were then sifted for internal consistency. The account presented here of the medical system represents information provided by the majority of the native doctors. Private or eccentric ideas, where recorded, are noted with the informant's name.

Among the Walbiri there are no prescribed rites and ordeals through which a doctor must pass in his novitiate, in contrast to the situation at Kalumburu (chapter 4). The office of doctor is dependent on the possession of the *mabanba*, and this is usually inherited. Shorty Tjangala has been busy with sickness since he was a boy being taught by his doctor father. One night when his father was nearly "finished," the *mabanba* was transferred to Shorty; he saw it for the first time, transparent as glass, soft as rubber. Barney Tjangala's father was a doctor before him, and he himself became a doctor as a young man. The story of his *mabanba* is a flamboyant one, as might be anticipated from Barney's personality. While he slept, a star shot from the midnight sky, pierced his side, and deposited *mabanba;* he showed me the patches of depigmented skin on his chest left by the sparks. His perception of the threat to his status by modern medicine is also to be found on his chest; the surgical scar made by the white doctors in Alice Springs (for the relief of empyema) represented to him an attempt to steal his *mabanba.* Maurice Tjungarai was taught medicine as a boy by his father, the aged Tjapaltjari; according to Maurice, his father would take him to see sick people and say: "You're a doctor like me. Try to rub 'em like me. Sing 'em like me." George Tjambitjimba, on the other hand, acquired his doctor status when a grown man working on a Mount Doreen cattle station. The *mabanba* came and he felt it jump in his belly. An old doctor came and confirmed its presence, because he heard a ticking sound inside George's belly. The apprenticeship was brief: "We go see the sick people, George, and try you out."

The characters of the Walbiri doctors fit the typology of altruistic, mystic, and sociopathic suggested in chapter 2. There is no suggestion that they earned their position through any longstanding personality disturbance—neurotic, psychotic, or hysteric—as suggested for the shamans of the arctic regions (vide the work of Ackerknecht 1942; and the discussion of Devereux and Opler 1961). One of the Walbiri doctors might be designated an aggressive sociopath and another suffered an involutional paranoid state. But the latter has not functioned as a doctor since his psychosis became apparent, and he is not included in the series of this chapter. He is described as a member of the "exceptional family" in chapter 10.

These Walbiri doctors are probably no more impelled by motives of profit or power than are modern doctors. At the same time there is no point of paying their character undue respect: they are not all "men of high degree," in Elkin's (1945) phrase. Some are more resourceful than others, and some are more scrupulous. Rose (1957) emphasized their magical powers such as telepathy, clairvoyance, and extrasensory perception; Elkin (1945) more than hinted at them. I have not been impressed with the need for supernatural explanations of their activities. There seems no reason to dismiss categories of natural causation just because explanations of magical phenomena are not immediately apparent. The clues may be unintentionally or deliberately concealed, usually for some pertinent social purpose. This is a rationalistic approach, but it does not make the phenomena less valid and worthy of study, nor detract from the credibility of these doctors.

Social pressures at Yuendumu are strongly arrayed against the native doctor. The missionary, while displaying a supportive interest in the traditional culture, feels obliged to oppose segments of it that collide with Christian education. He told me, for example, that when he heard the distant tones of a bullroarer slinging his church service held in the bush, he had no choice but to tell the men that if the noise did not stop, he would reveal its source to the children. This put the men on the spot: the bullroarer's sound, ostensibly the awesome voice of the rainbow serpent, is produced by whirling a sacred board secretly in the bush. Hearing the voice of the serpent, women and children would normally leave the vicinity to leave the men to their mysterious business. The lay superintendent, so far as he was able, bought up the local stock of poison or sorcery sticks, described in chapter 2. The sister in charge of nursing services for this region leads the strongest opposition of all. She sees bungling therapy that she rightly condemns and ridicules; she has many examples to relate. One native doctor, she says, had a boil on his thigh converted to a carbuncle by the sucking of a fellow practitioner. Another doctor blew into the ear of a child with otitis media. In her belief, Barney Tjangala exceeds the other doctors in his persistent zeal; she suspects that several babies brought to her in a shocked condition have been subject to his interference. He has the Walbiri counterpart of the "furor therapeuticus" found in some modern physicians.

The Walbiri themselves, though far from forsaking their doctors, patronize the settlement sick bay as well. At least half of the native doctors rationalize their situation as a decline in the potency of their assisting totem, the *mabanba*. George Tjambitjimba says that his *mabanba* was taken by Pintubi doctors, who have most of them now. Maurice Tjungarai says he lost his to an Aboriginal doctor during an illness that he contracted from a devil animal in the Lake Nash country on the Queensland border. Others say that their *mabanba* is weakened by the white doctor's pills, or worn out with curing the sick, or gone home to Nunggaitji, *mabanba* country out west where the Pintubi people live.

No new doctors are being trained. There appears to be only one novice or postulant, Tommy Tjambitjimba, aged thirteen years, styled "Dr. Hargrave" at the settlement because of his aspirations —after John Hargrave, distinguished Northern Territory physician who specializes in leprosy. He does not appear to interest the other doctors; his status is doubtful in the general social disintegration. His knowledge of Walbiri medical lore is negligible and his main activity appears to be giving comforting rubbings and suckings for pain. During my visits to Yuendumu he appeared disturbed in personality: speechless before white people, inattentive at school, dull and dreamy about the settlement. Was his dedication a form of altruism? A transition of the sort confronting tribal Aborigines cannot be accomplished rapidly, nor without its crop of maladaptation and maladjustment. It is a vastly complex process for the abstractions and assumptions such as I shall outline in this chapter to be replaced by modern abstractions that include external government, Christianity, British-style law, industry, and modern medicine.

A few of the more successfully bicultural individuals are beginning to function as archivists, preserving under some encouragement the language and arts of the people. Several Yuendumu doctors, the repository of beliefs reported here, are making effective contact with white people. Their elder statesman, Tjapaltjari, makes every effort to establish rapport with interested investigators. Shorty Tjangala is an expert maker—and seller—of wooden artifacts. The brush windbreak outside his camp is stacked with native tools like a carpenter's tool board. Barney Tjangala and Barney Tjapannanga together work a low-grade copper lode in a mine out in the bush. I have known Barney Tjangala to suck out "bad blood" from intact skin and before the skin was dry climb back into his trench to fossick the green rocks. Maurice Tjungarai is a mechanic in the settlement garage; being younger, he is less secure in tradition and will be more subject to the tensions of marginality—so often solaced in Aborigines by alcohol.

These Walbiri doctors continue to practice, though clandestinely, and the people turn to them in times of stress. This is a pre-

dictable pattern, one that modern medicine and law should anticipate. The Walbiri doctor is at the center of affairs in times of
sickness or social crises, assisted by his familiar spirit or totem, the
mabanba. He usually interprets and so manipulates the situation in
one of four ways, two of which are patently "legalistic" in the
modern sense, and two "medical." The legal interpretation involves
retaliatory sanctions by the *millelba,* the soul and spirit-counterpart, and by the *tjanba,* the executioners or social avengers appointed by the elders to punish transgressions. The medical interpretations involve either possession of the victim's body by *mamul*
and other evil spirits or introjection of solid foreign objects, the
yarda, through sorcery. The doctors are the socially appointed experts in interpreting the drama of sickness in these terms.

Mabanba, THE DOCTOR'S FAMILIAR

Mabanba are conceived of as small beings, the size of a thumb-
nail, that live in the doctor's body. Invisible to the uninitiated, they
appear to the doctor as clear or white in color, like stones or crystals of quartz. Magic stones or crystals are widespread in Aboriginal medicine, for example, the *tjagolo* of the Kimberleys (see chapter 4). But the *mabanba* at Yuendumu are soft like gum and possess
animal qualities. All the doctors affirm that *mabanba* have a little
voice that makes a ticking noise resembling that of a clock; everyone in the camp may hear it, but only a doctor understands its
speech. Though without limbs or wings, *mabanba* can travel
speedily through the air or under the ground. Their resting position is in the doctor's belly, arms, chest, and head, where the elder
Tjapaltjari depicted them lying along the "strings" (fiber tracts?)
of the brain. I have seen the doctor extract them for action by
"pulling" them, rubbing and stroking his body in the presence of
the patient. They function as the embodiment of the doctor's art
in diagnosis, therapy, and prevention.

While *mabanba* are usually started on their diagnostic errand by
the doctor pulling and casting them, they may act on their own
initiative. George Tjambitjimba says that his *mabanba* flies about
the camp like a butterfly, eavesdropping until it detects the culprit
in a "singing" (incantation) whereupon it flies back into his head
to tell him. When the source of the illness (whether sorcery or an

evil being) is thought to be at some distance, the doctor places his
mabanba upon his *pigiri* (spearthrower) and casts it toward points
on the horizon. Each time the little messenger returns ~~unsuccessful~~,
the doctor catches it and systematically casts it again in a fresh direction. Eventually it fails to return, indicating that it has found the
source of the trouble. To this spot, perhaps two miles away, the
doctor may run and gather bushes for a therapeutic application to
the sick person's body.

Doctors also apply their *mabanba* directly to the patient's body
by rubbing or insertion. For example, after taking a poison stick
from the mouth of a victim of incantation, the doctor will plug
with his *mabanba* the hole in the belly through which the poison
stick entered. For *wongamara* (insanity arising from being sung),
the *mabanba* is inserted into the temples to search and destroy the
snake or scorpion that has been sung into the brain. Barney Tjangala says he owns two kinds of *mabanba*, one which he depicts
shaped like a liver fluke, the other like a worm. The plump one
looks into people to find the bad blood. The thin one enters people
for a few days to treat them. Barney gave an impressive demonstration of the art of sucking out bad blood detected in this way. Sucking the skin of my arm, he spat several ounces of bright blood
mixed with saliva on to a stone, then quickly turned the stone over.
Responding to a polite request, Barney revealed the small flake of
stone in his mouth that had been pressed by his tongue to cut his
palate.

The doctor may protect his people against danger and sickness
by use of the versatile *mabanba*. In the dead of night, *mabanba*'s
ticking warns him of the approach of a devil animal. The rainbow
serpent bows to its power in several myths. Alex Wilson, a part-
Aboriginal stockman, says that a waterhole at Vaughan Springs is
never used because it is inhabited by *wanayara*, the rainbow serpent. If the serpent ventures out to attack the people, he must be
driven back into the water by the doctor and his *mabanba*. At Jay
Creek there is a big hill, Elwada, with a waterhole where the doctor, Maurice Tjungarai, as a boy, saw *wanayara* rise. The immense
snake, searching for people to eat, arched from the water into a
bright cloud and back down to earth. Maurice relates with conviction the rainbow's destruction: "I pull *mabanba*, cut him all along

[margin, left top:] like Noah's doves!

[margin, left lower:] aggressive quality of habitat & man's defense

[margin, bottom:] perhaps already a feature of H.G (Colin Turnbull's *Forest* may be romanticized) & increased in hostileut.

the belly, he fall down dead in the same place." Barney Tjangala pulls his *mabanba* to cut off the rain and scare the cloud. George Tjambitjimba pulls his *mabanba* to cut off the chill wind that smothers people in red dust. The protective functions of *mabanba*, though wide, do not apply to every contingency. Some are outside the scope of the doctors. Rainmaking itself is a specialty, the province of a separate official, the rainmaker *napajukulba*. The cooling of the too-fierce sun in summer is traditionally done by the old people placing a *purudja*, a miniature baby's cradle, in the path of its rays at sunset, to reduce the sun's power on the next day.

In the account of northern (Hooker Creek) Walbiri by Meggitt (1955), the Aboriginal doctor is said to have two kinds of objects in his body to carry out his functions, a crystal and a lizard. But the southern Walbiri doctors at Yuendumu are unanimous in that they have but one, and that is enough: the versatile *mabanba* of The Dreaming. *Mabanba* embodies the omnipotence of doctors, as the object psychology of the people requires, and organizes it into a comprehensive system.

INTRUSION BY EVIL SPIRITS

Walbiri thought renders concrete the idea of evil by transforming it into devil animals or malevolent spirits capable of intruding into the body to produce sickness, madness, and death. Here the Walbiri show their accustomed ethnocentricity. With one exception, the Walbiri doctors disclaim that there are any devil animals belonging to their country. They belong to Pintubi country to the west, or to Lake Nash country to the east. But because Pintubi people are now coming to live in Walbiri territory, bringing their disease spirits with them, Yuendumu Walbiri do not venture near Pintubi camps at night. The one exception I heard to the ethnocentric view came from the aged Tjapaltjari, who recalled that in the old days there was a Walbiri devil called *tjakorrolba*. He depicted it in the sand as a limbless being with a large head of many horns; it was a quiet devil that did not make the people sick, but scared them as it walked the camp at night.

The devil animals feared by the Walbiri are named *mamul, ginggi, tju-tju, kokolba,* and *kadili-kadili,* all differing in appearance and unpleasant habits. They are the figures of a complex mythology to explain disease. *Mamul*, for example, is a dingolike being that burrows furiously under the ground, bursting out to bite his victim's belly and snare his kidney fat. The doctor's job is to restore the kidney fat, replacement of which leaves no mark, any more than its removal does. Babies are favorite subjects for *mamul*'s kidney-fat snatching. The aged Tjapaltjari recalls that in his days of active healing practice, he would project his *mabanba* under the ground with a blow from his spearthrower to find *mamul* and bring back the kidney fat while he, Tjapaltjari, held the victim. Sometimes *mamul* changes his form to that of a worm about a foot long so that it can enter the victim's thighs and pass into the abdomen to attack the kidney fat. The two relatively sophisticated part-Aboriginal station hands at Mount Doreen, Jack Cusack and Alex Wilson, claim to have seen a doctor extract *mamul* by sucking the sick man's mouth. It was night in the camp, but the doctor held it up like a tapeworm for all to see before he dropped it in the fire.

In contrast with the stealthy devil animals, large and fierce man-eaters are described. *Kadili-kadili* has its lair in a limestone cave at the boundary of Walbiri country. It can travel underground with two or three terrible companions. Those who venture from Walbiri country and fail to return have probably become its prey. It can drag a man from his horse and devour him. Jack Cusack related that Walbiri men who drove or muster with him in this country will not leave his side for fear of it.

Dr. Kidson and I obtained a large quantity of information about malevolent spirits. It need not be elaborated here. The distinctions between these embodiments of evil were not essential, and the details perhaps subject to embroidery by individuals. Their psychological significance seems that they represent the idea of evil, non-human and unpredictable, the adversary of man, waiting to attack him.

INTROJECTION OF SOLID OBJECTS

Equalling the importance of nonhuman evil as a source of sickness for the Walbiri is human malevolence or sorcery, expressed by incantation with the aid of *yarda*, the poison stick. Belief in the power of incantation is so strong in the Walbiri that the doctors were reluctant to discuss the formulas with me because of their fear of harm resulting. Only when some professional relationship developed, as between Walbiri and Sydney doctors, was information revealed.

The common *yarda* or poison stick is a mulga wood blade three to nine inches long, with pointed ends. Transverse markings indicate the time sequence for its action: four marks means that four days will elapse before death or sickness ensues. On the first day such a stick is sung into the victim's belly, on the second and third it travels through the body, on the fourth it lodges in the heart. A hole burned beside the fourth mark represents the grave.

Poison sticks of special power and danger were rumored by the Walbiri. After much conversation and many requests, Shorty Tjangala took me away from the camp to inspect such a *yarda*. We found it wrapped in rags, hidden in dead brush in the porcupine grass under a lone corkwood tree. The doctor unwrapped it with great care, alarmed when I crossed its point or essayed to touch it. Its dagger-shaped blade of pearl shell presumably came from the coastal trade route and is attached to a thirty-inch length of red Walbiri hair-string by a mass of *palja*, the spinifex gum. The doctor explained that the hair-string encircles the singer's left arm so that his blood injects the *yarda*'s poison. He was painfully anxious lest by showing it he harm me, and it was pointless to invite him to sing the *yarda* song for the benefit of my tape recorder and, ultimately, for the archives.

In a secluded ceremonial camp at Yuendumu, guarded by two old men, I saw a treasury of sacred objects. Secreted in one tree was a bag containing a cord headdress, resembling that of the Arabs, together with ten kangaroo fibulas, used only for singing the kangaroo to make him lie down, according to the informant. Human ulnas are saved for a parallel purpose, but were not shown to me.

The possibility of private incantation by individuals with a grudge gives rise to widespread fear and suspicion. The victim is said to learn of his fate by means of the passage of a rumor through the group, so that everybody is familiar with his predicament before the whispers reach him. But the Walbiri doctors are quick to stress that they are associated only with judicial singing, sanctioned as penalty for transgressions such as adultery or sacrilege. A characteristic of Walbiri sorcery belief is that it is not regularly attributed to nameless malefactors outside the tribe. It is a form of interpersonal activity by aggrieved individuals, creating a climate of insecurity, suspicion, fear, and revenge. When more closely studied, its importance seems to lie less in its actual occurrence than in the fact that it provides the favored rationalization of human anxiety. A factual study of sorcery sequences as they actually occurred is presented in chapter 6.

THE SPIRIT-COUNTERPART, GUARDIAN OF THE SACRED OBJECTS

Each Yuendumu man has a twin or spirit-counterpart of the same kin and physiognomy living and hunting in the cave country in the hills, together with his wives, children, and dogs. These spirit-counterparts are called *millelba*. Being invisible, *millelba* wear no clothes; only their dogs and their camp fires at night can be seen. The Ngama caves near Yuendumu, containing sacred paintings, are populated by *millelba*, who are present also in the "special business," or ceremonial, camp.

Here is discernible a socially significant belief: *millelba* are the moral figures in The Dreaming. Their chief concern is the custody of *yarindalba*, the sacred ceremonial objects,[1] and the tools used to make them. Sickness is inflicted by *millelba* to enforce respect for the sacred engraved boards. If a man trespasses into country where the sacred objects are concealed, his *millelba* watches him from the rocks, and may sing the Ngama cave-painting snake, Tjugurba Wana, to bite him as punishment. This punishment is usually limited in severity; after the *millelba* considers it enough, the snake is revoked. It is an explanation that is applied to injuries that appear self-evident to Western eyes.

George Tjambitjimba disclosed that he was chopping a mulga tree near the caves to make himself a boomerang. A sudden pain in the shoulder made George realize that the tree he was chopping was *millelba*'s shade tree, and that *millelba* had sung the snake into his shoulder. George was three weeks in Alice Springs hospital having injections into his shoulder before *millelba* relented and removed the snake. On another occasion, Left-hand Tjupurula was touching

---

[1] Commonly called in Australia *churinga*, after the Aranda (of Alice Springs) term for them.

up the cave painting of the snake, a privilege that belonged to the other patrimoiety; he should have known better. Left-hand Tjupu-rula fell sick, a sickness that was lifted by *millelba* in forgiveness two weeks later.

The native doctor who diagnoses an ailment inflicted by *millelba* makes no effort to treat it. It is a justly imposed penalty for dese-cration against the sacred life by *millelba*, spiritual projection of Walbiri religious conscience.

THE APPOINTED EXECUTIONERS

Another law-enforcing agency of sickness or death envisaged by the Walbiri, and the final one to be outlined here, is the *tjanba*. *Tjanba*, at Yuendumu at least, are mortal avengers, comparable with the *kurdaitcha* of the Aranda people around Alice Springs. If any support were needed of the assertion of Tindale (1961) that the Walbiri are an emerging dominant group embracing more than one original tribe, such as the Ngalia from the southward, it may be recognized here. In their *tjanba* practice the Yuendumu people show southern affinities. In the northern Walbiri, recorded by Meggitt (1955) at Hooker Creek, *tjanba* are nonhuman devils. At Yuendumu, *tjanba* is a role assigned to men elected by the elders to carry out a judicial incantation or, sometimes, execution.

Tjanba participation in Yuendumu ceremonies, for example at initiations, ensures that his dread function and appearance are fa-miliar. At Yuendumu, a *tjanba* camp is situated at one edge of the secluded mulga scrub containing the "secret business" camp and initiation arena. Here the three to six appointed *tjanba* men make their private preparations. A headdress of brush and eagle feathers, knee boots and gloves of emu feathers, and ochre and charcoal em-bellishments upon the naked trunk comprise the costume. Entrance at the ceremony is late, contrived for the greatest possible effect of awe. The *tjanba* camp has special sacred objects, the most charac-teristic being the small daggerlike bullroarer *mana baganu* used for harmful incantations. Some *tjanba* songs recorded for us by Phar Lap Tjapangati prickle with fear: "*Tjanba* man comes from far away/he's close to you now as that tree." One song proffers good advice: "*Tjanba* stalks you/sing the feathers off his shoes." Much in the way that Western boys come to terms with violence playing cops and robbers, little Yuendumu boys play *tjanba,* dressed in a modified version of the regalia.

In the serious *tjanba* business of execution, the doctors' stories are consistent. A normally clad confederate lures the victim into the bush. The *tjanba* men, shod in shoes making them invisible in The Dreaming and disguising their footprints on the ground, lie in ambuscade. Execution still occurs in this way. The missionary at Yuendumu, Mr. Fleming, recalls that ten years ago, Jim, the son of Tjapaltjari, was murdered in the bush by *tjanba.* When the boy's body was exhumed, it was found that his neck had been broken. The story was given out that Tjapaltjari had made a serious mistake over a ceremony so that the life of his son was forfeited. Such is the dread of *tjanba* that rumor of their singing may be almost as effective as their onslaught. By repute, they attack a sleeping man, and without waking him, dislocate his neck; the man awakens and goes about his business, succumbing a few days later when he learns what has happened to him. The aged Tjapaltjari related that in bygone days a doctor might adopt the *tjanba* costume to enter hostile country alone and unseen, turning back only if a snake crossed his path. But individual use of the *tjanba* role is improper in the view of the other doctors, who deny that it can be practiced by an individual to further his malice or vendetta. In their view, the *tjanba* is the executioner of the council of elders in its employ of death or sickness as its penalties.

DATA IN SEARCH OF A THEORY

The study of a culture's medical and legal patterns is fruitfully approached through the functionalist tradition in anthropology, associated with the theories of Radcliffe-Brown, Evans-Pritchard, and Malinowski, that held that social units are kept stable by sets of complementary institutions (Radcliffe-Brown 1952). Alternatively, the relationship of these cultural patterns to the personality may be scrutinized, as in the work of Kardiner (1945), Benedict (1934), and their many successors. Again, a psychoanalyst would be impressed by the mental mechanisms utilized by this people to contain the conflicts that occur between inner drives and the world they live in. In these mechanisms, the projection of solid objects and their internalization predominate. The mechanisms are perhaps of special interest to object psychology: the solid objects personify both superego functions (*millelba* and *tjanba*) and id functions (*yarda* and *mamul*).

The clinician finds that even sophisticated Aborigines in time of sickness live in a world of assumptions about incantations, introjected solid objects, doctor's familiars, malevolent spirits, moral spirit-counterparts, and appointed avengers. Western medicine is revolutionary, constantly innovating, with a broad growing edge represented by a range of scientific disciplines. Hence one cannot look to modern medicine for a steady yardstick to evaluate primitive medicine; the interpretation of these phenomena inevitably varies according to the scientific theory of the day and according to the particular scientific discipline employed for the purpose.

But since we shall learn more about the medicine and law of the Walbiri of the desert from a comparison with that of the Pela of the North Kimberley seacoast, it would be wise to defer our theoretical formulations.

CHAPTER FOUR

Medicine of the Coast

JULES HENRY, in *Culture against Man* (1963), developed the idea that "psychosis is the final outcome of all that is wrong with a culture." Without pursuing Henry's thesis here in a systematic manner, it is nevertheless instructive to begin a study of the North Kimberley Aborigines of Western Australia by describing a psychosis that reflects the strains both of the culture and the culture change.

Umulumbri, a native doctor and songman, was suffering from an involutional paranoid state when I visited the North Kimberley region of Western Australia in 1963. He was aged about sixty years, six feet three inches tall, and of distinguished appearance, but thin and morose. He was one of the few who did not smile for the camera; as I write I am looking at his photograph showing his withdrawn, peevish frown. He had changed in personality a few years previously, giving up his participation in social activities and ceremonies. I had noted in my casebook:

> Some nights he complains that something pokes him in the back while he sleeps. He thinks it is an evil charm, a stone that somebody has thrown. He then raves all night. He brings out his spears and threatens everybody in the camp. He accuses the others of talking about him, swearing at him for being a bad man with women. He accuses them of casting *tjagolo* [magic stones] at him. Last year without warning he fled to the hills, keeping a course over stony country so that he would not be tracked. It took the search party days to find him and bring him back to the village. The village people call him *wambaba* [mad]. They behave unresponsively when he is in his violent moods. He was not like this before in his life.

During talks in the village I was able to establish some rapport with Umulumbri. I used an interpreter of the Pela language since his English was very limited. The villagers were broadly correct in their diagnosis of *wambaba;* this was a case of involutional paranoid melancholia. As might be expected, primitive people usually have little difficulty distinguishing paranoid illness from complaints of sorcery. The disturbed symptoms responded to my tranquillizing medication, chlorpromazine. He began to eat and to socialize more. Behind the statement of a medical diagnosis, one tried to formulate the adjustment problem of an Aboriginal leader deprived of his former social adequacy and offices because of the alien intrusion. Wittkower (1969) has emphasized role deprivation as one of the stress factors in transcultural psychiatry. Spanish Benedictine monks in 1908 established a mission in the North Kimberley region of Australia, and after some changes in site, consolidated it at the Kalumburu pool. The seven original tribes of the area, described by one of the missionaries (Hernandez 1940; 1941; 1961), are now disbanded and its members congregate at the mission. Most people know their old tribal affiliations, but the main distinctions are between Kulari people who derive from the northwest, Kuini who come from the southeast, and the Walambi from the west. For convenience, I shall refer to them collectively as Pela, the name of the most widely spoken vernacular. No roads reach the mission through the maze of rocky gorges that separate it from the northern towns of Western Australia. Inland lies mesa country, desolate but beautiful. The nearest white settler is twenty miles away and his influence on the Aborigines is negligible. Despite this extreme isolation from other European Australians, the impact of the Spanish mission cannot be underestimated. It will be evaluated later in this chapter. Here, it is sufficient to say that after fifty years of mission contact, the kinship laws are in almost complete eclipse, and there has been no systematic tribal initiation for thirty years.

In order to appreciate this cosmology, some knowledge of the setting is needed. There is a pool called Tjindi, a traditional Aboriginal meeting place some five miles from the mouth of the King Edward River that flows into Napier-Broome Bay and the Timor Sea. The pool is a fine stretch of fresh water, which remains well filled through the dry season. It is set in an alluvial plain covered by savannah woodland supporting prolific bird and animal life. Camping beside the pool, in the shade of the baobab tree, the visitor is awakened by screaming flocks of white parrots, swims among the inoffensive freshwater crocodiles in the heat of noon, and admires the stately pelicans at dusk. Kalumburu tradition maintains that the pool is the abode of Ungur, the rainbow serpent, who is mentioned at the outset because of the wide significance with which this people endow him and especially because he is the patron of the medical functions to be described.

There are six elderly native doctors, *punmun* men, at Kalumburu. I had leisurely talks with them around the village. Much of the discussion was not fruitful, inasmuch as they used the vague Pela conversational style usual when something serious is discussed. There were long delays when unauthorized men, women, or children intruded. Direct questions seemed to be evidence of improper etiquette and were ignored, or followed by further long pauses for reflection. A partial answer might come, as though the speaker had just thought of the topic. Information came in hints, rather than in a full straightforward statement. Sometimes when I had not comprehended, the old men seemed too polite to intervene and set me on the right track. I had some status in the community as a white man doctor, which possibly helped to establish a rapport. Gradually an account of the *punmun* man emerged, consistent with what I discovered of the cosmology of the Australian Kimberleys.

Umulumbri and the other *punmun* men are agreed that the basic (premission) concepts of the cause of illness among the Pela are sorcery (effected by the use of *tjagolo*) and attack by evil beings (usually *tjimi*). Subsidiary concepts include ghosts—*naui* and *malan* —and omens, such as *mamba*, the whirlwind. These concepts are strongly held by the older people, and, as will be seen, to some extent by the children. Physical illness and death—apart from trivial illnesses and, possibly, accidental occurrences of death such as drowning or shark attack—are interpreted as being caused in the same way. Accidents are usually attributed not to bad luck or bad management but to bad wishing and spells.

The Pela word *wambaba* and the pidgin word "crank" are used to mean mad or crazy. The Kalumburu idea of "crank" is an excited or assaultive individual who talk strangely, swears a lot, forgets his manners, opens his bowels where people live, knocks over his water holder, or runs off in fright to the bush. He behaves in a highly disturbed and incomprehensible way. *Wambaba* is also the word for feebleminded; the conditions of senile dementia and melancholia are apparently so rare that there is no Pela expression for them. For milder degrees of mental aberration the word *murugabu* is used, signifying deaf, with the implication "deaf . . . does not listen to what I tell him . . . silly, unreasonable." A still softer expression is *mi miwa*, to think wrongly, mistakenly. The word *mlml* conveys feelings of reluctance because of suspicion of harm or persecution; it is a common expression of emotional difficulty.

TJAGOLO AND TJIMI

Tjagolo and *tjimi* concepts represent events precipitating an illness. The predisposing and perpetuating causes of illness that are assigned more significance by modern medicine are of little interest to the Pela. The people at Kalumburu will not or cannot discuss a sick person's temperament or his mental conflicts. Their view of mental illness as something produced by an action, shock, or trauma, resembles the view current in Western culture until a mere fifty years ago and one still favored by television script writers.

Tjagolo are charms the size of marbles, with a special appearance —angular, shiny, or crystalline. They are commonly found in the bed of a water course. Pieces of horn, fishbone, wire, or glass also serve as *tjagolo*. I saw a toothlike variant called *ulumbulloo*, and a hooklike one, *wierung*. The six Kalumburu *punmun* men are conceded the powers of throwing *tjagolo* through the air to lodge in the body of the victim, and also the ability to remove such intrusions. Penetration by a *tjagolo* may produce local or general disease, mental illness, in fact any personal calamity. One ancient *punmun* man told me that the *tjagolo* after penetrating the navel may lodge in a vein, there heating the blood stream. The victim falls into a fever and may die, unless the *punmun* man removes the *tjagolo* from the body.

The use of the *tjagolo* may be reinforced by evil songs; less commonly, evil songs may be used irrespective of the *tjagolo*. It is virtually impossible to find information at Kalumburu about harmful incantations; most people there are at pains to deny that they are still used. Healing songs, *yarindi*, are openly and commonly sung and will be described as an aspect of management of illness along with the work of the *punmun* man and his servant, the snake Ungur. Belief in *tjagolo* is declining; it survives mainly in middle-aged and older people. In the past, *tjagolo* belief was associated with intertribal and interpersonal suspicion and revenge—motives still prominent in the Kalumburu Aborigine's mental life, but for which the occasion is altering. In this institutional setting, much of the interpersonal hostility is now channeled toward the mission, frequently in passive-aggressive ways. For hostility toward European Australians, sorcery is less appropriate than passive aggression. Sorcery requires dyadic belief, shared by both parties.

While *tjagolo* belief is in decline, *tjimi* belief is flourishing. *Tjimi* are evil spirits, comparable to gremlins, trolls, and goblins. They roam the bush singly and usually have their lair in a cave in the hills. They change their shape at will: a description of one includes long ears like a donkey's, the body of an eagle or of a flying fox. A big stomach, big feet, and horns like a devil's are popular features. *Tjimi* are known to walk through the village in the shape of a cat. The children relate that it is the willy wagtail, a little black and white bird that progresses in a series of inviting hops, luring the unwary to the hills where he becomes lost and goes mad. It is heard crying in the night "Oo—oo, oo—oo . . . come here, come here, I'll take you away." One little boy said "That's not *tjimi*— that's a bandicoot saying that." Another boy said "It's like the Devil from hell . . . the catechism tells you about hell . . . if you're a bad boy, chase women, and go fighting, you go to hell."

The failure of *tjimi* to decline at the same rate as *tjagolo* suggested to me that *tjimi* might be receiving reinforcement from Christian education about the Devil. But inquiry revealed no particular stress on damnation and the Devil in the mission. Nor did I find any specific mention in the Pela catechism compiled for the people by Father Gil (1934*a*). *Tjimi*'s flourishing survival suggests that it receives reinforcements related to social expedience. One of its more obvious functions is to instill fear, thereby limiting the range of the individual's unaccompanied movements. This tends to prevent children from getting lost or women from keeping trysts.

Tjimi's reputation for the levitation of men from spot to spot helps them by explaining how an individual comes to be in the wrong place, or altogether lost. Thus when a stockman on muster failed to return to his camp and the searchers finally found him sleeping under a tree in the wrong gully: *tjimi* had moved him there. Insofar as it was believed, the explanation saved the unlucky man's reputation.

The Pela feel toward *tjimi* an ambivalence similar to that we feel toward authority constituted to safeguard us. By day it is the butt of their jokes; silly occurrences are attributed to it, and the girls say there is a girl *tjimi* who bosses all the others. But by night it becomes a general phobia; the women are circumspect in not going out without each other's company and children in a dormitory established at Kalumburu could not sleep without a nightlight lest a *tjimi* approach unawares.

The displacement of *tjagolo* by *tjimi* is doubtless in the interests of Australian law and of the Christian ethic. Thus the scapegoat in the event of misfortune is not the unfortunate Aborigine who is accused of throwing *tjagolo*, but the ridiculous yet fearsome, blamable yet unpunishable *tjimi*. In chapter 6 I shall consider evidence to suggest that spirit intrusion and sorcery reflect complementary aspects of the machinery for law and order. Where behavior is policed by spirits, intrusion predominates; where it is policed by peers, sorcery is more important. This is a question of the balance between religious and temporal authority.

People at Kalumburu talk about several kinds of spirits, in the sense of ghosts. In Pela language (Gil 1934*b*), *naui* means a "holy" ghost, and is used to refer not only to the ghost of Jesus, but to the soul of any Christian that has left its body. *Malan* refers to the ghosts or spirits of the old "pagan" Aborigines. Ghosts are not seen by day, but are visible at night by the light coming from their eyes. They are met in strange country, even where a burial platform has not been seen for years. They are sometimes described as lights coming down from the trees; one man likened them to the headlights of an approaching car. Their aura imparts a sensation or reminder of death. Most Kalumburu people think that ghosts have the power to stop a man in his tracks, to paralyze, to put him to sleep or into a trance. A stockman returning from a cattle muster

during my visit reported that he had seen a ghost and that both he
and his horse had been paralyzed, deathly still. Just in time he
crossed himself like a Christian, and the horse was able to move on.

Natural phenomena such as whirlwinds and lightning are blamed
for making people sad and for bringing on various other moods.
Lightning is the sign of *tjimi:* women shout at the sky and threaten
it with sticks to drive it away. Rain is ominous to the Pela-speaking
people, putting out fires, preventing hunting and comfortable moving about. A Kulari *punmun* man gave me two of his rainmaking
stones, but asked me not to use them; he would not show me his
lightning stones, fracture of which might smash the houses at the
mission, he said. The willy-willy or whirlwind, with its capricious
trail of damage, is opposed by the *punmun* man, who may rush
after it with a stick. All such natural phenomena, with various elab-
orations, are blamed for producing personal difficulties.

THE ACTIVITIES OF DOCTORS

It is hard to form conclusions about the social care of the sick at
Kalumburu. Food in this coastal riverine area is admittedly plentiful, and is shared with those unable to provide for themselves. I
observed a threatening and irritable psychotic man in the village
being treated with tact and forbearance. But whether these kindly
attitudes were a feature before the arrival of the mission is uncertain. Understandably, such altruism might be too much for a nomadic horde. When questioned on this matter, some *punmun* men
thought that a man sick from a *tjagolo*, after initial treatment and
healing chants had been given, would be left to himself. On the
other hand, I found song cycles that are sung daily to a sick man. I
concluded that Kalumburu attitudes toward sickness are "enlight-
ened," but that these attitudes could to some extent represent an
artifact of the mission's work. The spartan rigor I observed among
the desert people is not conspicuous at Kalumburu.

The Pela have little information about herbal medicine. Such
usages either have been forgotten or never were of much importance in the manner of the classical empirical remedies in other
societies, such as cinchona bark in Peru. Instances were cited of
wambaba people eating charcoal—which is of empirical value in
alleviating dysentery. The household remedy for colds, stomach

ache, or minor complaints was an infusion of the bark of *baldja,* the black wattle. Native tobacco (*Nicotiana*) does not seem to have been used by the Pela; today they are greatly addicted to chewing plug tobacco rather than to smoking. The narcotic *pituri,* used in the desert for stupefying fish in small waterholes, was known but not used by this coastal people. The regional flying doctor, Dr. J. P. Elphinstone, visiting us at Kalumburu mentioned that the natives are aware of a vesicant resin from a species of *Grevillea,* which when surreptitiously applied to a blanket causes severe blistering of the person who uses the blanket. He has treated two cases in recent years. It is his experience that the medicine men are as much concerned with "black" magic (sorcery) as the "white" (healing). He noted, however, that only the former group of cases connected with sorcery were brought to his notice.

No Pela Aborigine remembered the use of effigies for sorcery and exorcism, yet I have the assurance of the elder Father Rosendo Sosa at the mission that these once had their place in their ritual. Kalumburu men keep a mass of spinifex resin and beeswax, called a *midji,* for hafting spear points to the shafts. (Manufacture of quartz or commonly glass points by pressure-flaking is an advanced art at Kalumburu.) A man may shape his *midji* into a likeness of a female doll, adorn it, and use it for love magic. Father Rosendo remembers one "exorcism" effigy (its present location is uncertain —it may be in the Frankfurt Museum), which functioned as a sorcery effigy in reverse. Into it the *punmun* man inserted wires "taken" from the hurt part of the subject's body. The Father recalls the effigy as being stuck all over like a porcupine. But the Pela who were likely to remember denied it. Either they had forgotten, or the effigy could also be used for witchcraft and the taboo on discussing it was too strong.

Aboriginal physical therapy at Kalumburu is fast becoming obsolete, but I found applications of matted grass concealing a *tjagolo,* and the *rungala,* a flat stone applied to headaches. Various forms of physiotherapy include massage, sucking of skin, and blowing of air to cool a man whose blood is heated by a *tjagolo.* Bloodletting is used; Father Rosendo recalls a bloodletting at the patient's temple by which he became seriously exsanguinated from spurting of the temporal artery.

Each *punmun* man has a healing theme or "signature song" called his *palga*. These songs are frequently combined with ceremonial dances. A Kulari *punmun* man translates his *palga* as follows:

> I caught that *palga* from the place called Kwala.
> I'm a doctor man.
> I'm always doing something.
> I'm a doctor man.
> I found that *palga*.
> I know what to do with it.

During the performance of his *palga* or doctor song, the *punmun* man waves his *palga* stick, an engraved ironwood blade about eighteen inches long. The Kulari have a fine Norse-sounding myth for the way their *punmun* man acquires his *palga*. The details and place names vary for the individual *punmun* man. Thus, Umulumbri, a Kalari *punmun* man, told me of his canoe visit as a young man to Graham Moor Island, twenty miles out in Napier-Broome Bay. There the road led him to the mountain Radan, but a stone door barred the way. At the throw of his *tjagolo*, the door opened to reveal the secret valley of Ni-Walera. A big mob of ghosts was having a corroboree—not *naui* or holy ghosts but pagan ghosts, men *malan* and women *tjilinya*—and from them he learned his *palga* ceremony and received his *palga* blade. Closing the door of Radan again with his *tjagolo*, he returned to his people to show his song and his stick. The ironwood *palga* blade given me by Umulumbri illustrates the story with its engraving of the road to Radan, the stone door leading to Ni-Walera and the place of ghosts, and the dancing *malan* and *tjilinya*.

The Pela deny that incantations to produce sickness or bad luck are still used. These evil *yarindi* are as illegal as *tjagolo;* they are classified as being top secret. Their content will almost certainly never be discovered. This sort of singing is "officially" dead—disapproved by the welfare officer who controls the pension and by the missionaries who control the food. The same taboo applies to ceremonies. The Pela are open about dances designed for entertainment, but dances accompanied by magical, religious, or sexual ritual are concealed.

However, there is no mystery about the good or healing *yarindi*. Thus, a sick Kuini tribesman may hire someone to sing a song

cycle, which continues from the onset of his illness right into convalescence. The Kuini men place a *yarindi* stick on the supine patient from sternum to pubis, encircle him, and chant the *yarindi*,
accompanied by clapping-sticks and dronepipe. Healing *yarindi*
translate very like the bedside expressions of the French physician
Coué:

> We sing to make his bone and meat fresh again,
> To cool him down, sing away his pain,
> To make him fresh, lovely, better,
> To get him up in the afternoon,
> Grrr . . .

The "Grrr" is a high-pitched descending warble supposed to de-
note the action of getting up. It seems derived from the sound of
a bird arising and fluttering away. If the patient does not get up,
and requires more singing, the song continues next day:

> That man is feeling better yet,
> He walks, he walks along.

This is repeated as needed, and then later:

> That man goes fishing now,
> And comes back from fishing.
> He's better now,
> And won't get sick again.

And, during further convalescence, a further chant:

> That man goes running now,
> Runs and runs, chasing the kangaroo.

There are medical expenses. On recovery, a patient pays his
songmen for their services with a gift of tea, sugar, or clothing, or,
in the older days, fish, turtle, oyster, or other food. Predictably, he
pays the *punmun* man first.

DOCTOR AND SERPENT

The *punmun* man maintains a lifelong association with Ungur,
the mythical serpent. He begins his calling at about the age of ten,
before initiation, when he is selected for a ceremonial internalization of the serpent. The first account to be given maintained that
the boy ate the eggs of Ungur, but two *punmun* men described the

procedure more exactly. The scum that floats on Tjindi, the Kalumburu pool, is Ungur's spittle. This spittle is skimmed by the initiating *punmun* man and rolled into an egg—also referred to as a *tjagolo*—which is inserted into the novice's navel. The boy knows that the water serpent has hatched and is growing by the cold feeling in his belly. He must not take hot food or drink, which would displease the growing serpent. It is the acquisition of this assisting totem that invests the future *punmun* man with his special position and power. The aspirant's father pays the elder *punmun* man for the apprenticeship that follows; a suitable payment might be the gift of a kangaroo.

The *punmun* man proclaims his relationship with the serpent by a system of personal myths, creating for himself both a medical tradition and a mystique. He makes it known that he can summon Ungur to do his bidding: one end of a reed or bamboo containing a *tjagolo* is inserted in the *punmun* man's navel, while the other is used to call for Ungur in his pool. When the reed stirs Ungur's flesh the serpent rises from the water and creeps on to dry land. Transforming his back into a canoelike hollow, he may take the whole group of *punmun* men aboard. They paddle away into the sky "long way—maybe to Darwin" before returning to the pool. When an act of hostility requires that *punmun* men of opposing tribes fight, each summons his Ungur from its pool, mounts astride, and swims into the sky where they do battle. When the loser's ribs are crushed, snake and man fall dead from the sky. Levitation seems essential to *punmun*-Ungur myth.

As I understood it, the essence of the medical organization of the Pela is the belief that the doctor is associated with the healing symbol, the spirit serpent. He is the intermediary between the healing serpent and man in the event of illness. The little charms, *tjagolo,* are analogous with the serpent's egg, which entered the doctor's navel during his initiation. The *punmun* man has a monopoly of the best *tjagolo* because he alone can safely dive into Ungur's pool to look for them. Any person who is hostile enough can throw a *tjagolo;* but to the *punmun* man is given the healing office by virtue of his partnership with Ungur. I shall refer to the apparent universality of the serpent as a medical symbol in chapter 5.

The question is often asked by Western observers of primitive society: How is the deceit practiced by the native doctor in creating his mystique and in conjuring his medicine stones compatible with his sincerity? The Spanish missionaries are interested in this paradox, themselves having little doubt that although the removal of a *tjagolo* might depend on deceit the *punmun* man himself has sincere faith in the act. They put it: he himself is deceived by his deception. A sick *punmun* man will consult another *punmun* man for removal of the *tjagolo*, an act that he knows is one of legerdemain. They suggested that it is like a sacrament, and that is what matters. If faith and hope are healing emotions, the *punmun* man mobilizes them as do priests and therapists in other cultures. In doing so, he uses elements common to all psychotherapeutic systems, coupled with the scientific knowledge available to his culture. *Punmun* man and snake are being superseded, especially in this era of introduced diseases and of the modern medical skills needed to combat them. But in the alien contact they are being superseded prematurely, lost before an emotional trust in modern medicine has been formed.

THE KALUMBURU MISSION

I should now describe in more detail the alien-contact situation as I saw it in 1963, in order to indicate the level of anomie and its effects on social character and modes of adaptation and adjustment, before returning to a consideration of medicine and the law in this changing situation.

Nutrition and cleanliness at Kalumburu are reasonably good for a nomadic people introduced to sedentary living. The effects of yaws and leprosy are visible, but their present incidence is low. The disease of particular significance is actually a hidden one: hookworm. Thus my colleague Dr. William Pitney found in the year previous to my visit that of the 187 blood films from adults that he examined 58 (31 percent) showed iron deficiency. Some of the hemoglobin values were quite low (Pitney 1962). Unless a fieldworker possesses this information, he could mistakenly interpret some behavioral features, particularly apathy and lack of initiative. The congregation of people at the mission increases the hazard of hookworm, which is transmitted through fecal contamination of the ground during the wet season. Nomadic life afforded some protection against contagious diseases.

My arrival by air gave me the opportunity for a bird's eye view of the settlement. I was impressed by the orderly arrangement of the monastery, the adjacent village, the abundantly productive kitchen garden and orchards, and the peanut plantation. Domestic animals are kept in the vicinity of the village and a wide plain for the beef cattle runs beyond. Subsistence, supplemented by fish, shellfish, and turtle from the sea, could not be more generous for the inhabitants. So well have the Spanish missionaries established a viable settlement that it seems ungenerous to draw attention to the inhabitants' personality problems consequent upon the social disorganization. Australian missions are all too easy to blame for difficulties such as dependency and institutionalism; it is easy to forget that without their protective canopy many local populations may not have survived—did not survive, in some cases—Western contact at all.

After Western contact, the infertility of the Pela-speaking people, as of full-blood Aborigines elsewhere, reached such proportions that by 1955 it was generally believed that extinction was fast approaching. In the early 1950s, deaths at Kalumburu outnumbered births by nine to one (Perez 1958). During this period the visiting German anthropologist Lommel (1951) proposed his theory that Aboriginal infertility was psychosomatic. He held that contact with white culture had destroyed the Aborigines' concept of the universe, the ensuing apathy and depression being reflected in the declining birthrate. Lommel's theory of psychic genosuicide was open to question on medical grounds, had these been better appreciated at the time. While it is true that mental depression is associated with amenorrhea and infertility in women and diminished libido in both sexes, it has to be severe in degree. There were other adequate causes of a physical nature, the more obvious being the endemic diseases—hookworm infestation and anemia, subnutrition, gonorrheal cervicitis and salpingitis. By 1955 this trend was arrested by health measures, and the years since then have seen a population recovery. Of the twenty-six children in the school at the time of my visit in 1963, nine were in grade one, and one in grade seven, the highest grade. Whatever the contemporary problems at Kalumburu, infertility is not one of them.

Housing divides the population into three socioeconomic strata.

Twenty European-style houses supplied with electricity and fenced yards are inhabited by the progressive families. A block of thirty single-room iron huts, shaded by the mango orchard, is occupied by a mixture of Kulari and Kuini people of lesser Westernization but who have a close dependency upon the mission. Two other groups are housed in shacks about a mile on the Kulari and Kuini sides of the mission respectively. These groups, though mainly relying on the mission for food, still go away foraging and hunting with their dogs for months at a time. As for the other, reliance on mission-grown food has replaced hunting and food gathering; rifles are used for the occasional kangaroo hunt, and a modern net for fishing in the sea.

PERSONALITY PROBLEMS

An atmosphere of apathy, dependency, and institutionalism pervades the settlement. Some of the younger progressive men, capable of leaving their less successful relatives behind, seem to prefer the new way of life and do not regret the passing of the old. But in the village it is striking to observe a lost and unoccupied appearance in people of middle age, despite every effort by the missionaries to encourage Western habits of industry. From time to time a few Aborigines, like Umulumbri, reflect their loss of purpose in psychotic behavior; many show what could be defined as personality disorders, which take two main forms, passive aggression and sick-role behavior.

Unable to oppose mission authority directly, people express their aggression in circuitous ways. One missionary is careful to avoid showing his fondness of a favorite horse. He reasons that he will become unpopular from time to time as he insists on standards of performance; to show a "weakness" for anything would provide a point through which he could be attacked. The missionaries complain that there is little incentive to learn in school and little application to work afterward. There is little desire to learn a special occupation—to be tradesmen or nurses. The missionaries are painfully aware of the disappointing development of qualities that might lead to socioeconomic self-sufficiency. Said one ruefully: "It's not much to show for fifty years' work here."

Another contemporary aspect of personality organization is

hypochondria, or sick-role behavior. The Pela language expression *mintjal ninga* means "give me something to take." It forms a common presentation of Aborigines at the sick bay. Supporting complaints are not volunteered, but if the nurse suggests complaints, the applicant will cooperate by admitting complaints from top to toe. This use of the sick bay is not strictly comparable with neurotic attendances at a Western clinic. Nor is it merely a social visit to bring variety into the monotonous days. It has a ring of pauperism, in which the Aborigine seems concerned to get whatever is being handed out. Sometimes the nurse has to attend to half the population of the village each morning. Of these people, half might come for minor first aid, half for *mintjal ninga*. The really sick people might not come at all. She does her best to discourage the *mintjal ninga* faction, but since this is an attitude to life that deeply permeates the village it is not really to be denied. It expresses too well the villagers' peevishness and passive aggression.

The activities of the *punmun* men, and of the songmen with their healing chants, are in a phase of disorganized obsolescence. Singing and dancing are pursued with an extraordinary tenacity. Many of the songs are connected with healing chants, but rarely is full ceremonial observed. When the doctors perform their stately *palga* dance, with the enormous arched headdresses of string representing Ungur the serpent, it is an impressive spectacle. Mostly the dances are poorly organized and comprehended. Many times I sought from bystanders what the dancer was expressing, only to hear in reply "That's George." George himself is only vaguely aware of what the dance originally represented, of its symbolic significance and the place it held in the scheme of things. For some Aborigines singing and dancing go on for most of the night, leaving performers too tired to work the next day. It forcibly reminded me of obsessive television viewing; like this pastime, it has become a time-structuring substitute activity for ill-employed people.

With continuing detribalization at Kalumburu, anxiety is coming to be experienced in the diffuse way of Western peoples, driving toward some change in adjustment—even if only the adoption of ill health as a rationalization of inadequacy. Despite the idyllic leisure and plenty, and the grave courtesy shown by Aborigines to white people and indeed generally to each other, the Kalumburu village is not the tranquil place it appears. Suddenly a spark ignites a conflagration. The village comes alive with tension and animosity. Illegally owned spears are brought out from the bushes. Corroborees are cancelled because disputants will not dance with each other. The intervening missionary is fobbed off with a vague statement of the obvious—"Maybe something wrong"—by dissentients who cannot cooperate with him through fear of sorcery and revenge.

This pattern of routine evasion of personal confrontation punctuated by periodic explosions of tension and rioting I found to be a characteristic of Aboriginal camps. I had the opportunity in other places to observe camp riots. To some extent, they reflect camp conditions of lack of personal space and privacy and the consequent irritability and intrigue. But they also seem related to a preferred social character of many groups of Aborigines: the placing of a high value on tolerance and peacemaking. They are reluctant or unable to air their grievances or to confront antagonists a little at a time. Confrontation is evaded until a trivial event revives pent-up resentments. Coalitions then form around old grievances until half the community is brawling.

"Modal" character studies have fallen into disrepute—perhaps temporarily—but it is tempting to make correlations between child-rearing practices and social character (or as Kardiner [1945] terms it, basic personality) at Kalumburu. Many observers comment that people there are governed by fear rather than guilt, that there is absence of industry unless supervised and improvident lack of planning for the future. They find it reasonable to relate these traits to the indulgent neglect of discipline in childhood training. Fond and affectionate, parents are reluctant to hurt their children by setting limits to their pleasure. The nurse complained that one mother took away her infant with pneumonia rather than have it cry from the penicillin injection. Children are not weaned before the age of four or five, though at this age the slack breast contains little or no milk and is given for pacification. The teacher finds it impossible to set homework because of the parents' attitude.

Is this traditional Aboriginal socialization—or anomie? It is right to raise the question of how far the social character of which the missionaries complain is an artifact of settlement existence and the release from traditional responsibilities. It is fair to point out that these Aborigines, when compared with one another and not with whites, show as wide a variation in personality as any white population. I found them genial and morose, loquacious and taciturn, bold and timid, rough and gentle, active and sluggish, differing one from the other. This is a matter of perspective: the ethnographer interested in social character, and using a collective focus, tends to see similarities; the clinician, with an individual focus, tends to see differences.

It is inevitable for missionaries to measure people by Western standards, since they are trying to guide them toward Western ways. They find it particularly hard to accept the sexual practices, which by Western suburban standards are excessive and perverse. The children play sex games at the age of four, with realistic looking "intercourse" including pelvic thrusting.[1] A lively fourteen-year-old girl in the convent is the despair of the nuns; despite almost constant supervision and all the persuasion and punishments available, she manages to find intercourse whenever alone for a few minutes, whether in the laundry or kitchen, and is sometimes caught in the act. Nubile girls run after mates of white or mixed blood—rare at Kalumburu—who represent a higher social status. A group of young lads marched off naked to the bush and pretended the trees were women. Once again, it could be asked whether the emphasis on sex was an artifact of settled camp life.

Pela attitudes to sex and work, seemingly opposed to the development of Western social habits, have ceased to be a challenge for some of the missionaries. Some have accepted failure with resignation and disappointment. The disappointment is the more painful in that these missionaries are an unusually devoted group, giving up years of toil in a strange land. Spain has little connection with Australia. After the mission was attacked by Japanese bombers in 1943, one Father was found dead in a trench, his body sheltering two Aboriginal children. I could feel sympathy for a missionary's outburst: "If it wasn't for my religion, the whole lot could go to

---

[1] The significance of infant sex play for psychosexual development and subsequent personality has been examined by Dr. John Money (1970) in a subsequent expedition to Arnhem Land.

buggery!" His religion meant little to most of the Aborigines; the medicine and law that he represented was barely beginning to show its intended social effects. Umulumbri's psychosis in some way reflects the deeper state of mind of his people and the source of the frustration of the Christian missionary.

CHAPTER FIVE

Primitive Concepts of Disease:
A Reformulation

THE SYSTEMATIC STUDY of primitive theories of disease is said to have been established by Max Bartels' *Die Medicin der Naturvölker* (1893). Bartels enumerated the eleven main concepts of disease held by primitives thus: demons; ghosts of the dead; animals or ghosts of animals; sucking or consuming by a demon; a foreign substance in the body; poison; displacement or loss of principal parts of the body; bewitching or cursing; the will of the gods; ill winds; the evil eye. Apart from the evil eye, which seems to be an Old World idea, most of these concepts of the origin of disease are represented in one form or another in the primitive societies of Australia.

A promising step in the study of primitive disease concepts might have been the correlation of the different concepts with aspects of the local culture and ecology. At the turn of the century, medical interest was growing in epidemiology not as the study of epidemics but as the science of the distribution of diseases within populations and within spatial zones. This interest was quickened by something more than scientific curiosity: in order to plan for the improvement of people's health, accurate and precise data of the relationship between disease and environment were needed. But lacking this incentive, theoretical anthropology at first made little use of epidemiological methods, focusing instead upon historical connections. In 1932, Clements published the monograph *Primitive Concepts of Disease* based on his survey of the world literature concerning aboriginal concepts of disease. Clements' stated aims (p. 185) were "to offer a scheme of classification for the disease concepts of primitive people; to obtain a fairly complete geographical distribution of the classified concepts; and to frame certain conclusions as to their relative antiquity, probable origin, and historical connections. Such a study affords a good opportunity for the application of general methodological principles, thus involving one of the most basic questions of modern theoretical anthropology—the interpretation of cultural similarities and the convertibility of distributions in space into time sequences."

In his monograph, Clements drew attention to three universally accepted categories of disease causation: natural causes, human agency, and supernatural agency. All three categories occur among both civilized and primitive people, but Clements considered them too broad for his purpose of investigating historical connections, and put them aside in favor of five main classes:

Sorcery. Here are grouped all those theories that ascribe sickness either to the manipulations of persons skilled in magic or to the operations of human beings who exercise some control over the supernatural world.

Breach of taboo. All theories that explain sickness as a punishment sent by the gods for breach of religious prohibitions or social prohibitions having divine sanction are included under this heading.

Disease-object intrusion. Under this heading are listed all theories attributing disease to the presence in the body of some malefic foreign substance.

Spirit intrusion. This class includes all those etiologies that hold that disease is due to the presence in the body of evil spirits, ghosts, or demons.

Soul loss. This class includes all theories attributing sickness to loss of the soul, whether abstracted by ghosts or sorcerers or injured in its nocturnal ramblings when out of the body during sleep.

The "basic questions of modern theoretical anthropology" in which Clements was interested concern whether disease concepts are historically connected through the process of cultural diffusion from a common source or whether they have independent and spontaneous origin in different parts of the world. The *principle of diffusion* suggests that concepts of disease are historically connected, derived from a single source or point of origin—as one might envisage a type of agriculture, for example, originating in Southeast Asia and diffusing into China. Thus a disease concept such as the idea of taboo might travel as a culture trait from Mesopotamia across Persia to India and so into Oceania. The *principle of independent origin,* on the other hand, suggests that these disease concepts represent ideas that occur universally, due to the fundamental psychological similarity of mankind. Such are the "elementary ideas" or *elementargedanken* of the late nineteenth-century German anthropologists. Thus, all peoples appear to believe in spiritual beings, conjecturing them as the explanation for the difference between live bodies and dead bodies or as the inhabitants of dreams. If people believe in spirits, they logically attribute to them the power of producing disease.

Clements plotted on maps of the world the distribution of disease concepts recorded in the ethnographic literature. He interpreted the maps as favoring the principle of diffusion rather than the principle of independent origin. He supported the notion of a historical linkage between similar concepts in different parts of the world, rather than of independent and parallel emergence. For example, he interpreted the absence of spirit intrusion from extremely primitive cultures, such as the Australian, as reflecting their long isolation and consequent diminished opportunity to be reached by waves of diffusion. He argued that the absence of spirit intrusion in these cultures is explained by the assumption that it was developed and diffused after these cultures became isolated, rather than that some psychological peculiarity prevented spontaneous derivation of this particular disease concept. Unfortunately for Clements' interpretation, the data available to him at the time were not complete enough: spirit intrusion is in fact widespread in primitive Australian society. Chapter 7 describes a very highly developed form in Australia not before reported, as a culture-bound syndrome.

The survey by Rogers (1944) of disease concepts in North America developed and refined the theme of Clements. (Epidemiology and culture history seem not yet to have cross-fertilized. The epidemiological interest in the relationship of disease to environment is still not in evidence.) Rogers too was concerned with the "relative antiquity" of various disease theories. Using Clements' method, he offered a more detailed map showing the distribution of disease concepts in North America. Rogers now divided the primitive disease concepts into two categories, having some advantages over the lists previously prepared:

Proximate disease causes: object intrusion; spirit intrusion; soul loss

Remote disease causes: black magic; dreaming; breach of taboo; divine wrath.

Rogers considered the proximate types of disease theory as psychologically more elementary and probably older historically than the remote doctrines. However, he suggested caution in interpreting historically the distributional data because of the uncertain patterns of coverage and the complexities of the subject.

The culture historians in this tradition deserve credit for advancing the systematic study of primitive disease concepts. However, they paid insufficient regard to certain other factors now emphasized as important to cultural history—such as independent invention, ecological adaptation, and biological (phylogenetic) evolution (Rouse 1962). And in the light of the contemporary development of epidemiology, certain features of the clinical method must be applied to a study of disease distribution. These features include sampling; disease entities; the effect of environment; and parsimony of hypothesis.

Sampling. This should be adequate and representative. The ethnographic record available to the earlier workers suffered from inadequate coverage of many parts of the world, which led to serious errors in inference.

Entities. These should be sufficiently distinct to serve as units of analysis. Hallowell (1935) pointed out that primitive disease concepts were not capable of being manipulated as independent unitary traits because they regularly overlapped.

Environment. Factors in the human ecology peculiar to the region have to be scrutinized for their influence upon disease frequencies, concepts, and treatments.

Parsimony of hypothesis. Occam's razor should be employed, so long as it does not do violence to the data. It is preferable to ob-

serve an economy of hypothesis than to abstract data to fit preconceived theoretical ideas. When these principles are heeded,
hypotheses about primitive concepts of disease are still possible,
though they are less elaborate than those contemplated by earlier
observers.

Using the material presented in the previous two chapters concerning the people of the desert and of the sea coast respectively, a
limited hypothesis may be offered relating to what I may call *the
common infrastructure* and *the regional superstructure* of primitive
concepts of disease.

THE COMMON INFRASTRUCTURE
AND THE REGIONAL SUPERSTRUCTURE

As the pool of ethnographic data grows (as for example, spirit
intrusion is found to be prevalent in Australia contrary to the information available to earlier workers), it appears that primitive
cultures around the world show definite constants or regularly
recurring features in their concepts of disease. Sorcery and spirit
intrusion, for example, seem practically universal. There are different blends or formulas, it is true, but fairly constant elements are
present. These constants, found in many parts of the world, form
what I have termed the common infrastructure of primitive concepts of disease. Among cultures which are highly isolated or
"primeval," in the term of Clements, with little evidence of waves
of diffusion, the simplest explanation of the common conceptual
infrastructure is that it originated from the "elementary ideas"
common to mankind. These are the *elementargedanken* assumptions
of people who lack the science to appreciate the correct, but hidden, cause-effect relationships in illness.

Primitive cultures around the world also show distinctly variable features in their concepts of disease. The set of assumptions
that characterizes the disease concepts of a community, and distin-
guishes it from others, may be called the regional superstructure
of primitive concepts of disease. The determining factors for these
variations in causal explanation should be sought in the specific
features of that region and community. Here one must look to the
natural habitat and ecology, to the way of life consequent on that
ecology, and to further factors arising from the situation and from

the social group. Some of these factors will be illustrated in this chapter by reference to the Australian data before us.

Walbiri and Pela, our two paradigms of Aboriginal institutions of medicine and the law, share a common infrastructure of concepts of disease not only with each other but with unrelated societies across the world. In brief résumé, each emphasizes the concept of intrusion of solid objects effected through the magic of sorcery, malefic rites, and songs performed by an ill wisher. Each society emphasizes the intrusion into the body of spirits or occasionally its possession (control) by intruding spirits. Of the varied spirits in criminated, some are related to human form, others to animals, others to completely nonreal species. Both Walbiri and Pela medicine recognize disease produced by breach of taboos or sanctions. Each is impressed by the serious effect of the loss of vital substance —the "soul"—from the body. (The reason why kidney fat, rather than the heart or liver, is widely regarded as the seat of the soul in Oceania is a regional variation that is interesting to conjecture. I doubt if its gleaming white appearance gives it this special glamor, though this could be a factor. My conjecture is that Aborigines have observed how the kidney fat, unlike the other organs, is a variable commodity—conspicuous in well-fed persons, greatly reduced in starved ones. The variation in this organ is therefore related to the health of the individual and to the fluctuating abundance that characterizes the ecology of Australia. But here we anticipate the second part of the hypothesis concerning primitive concepts of disease, the regional superstructure.) Of significance is the fact that these Aboriginal societies, isolated from the rest of mankind for so many millennia that Clements refers to them as primeval rather than primitive, share the same infrastructure of medical belief that is held by primitive man elsewhere.

Though the healing of disease and the maintenance of social stability are universal problems, the solutions adopted are not universal. We should expect to learn more specifically about a particular society from the variables (the regional superstructure) than from the constants (the common infrastructure). When the variation in medical belief between Walbiri and Pela societies is brought to our attention, several determinants of this variation may be considered. Since it is not likely that the expanse of desert between them was such a sheer physical barrier to cultural diffusion that one tribe could not borrow ideas from the other, it should be considered whether the difference in natural habitat and human ecology is such that medical concepts in one zone are inapplicable in the other. Or alternatively, whether there is such a difference in the respective ways of life, including the socialization of children, that ideas in one are irrelevant in the other. Or, to consider a common clinical occurrence, whether a local prophet succeeded in getting an idiosyncratic idea adopted in his small isolated community.

Unfortunately for any diffusionist concept of a physical barrier imposed by the expanse of desert country between the Walbiri and Pela peoples, there is an overland track. The track, or network of tracks, represents a trade route that linked the coastal dwellers with the people of the desert. It permitted social and cultural exchange between desert and coast such that if one society had a cultural feature that the other could profitably adopt, diffusion could occur. Evidence of this trade may still be found, but the traffic seems to have been limited to items of religious or ceremonial significance. I described how a Walbiri doctor led me to a lone corkwood tree in the desert to disclose the cache of a powerful sorcery implement: it was a cutting blade made of mother-of-pearl, which could have come from nowhere but the coast. This doctor had it attached to a length of hair string by means of the hard gum (plastic when heated) prepared from grass in this desert region. The hair of the string had the reddish lights of the Walbiri, not the black of the coastal Pela. The cutting blade was designed for use in the magical kidney-fat surgery important in Walbiri lore. At the coast, a *punmun* man showed me his stones for use in rainmaking ceremonies. They were mineralized quartz specimens of a kind found in the arid hills of the desert. Each doctor knew that his ceremonial object had been imported from the other end of the trade route. The trade was limited to this kind of exchange and not reinforced by the economic advantages of the kind that promoted the well-known *hiri* and *kula* trade rings of Papua and New Guinea (Malinowski 1922).

It is possible that the trade route was so little employed that the desert functioned as a partial barrier between Walbiri and Pela. But a more probable explanation of this regional difference in concepts of disease is that disease theory and treatment, like a tree or plant, is highly sensitive to the locality. It should be possible, no doubt, to relate the regional differences to preferences for social behavior, in the manner of Kardiner's concept of basic personality or Wallace's concept of modal personality. These concepts are currently fraught by controversy, though they may be more applicable to small isolated communities than to highly stratified modern ones. But it may not be essential to our hypothesis to utilize theories of personality, for it seems a reasonable inference that the development of different medical concepts is traceable to factors in that spatial zone, biological or situational in character, the realm of human ecology. Nature, as well as culture, determines the hunting-gathering way of life.

Three aspects of the regional superstructures of Pela and Walbiri medical concepts may serve here to illustrate the contrast between them: the use of the snake as a medical symbol, the use of healing chants, and the emphasis placed by the doctors on individual comfort as opposed to social control. Each characterizes the Pela system as contrasted with the Walbiri. I want to comment on these three aspects, not because of any optimism I have that they are significant for archetypal configurations in the psychology of the people, but for the more limited purpose that they suggest the importance of ecological adaptation, rather than of cultural diffusion, in primitive concepts of disease.

The Snake as a Medical Symbol

Though the rainbow serpent is prominent in most Aboriginal belief systems, its significance is not consistent among the cultural blocs. Its ritual significance in Arnhem Land has been documented in detail by R. M. Berndt (1951) for the Kunapipi cult. The cult includes rites of fertility and male "pseudoprocreation," in which youths are ceremonially "killed" by the men and born again as their sons (see chapter 9). The snake is not invariably the symbol of healing or of disease; in northeast Arnhem Land these have other symbols, the *gulun* and *marngitj* described in chapter 2. In the Walbiri desert country, the snake is pictorially represented at several sacred sites, such as the Ngama (mother) cave thirty miles west of the Yuendumu settlement and the Wanayara waterholes, its mythical home thirty miles to the north. Among the Walbiri it is not the doctor's symbol or assistant; *mabanba,* a being with no counterpart in natural species, is the Walbiri doctor's healing symbol or "assisting totem." It stands in opposition to the serpent, which is rather the agent of disease and suffering.

By contrast, the Pela *punmun* man has a closely cooperative relationship with the serpent. An analogy is irresistible with the serpent of Aesculapius, which was in early classical times the emblem of the beloved and divine physician and which became, together with the rod or staff, the symbol of modern medicine. Schouten (1967) analyzed the role of the serpent as the symbol of medicine, and it is tempting to extend the applicability of his analysis to this Aboriginal culture. In the ancient world the serpent was looked upon as chthonic (that is, of the earth or the underworld), living in caves and crevices, preeminently the animal of the underworld and the realm of the dead. Medical belief concerning the serpent hinges upon the association of the serpent with the earth "which renews itself year after year, and, as it were, constantly snatches life from annihilation, by virtue of which it was looked upon as the paramount savior" (Winton 1969: 237). The association of the serpent with the earth made it an independent symbol of life ever renewed and thus of restored health. In the eyes of the ancients, the serpent was not so much a symbol of the medical art as of the healer himself. Aesculapius, it would seem, was at first a chthonic deity worshiped in the guise of a serpent.

The serpent is a generous symbol for native doctors. He heals. He is a phallus, symbol of joyful union of sexes. He disappears into the earth, the underworld from which life comes, and into which death goes. He is the rainbow, harbinger of the wet season and the earth's renewal. His curving form in a cave painting resembles a regional route taken by nomadic people. He is a road to the mythical past, the creative epoch when the skies were still open and gods and men walked the earth. The *punmun* man of the Kimberleys wears a beautiful headdress during his stately doctor's singing-dance or *palga.* It is made of hairstring wound on a framework of sticks, like a spider's web, and resembles the sacred *waninga* string ornaments of central Australia. In its *palga* form, it appears to represent a snake or a rainbow. Levi-Strauss (1963) ingeniously suggests that the undulating shape of the serpent, depicted on cave walls, resembles the rainfall graph of the monsoonal climate. The medical symbolism of the snake applies in many cultures which are historically unrelated to each other.

The assumption about *mabanba*, the little being that embodies the desert doctor's art, has no immediate counterpart in Pela cosmology and little in common with the rainbow serpent. The clinician will observe interesting implications in it. *Mabanba* has some functions in common with the amulet or charm, which is a real, if symbolic, object. It resembles the soteria, described by Laughlin (1956) as the converse of the phobia, an object invested with the power of supplying protection and comfort. But soteria—for example the rabbit's foot—are external real objects, substitutes for the security that should lie within. Some psychiatrists will suggest that the nature of *mabanba* may be appreciated by recourse to the psychology of object relations. The British school of psychoanalysis led by Melanie Klein has directed attention to an early form of perception by the child, whereby things are retained in two ways that are called respectively memory and internal objects. By this conception, the Walbiri father-doctor is retained in the form of little objects that conduct themselves in effect like doctors. There is no need for the repression of these good objects from awareness; on the contrary, they have to be available in an emergency to represent the healing art and the power of father-doctors.

The concept of introjected objects—whole objects and part objects—and of the paranoid and depressive positions of the first year of life lends itself aptly to the understanding of Walbiri concepts, in particular to the extraordinary emphasis placed upon introjected objects. It is comparable with the "oral system" proposal of Whiting and Child (1953), to be mentioned shortly.

The Healing Chant

The use of the serpent as a symbol of healing is not the only aspect of the Pela medical superstructure that bears more resemblance to totally unrelated cultures (such as Classical Greece) than to the culture of the Walbiri. The emphasis on the formal healing chant is another. The song has healing attributes in many primitive societies. Navaho ceremonial patterns, described by C. Kluckhohn

(1944), include healing chants that associate singers and healers. Like the Navaho, the Pela hire singers of elaborate healing songs. Healing chants occur in other Aboriginal groups; the culture-bound syndrome *malgri* of the Lardil of the Gulf of Carpentaria, described in chapter 7, is treated by a healing song. But the Walbiri doctor seems less concerned to provide his patient with interminable comforting songs, so far as could be ascertained.

The fact that completely disparate cultures discern similar healing qualities in the serpent, and exploit the comforting magic of music and song, hardly implies a cultural diffusion—in this case between Pela, ancient Greece, and Navaho! But it may suggest that there are basic ecological factors in common. To begin with, each ecology has snakes! This is a hypothesis to which attention might better be directed, than to cultural diffusion.

CARE OR CONTROL?

To a clinician, a striking difference between Pela and Walbiri doctors lies in the "tenderness" or "toughness" of their respective attitudes toward patients. The Pela doctor seems more oriented toward individual care, while the Walbiri doctor seems more oriented toward social control. A modern analogy springs to mind by comparing the attitudes of doctors in the private practice of psychiatry and doctors practicing military psychiatry. In military psychiatry (Glass 1955) the needs of the group often precede those of the individual. The distinctively Walbiri belief in *millelba*, the spirit-counterpart, should be examined in this light. Belief in a soul, or spirit-counterpart, is almost universal; the Walbiri belief is in the existence of a "twin" or "mirror" spirit-counterpart. Its explicitness suggests to the clinician the phenomenon of autoscopy, described by Schilder (1950) and documented in clinical literature (Arieti and Meth 1959). In this syndrome, a patient's double may suddenly appear in a a visual form, as in a dream. In one classical case, a barber would step aside to let his double carry on with the shaving. The majority of reports of autoscopy are associated with cases of epilepsy or migraine. Schilder viewed the condition as a projection of the body image, and in fact it shows closer resemblance to the hallucinations that occur in disorders of the temporal lobe than to those of schizophrenia.

If it is conjectured that some tribesman was affected by this clinical syndrome, and conditions in the group were suitable, spreading acceptance of the experience might follow, reinforced in this instance by a consciencelike concern for the sacred life and social sanctions. Belief in a form of autoscopic control of the self by the self ("Big Brother is watching you") combines well with close control by peers, necessitated by the problems of survival in the desert habitat. This might be termed a "folie communiquée" theory of the origin of medical belief or legal control. (See also chapter 8.)

Psychoanalytic theory offers insights that illuminate the clinical and organic. The American workers Whiting and Child (1953) adapted the psychoanalytic theory of psychosexual development to determine whether the kind of socialization experienced in childhood bore any relation to the sorcery belief adopted by the culture. In their study, they entertained five "systems" to describe the child's socialization experience—oral, anal, sexual, dependency, and aggression. The hypothesis was that harsh, fixating experience in a given system in childhood might be associated with a cultural interpretation of illness and misfortune in terms of that system. We may ask how their hypothesis fits Walbiri and Pela cultures, in which we have remarked a difference in the ratios between medical care and control.

Whiting and Child's procedure was to rank cultures by their propensity to produce satisfaction, or conversely anxiety, through cultural childrearing practices arising from each of these five socialization systems. Thus anxiety associated with oral experiences might be reflected in the culture's tendency to ascribe illness to eating something dangerous, or, by extension, to verbal spells. Anal system anxieties might be reflected in explanations tracing sickness to manipulation of exuviae—feces, hair, nails, and other body detritus. Sexual system anxieties might lead illness to be ascribed to sex transgressions or to sex excretions such as menstrual blood and semen. Dependency system anxieties might be associated with illness being attributed to loss of one's soul or to possession by a malevolent spirit. Aggression system anxieties might lead to illness being represented as the result of punishment for disobedience to authority figures and, by extension, to the spirits.

Walbiri explanations of illness prominently involve the oral system (incantation and intrusion or swallowing up of the *yarda*), the dependency system (control by *millelba*), and the aggression system (attack by *tjanba*). They less prominently involve the anal and sexual systems of socialization. Acquaintance with childrearing in the desert confirms that childrearing anxieties are highly likely to be associated with the oral, dependency, and aggression systems, and less strongly with the anal and sexual. It will be seen later, when we concern ourselves with tribal women (chapter 9), that menstrual blood is conceptually linked with illness—but less because of the association of menses with sex in the sense of erotic satisfaction than because blood and hemorrhage have aggressive significance in Walbiri cosmology. Anal system explanations are not conspicuous in the desert. This is in contrast with New Guinea villages, where anal and exuvial ideas are preeminent and most sorcery begins by "taking dirt." This reflects, ecologically, the contrast between the comfortable hygiene of nomadic life and the precarious hygiene of living in a village. Villagers are inevitably more concerned with feces and its concealment.

This recital of comparisons and variations between Pela and Walbiri medical systems—and unrelated systems at the far corners of the earth—is not intended as the basis for conjectures about the structure of the mind, in what was a time-honored anthropological-psychiatric tradition. All that is suggested is that Pela and Walbiri medical systems serve different realities. Inevitably, they share the common infrastructure of concepts, such as sorcery and spirit intrusion, found all around the world. But the regional superstructures of distinctive variables reflect differences in the situations to which the people have to adapt. In our example, this is basically the ecological difference between the comparative reliability of the sea coast as a source of food and survival and the fluctuating and unreliable abundance of the desert. These factors are the constraints in the environment that regulate the way of life. Just as the personality structure of a man is responsive to what he has to do to achieve his subsistence, so medical and legal systems, and the attitudes and behaviors of doctors, are sensitively attuned to ecological forces.

CHAPTER SIX

The Victim of Sorcery

DESCRIPTIVE DATA concerning sorcery and spirit possession are unsatisfying where clinical data could be obtained. The Aborigines of Mornington Island in the Gulf of Carpentaria provided an unusual opportunity for access to information on this desirable level. A team of medical research workers from the University of New South Wales chose Mornington Island for its survey of mental health in an Aboriginal community. The entire population of about six hundred was studied by means of psychiatric examinations coupled with self-rating questionnaires of symptoms, based on the Cornell Medical Index. These data were correlated with measures of genetic constitution and of cultural identity. The findings are presented in a companion volume entitled *Cruel, Poor and Brutal Nations* (Cawte 1972), which differs from the present book in being an intensive study of a single population, using epidemiological and statistical techniques.

In the course of our medical work on Mornington Island, good rapport developed with key informants, and indeed with the community at large, so that information about indigenous concepts of medicine and law were forthcoming, of a satisfactorily first-hand, clinical, kind.[1] Illuminating as it was for primitive medicine, this information fell outside the scope of the epidemiological study reported in *Cruel, Poor and Brutal Nations*, which utilizes the conventional modern categories of illness. Nevertheless they furnish

[1] I am indebted to my collaborators in that research, particularly Dr. Barry Nurcombe, Dr. Michael Friedman, and the Reverend Douglas Belcher for assistance in compiling and interpreting some of the data reported in this chapter and the next.

us in this volume with a clinical perspective upon sorcery for this chapter, and on spirit intrusion or *malgri* for the next.

It is necessary to sketch the historical and ecological setting of these Aboriginal islanders, before examining the sorcery events produced by their society. The first white men to see their fore-fathers were Dutch explorers sent from the East Indies early in the seventeenth century. Carpentaria is an early Dutch name for what is now West Irian, and the Dutch navigators, believing that the Great South Land was joined to this land to the north, considered they were exploring the Gulf of Carpentaria (New Guinea). In 1623 the yachts *Pera* and *Arnhem*, under the command of Jan Carstens, were despatched from Amboina. Carstens, with eight of the *Arnhem*'s crew, were murdered by the natives of New Guinea. The *Pera* continued into the huge gulf, and upon return to Amboina gave this, the first known report of our subjects: "In this discovery were found, everywhere, shallow water and barren coasts; islands altogether thinly peopled by divers cruel, poor and brutal nations; and of very little use to the [Dutch East-India] Company." (quoted by Flinders 1814: xi)

Little satisfactory information is obtained from the accounts of the early Dutch discoveries, either about the lands or the peoples. This "has usually been attributed to the monopolizing spirit of their Dutch East-India Company, which induced it to keep secret, or to destroy, the journals." (Flinders 1814: xiv)

Flinders himself was the next European navigator to make con-tact with the Aborigines of the Gulf of Carpentaria. In 1802 he named the Wellesley group of islands in honor of his patron, the Duke of Wellington. The largest island he named Mornington and the second largest Bentinck, after British statesmen; the former is the home of the Lardil Aborigines, the latter the home of the Kaiadilt. Flinders was obliged to careen H.M.S. *Investigator* on Bentinck Island to examine some rotten planks, and had the oppor-tunity to see the Kaiadilt, but was unable to come to close quarters with these wary islanders.

The Wellesley Islands are set in such a backwater for trade or commerce that until recently they have been ignored by industrial society. There was no regular contact with Mornington Island until in 1914 the Australian Presbyterian Board of Missions, with the help of missionaries from Dunedin, New Zealand, established a mission. Little was known of the Kaiadilt until much later; they are in fact the last group of coastal Aborigines to come into regular contact with white Australians. In 1948, grossly stressed by ecological privations and consequent physical and mental illnesses, they were induced to leave their own island to migrate to Mornington. Unless they had done so, it appears that their survival was open to question. This sequence, which in coldly scientific terms may be viewed as an experiment of nature on the effects of human overcrowding in the presence of limited resources (see Hamburg 1971) is documented in *Cruel, Poor and Brutal Nations*. It was felt important, in that book, to measure the effects of such stresses upon man's physical and behavioral responses, of which sorcery is one of the more fundamental in the eyes of the protagonists.

Sorcery is the hardest aspect of primitive medicine to investigate objectively and with thoroughness, surrounded as it is by clouds of anecdote with the genuine sequence relatively unapproachable. Nearly everybody in the community will talk about it, but few will openly admit practicing it; to do so would invite retaliation sooner or later. Some people hint or let it be understood that they possess dark powers, but this is risky. Traditional doctors who admit they have used it stress that they used it for sanctioned judicial purposes—to maintain law—and not to promote private feuds. But I have usually found in each tradition-oriented society an individual who would eventually direct me to a cache of sorcery objects, or reveal them one by one. I sometimes suspected that he had manufactured them and was their chief user, but it would have been tactless as well as fruitless to enquire more closely. I not infrequently uncovered in this way objects the existence of which amazed administrators who had lived closely with the people for thirty years. Even with these little discoveries, the problem rested: how to make an adequate medical study of a social process that was so closely linked with sickness, yet was fundamentally secretive.

There are two approaches to the study of the phenomena of sorcery: the ethnographic by an anthropologist or social scientist and the clinical by a physician. Most accounts reflect the social science approach, dovetailing the descriptions of informants with a knowledge of the wider social process. The social scientist offers medicine valuable insights here. Thus Whiting and Child (1953) correlate childhood socialization experience with sorcery practices in that culture. Other anthropologists, notably Kluckhohn (1944), draw attention to the functional value of sorcery in providing a stateless society with machinery for law and order. Beatrice Whiting (1950) finds sorcery to be prominent in social systems emphasizing peer group control as contrasted with political or religious control. My studies show the Australian native doctor privy to a system which includes sorcery and which exploits the occurrence of illness as a means of social control.

The clinician's approach is distinct. Learning of a complaint of sorcery, he may view the victim as he might a patient, alert to his health, personality, and interpersonal transactions. He naturally focuses the victim's role, while becoming involved with all the protagonists in an attempt to find out what is going on in the particular case.

It seemed that in order to achieve a clinical understanding of sorcery I should study the actual cases occurring around the time of a visit to an Aboriginal settlement, while not ignoring any general ethnographic information that should be offered. At Mornington Island I kept a record of the phenomenology of sorcery. I examined it from the standpoint of possible social function. I studied individual subjects in order to make a clinical or psychiatric appraisal of their personalities and social transactions. Having done so, I addressed myself to three questions. What sort of people are sorcerers? What sort of people are victims? What are the common social contexts? Answers to these questions are of interest to the local administrator and, equally importantly, germane to the scientific description of sorcery.

SORCERY—TRANSITIVE AND INTRANSITIVE

At an early point in my study of cases of sorcery, I found it useful to distinguish between "transitive" forms, in which a sorcerer is identifiable, and "intransitive" forms, in which no such activity is evident. The official versions of sorcery provided by Lardil informants are always transitive—a sorcerer has been at work. For example, a Lardil woman for years had an ulcer on the sole of her foot caused by leprosy. The belief was current that her father had jabbed her footprints with a poison dart to punish her for running after young men and neglecting her old father. The official Lardil versions correspond in the main to the well-known anecdotes in the literature, such as that of bone-pointing magic by Warner (1937) and by Basedow (1927) used as the illustration of voodoo death in the classical paper by Cannon (1942). In anecdotes of this type, the victim is aghast to discover that he is being or has just been "boned" or "sung" by a sorcerer, and he falls into a state of suspended animation resembling the Western depressive stupor. He declines to eat or otherwise help himself and awaits forlornly his fate while his relatives, having withdrawn their support and encouragement, concern themselves with his burial rites. Their ostracism presumably reinforces his despair and hastens his demise. That such sequences exist is not disputed; indeed, I have occasionally been called upon to treat Aboriginal patients with histories and symptoms of this kind.

If death occurs under such circumstances, what is the mode of dying? The physiologists Cannon (1942) and Richter (1957) both suggest a cardiac death. But whereas Cannon suggests a state of excitement of the sympathetic nervous system, with the heart ceasing in systole, Richter from rat-immersion experiments suggests a parasympathetic predominance, with the heart ceasing in diastole. The cessation of the heart is not necessarily due to myocardial infarction. Wolf (1971: 329), evaluating the information concerning psychosocial forces in sudden death, concludes "the evidence reviewed supports the thesis that fatal cardiac arrhythmias, with or without associated myocardial infarction, may often be attributed to undamped autonomic discharges in response to either afferent information from below, or to impulses resulting from integrative process in the brain involved in adaptation to life experience, or both. . . . Regulatory inhibition appears to be diminished in situations that are interpreted as overwhelming and without hope, such as total social exclusion and other circumstances characterized by hopeless dejection or sudden fear. At such times, the loss of regulatory inhibition may provide a mechanism of death."

Referring to the apparent contradiction between the sympathetic emphasis of Cannon and the parasympathetic emphasis of Richter, Engel (1970) suggests that the unexplained cardiac deaths associated with fear occur during the uneasy transition between these two extremes. But I can think of no way of studying this problem in Aborigines and, despite the popularity of this subject, there is no evidence that unexplained cardiac death is commoner in "voodoo-ridden" people than in modern society. Sudden unexplained death following severe stress seems universal, in animals as well as man.

By contrast with the anecdotes that I heard, the sequences involving complaints of sorcery that I actually observed in the field are chiefly of the intransitive variety. They may be described as sorcery sans sorcerer, magic sans magician. They usually involve an overt somatic or psychiatric disorder, or else a social situation seriously disturbed by tension and interpersonal manipulation. No sorcerer acknowledges himself or can be found in such cases, especially at the outset; the complaint of sorcery arises ex post facto, as a hypothesis offered retrospectively. (I should emphasize that whenever I have made a diagnosis of psychiatric disorder in sequences of sorcery, it is not on the basis of the sorcery complaint, but on the evidence of the full biography and the personality factors—taking into account disturbance of emotion, thought, activity, and interpersonal relations, as is proper before assigning some recognized psychiatric category.)

The distinction made here between the transitive and intransitive perceptions of sorcery may be unsettling to the Western observer who is familiar only with the accounts in the popular literature. It does not seem to worry the Aborigine. Dissonant aspects are retained in noncontradictory logical compartments. In fact this discrepancy may be regarded, in Festinger's (1957) term, as a "cognitive dissonance." The Aboriginal elders, like Gilbert's Pooh-Bah, succeed in reducing the dissonance by elaborating to an extreme degree the "corroborative detail intended to give artistic verisimilitude"[2] to the transitive view. Thus, a vast array not only of information but of material objects can be mustered in the village in support of sorcery as a transitive process. In being so help-

---

[2] *Ko.* Well, a nice mess you've got us into, with your nodding head and deference due to a man of pedigree!
Pooh. Merely corroborative detail, intended to give artistic verisimilitude to an otherwise bald and unconvincing narrative.   [*Act 2, The Mikado*]

ful, the Aboriginal informants resemble to us public personages, cited by Festinger, who publicly state something that could be at variance with their private experience. The greater the justification that can be found for the public statement, the less bothersome the dissonance will be.

THE MATERIAL TRAPPINGS OF SORCERY

The system of Lardil sorcery described by informants and backed by an armory of artifacts is classified here for convenience according to the paraphernalia used in the ritual of the alleged enactment—breath sorcery, track (footprint) sorcery, net sorcery, excrement sorcery, and effigy sorcery.

Breath sorcery is known as *mulya;* in this form a man grasps his chin whiskers in his hand and blows sharply with a gesture toward his adversary, his camp, or his tracks. The gesture is accompanied by an uttered "Shu!" an exclamation commonly used in Lardil sorcery, equivalent in sound and in meaning to the English "Shoo!" By this act a breath, a shadow, a spirit, or a dream is transmitted into the other causing him to think or dream of being drowned or speared, or of something that may bring bad luck. The instigating occasion may be an insult or a theft; if he is aware of the act, the one who is cursed will fight back in resentment. Sickness arising from *mulya* is not necessarily regarded seriously; some of the elders suggest that herbal remedies such as the aromatic medicine grass or the milk from the sandridge flower are effective. Diluted, the curse may become a mere hostile gesture or conversational aside.

Footprint sorcery is called *laba-bridi*, literally 'track-you go to it'. The ill-wisher goes to the victim's tracks or to his knee prints at a waterhole and transfixes them with a spike called *djaduran*. The spike may be a small spear with which the sorcerer stabs the footprints as he walks along, or it may be a dart that can be left inserted in the footprint. Another characteristic Lardil device for footprint sorcery is the *bidibil*, a stick bent over fire to the shape of the crescent moon, or held in this shape by a hair string. Two or three *bidibil* across the track of a victim invoke Gidigil, the moon spirit, to induce sickness. The moon is emphasized in Lardil cosmology, possibly because it is vital to fishing. It may play a part as the penetrating spirit in the *malgri* sickness (discussed in chapter

7). In causing *malgri* its potency is judged by some to be greater even than that of the sea serpent, Thuwathu, the Lardil counterpart of the rainbow serpent.

Net sorcery is enacted with the *midjil*, the hand-fishing scoop net of Mornington Islanders, by the act of *bulda*, a swishing or flailing action in the direction of a person or camp in the distance. Only rotten disintegrating net is used. The power of the net makes the victim mad or kills him. Sometimes a flat stone, *birra*, is enclosed in the net and flogged on the victim's camp ashes or excrement, with the curse "*Shu ningga buggada*" ("You die"). A *birra* stone is round or crescent-shaped, like the moon in either case, and has a spirit inside it. The *birra* came in former times from the northern end of the island, but keeps shifting of its own accord around the island and is never found in the same place. If a man walked past a *birra* stone and his shadow fell on it his spirit was caught. The fishing net is also the instrument employed in Lardil levitation, a necromantic happening in which the ghosts of a man's deceased relatives (*mulgun*) transport him for a visit to the spirit home in the east.

Excrement sorcery, or *walga*, is familiar both to Lardil and Kaiadilt people and is not greatly different from that practiced on the mainland. In the urinary form, the dart *djaduran* or the stingray barb *meda* is inserted into the urinated ground, thus causing inflammation of the victim's genitourinary tract. The beak of the bird *djaberoo* is saved and sung to make it poisonous before it's jabbed into the urine patch. The case was quoted to us of a Lardil man whose penis was so covered with sores from this cause that nobody could cure him and he was sent to Palm Island to die. In the fecal variety an earth oven *djakama* is built into which the victim's feces are placed with bone and seaweed; the whole is covered with paperbark and cooked by adding fire-heated stones. In addition to pain in the anogenital region, this powerful sorcery was said to induce madness and death.

Effigy sorcery was also described. I encountered no human replicas, but was presented with a carved *darwal* or animal figure made of cork wood, locally known as *walpa*. The carving resembles a crocodile. Although not so prevalent as in some northern Australian rivers, crocodiles are present in the Mornington Island estuaries. Our specimen is riddled by marine or teredo worm, indicating it has been some time in the sea. The Lardil method is to make an effigy, curse the person to be harmed, and then throw the effigy into the water. For the *darwal* effigy the curse is "*Shu, shu, darwal eetha ngimban!*" meaning "The crocodile will bite or eat you!" A similar effigy is made of Thuwathu, the sea serpent, though no specimen was available.

The distinction between the traditional Lardil and mainland forms of sorcery is instructive. Indigenous Lardil sorcery as described here evidently lacks the magic operations, introjection of solid objects, pointing bones, and poison bullroarers commonly found in the mainland tribes (see chapter 3). Despite its faint New Guinea flavor, it is not referred to as *puripuri*, a term of Papuan or possibly Indonesian origin used collectively in Papua, Cape York Peninsula, and the mainland country just south of the Gulf of Carpentaria for all sorcery and more precisely for a poisonous substance. This substance is sometimes thought to be *moondi* fat—human kidney fat removed by magic operation—or sometimes the deadly sea wasp (*Chironex fleckeri*) prevalent in Gulf waters in summer. The putrefying matter is kept in a small container such as a tobacco tin. Articles in everyday use, from teacups to trousers, are always suspect of contamination by *puripuri* if they have been left lying about. Lardil informants consider that mainland people on the south shores of the gulf live in perpetual dread of *puripuri* and that there is a great deal of trouble over it; they are themselves more worried about it than about their own traditional forms that we have described.

PATTERNS OF SORCERY COMPLAINT

During one visit to Mornington Island, I was fortunate in being able to examine some ten cases in which persons complained of sorcery or recently had done so. Although described to me—at least initially by the Aboriginal participants—in terms of transitive sorcery, the striking feature of these cases was the presence of a somatic or a psychiatric disorder, or else a social context characterized by an interpersonal conflict of some severity. Sometimes these contexts were interwoven. The clinical diagnoses covered a broad range: paranoid schizophrenia; pathological personality; depressive state; hypochondriasis; organic brain deterioration; probable carcinoma. In the cases where an overt illness was not ascertained, family and transactional factors had seemingly led to a social impasse that appeared—to Western eyes—adequate precipitant of the symptoms complained of; the factor of "sorcery" seemed an embellishment.

These conclusions should now be illustrated by the Mornington Island case material. Cases showing psychiatric or somatic disorders are presented as brief vignettes; the others are described in more detail in order to specify the social contexts. The participants are identified by a convention of coded initials in the briefly worded cases or by fictitious names in the more detailed descriptions in order to safeguard professional confidence. They are representative of modes of sorcery. It is hardly possible to aim at statistical treatment of such a subject, so none is attempted.

Pathological Personality, Inadequate Type

A. O. presented himself to me, at the suggestion of the mission superintendent, complaining that a pain in his side prevented him from working. In the course of the interview some of his statements were taken down verbatim.

> I came back to the island three months ago because of this pain in my left side. Can't work with it. Lost weight. Sleep poor—I jump up with fright and my wind goes. I see the shadow of a man. I had this row with a man last October on Gregory Downs. He must have tried to *puripuri* me. I dreamed he done it to me, in my side. Old C. B., the doctor man from Mitchell River, took a marble from my side, sucked it out. Real rusty from being in so long. Still sore now. I couldn't go back to Gregory Downs.

Physical examination revealed no abnormality. Further enquiry showed that the episode complained of was not an isolated one; there had been so many previously that A. O. had never supported his wife or worked regularly. In most instances the work situation had been disrupted as a consequence of A. O.'s physical and social inadequacy.

Paranoid Schizophrenia

T. C. is an elderly Kaiadilt who lives by himself at the edge of the Bentinck camp. He taps his head and says that he has been

caught by *walga* (excrement sorcery). For several years he has
been regarded as mad by the villagers and for a time was so noisy
and destructive that they "marooned" him on Denham Island,
across the Appel Channel from Mornington Island. They provided
him with food but otherwise left him to his own devices. In common with some other psychotic tribal Aborigines described later
(chapters 10 and 11), he had been overactive in buffoonlike and
grandiose mimicry of the white man's activities, such as fence-
building and roadmaking. I was able to observe him and to interview him extensively with the aid of an interpreter. T. C. is blind
from the effects of trachoma but there is no evidence of organic
brain disorder; in fact his camp and fire are unusually neat. His
penile subincision is long for this society, indicating treatment procedures by his countrymen rather than the usual partial subincision
of initiation. T. C. blames excrement sorcery for his difficulties. He
says there is a spirit wandering around talking to him. Sometimes
he hears women coming to his camp offering to be his wife, but
they never arrive. Before the first bird call of the morning he hears
men running around his camp coming to kill him; he shouts at
them to go away and not disturb him.

In a discussion with the island council, comprising both Lardil
and Kaiadilt members, it was learned that the members of the
council were less convinced about the idea of sorcery than was the
patient. Methods of coping with T. C. suggested to the council included a regime to improve supportive social interaction in an
effort to combat his withdrawal, coupled with advice to deter
Kaiadilt children who teased him and threw rubbish at him. Tranquillizing medication was given to suppress excited outbursts.
When his case was reviewed six months later T. C. was steadily
improving. It was a great relief to the villagers and no doubt to the
patient himself.

Chronic Wasting Disorder: Carcinoma?

P. Q. was a mainland Aborigine who worked on Mornington
Island for several years before his death recently. The last year of
his life was marked by progressive wasting and weakness that was
not diagnosed but which would suggest—to Western medical

judgment—a progressive somatic disorder such as carcinoma or tuberculosis. To P. Q., and to his two companions Q. F. and M. M., the condition was caused by sorcery. The words of the two companions are quoted verbatim:

Q. F.: When P. Q. was over working on the mainland, his wife died. Instead of gathering all her clothes to put away in a swag to give to her uncle with gifts for all the relatives, P. Q. didn't bother. He thought he'd passed over these old customs—he was a tracker in the police force. He was careless. But the relatives caught him with the *puripuri*. P.Q. knew this, and he was always thinking about it. He thought he would leave town and come here to get away from it. But he was always thinking about it. Out with me on the cattle, his body would get hot and weak. He was losing condition, always thinking about that *puripuri*.

M. M.: P. Q. would say to me: "I don't know why I done this thing. I never sent my wife's clothes to those relatives and they thought I must have *puripuri*'d her. You're too young to understand these things. They must have took my trousers into water where that jellyfish is. They must have hired a 'working man' (sorcery practitioner) to *puripuri* my clothes." We tried to help P. Q. We tried reading from the Bible. We tried those mainland tricks, taking a bone or stone from his body and showing it. No good. P.Q. never stopped thinking about it till he died.

Accidental Death

C. C. described the disappearance of his brother Dadngewalu. A small party of men was fishing in the shallows at Sydney Island when a big splash and commotion erupted around Dadngewalu. All the others beat the water and drove the "thing" away. On a second occasion, Dadngewalu was again in the shallows off Sydney Island with a fish-laden raft when he and the raft were overcome in a manner that could not be explained. Next day his body was found on the shore and although bruised it had not been mutilated in any way. It was wrapped in paperbark and buried in a sand pit at a place called Labarugan between Sydney and Mornington islands. His death was considered due to effigy sorcery invoking the sea serpent.

Depressive State

Q. M., one of the depressed Kaiadilt people, blames his sad mood and general difficulties on sorcery—of the variety sometimes classified as "contagious" magic. A distinguished-looking man in his forties, he claims that his head sickness is caused through his excreta and discarded food, such as fish bones, being worked upon by his enemies. The events leading up to his miserable condition—including emigration from Bentinck Island, loss of social role, and domestic disharmony—need not be repeated here.[3] Q. M. now prefers to be in the company of whites because of his fear and mistrust of Aborigines. Because of his suicidal preoccupation and profound misery, and the surrounding social disorganization consequent upon them, he has recently been sent to a mental hospital. At present he prefers this to being at home. It is interesting that because of the history he gives of malign magical influences, he has been diagnosed in the hospital as schizophrenic. The opportunity to observe him at home suggests that this is probably a misdiagnosis, and that the ideas of reference represent the sorcery complaints common to his culture. His condition might be more aptly depicted as a chronic depressive state arising in response to gross stress.

A Disturbed Social Context: Domestic Infidelity

T. R., a Lardil father of three children, complained of a urethral discharge. He told the nursing sister at the mission that he had gonorrhea and although his symptoms did not support this—there was no pus or inflammation, and he had not experienced painful urination—he was so convinced that the nurse gave him penicillin injections. The village interpretation of his condition involved sorcery. An elderly mainland man with a reputation for a knowledge of bad magic had warned T. R. that if he should ever dream of him, he should wake up completely and warm himself at the fire or he would become sick. Predictably T. R. had dreamed of him and, having omitted to wake up and warm himself at the fire, was now sick. No blame for this could be attached to the older man, who in fact became the object of some attention and respect. T. R.'s agitation continued to mount until he was fainting with fright, crying aloud, and generally unmanageable. He continued to complain of gonorrhea to the nursing sister at the hospital.

T. R.'s relatives scraped together their savings for a fare to send

---

[3] This history is described in detail in *Cruel, Poor and Brutal Nations* (Cawte 1972), especially in the Epilogue.

him by aircraft to a doctor in Cloncurry, the nearest town of any size, over two hundred miles away, where there was a white doctor who had previously treated him and who might understand his condition. The pilot of the aircraft for his own convenience took the patient on to the next town, Mount Isa, and had him admitted to the hospital there. Physical examination revealed no gonorrhea and he was returned to the island in a week. By this time he seemed more settled and after another month was well enough to return to work.

Shortly after, when I took this history from him, another dimension emerged. He confided that he thought he had gonorrhea because he had associated with an attractive young Lardil woman in the village. It had happened only once; he thought the girl just wanted to find out what he was like. She no longer came near him. He feared that his wife would find out. Though he had not wanted to marry his wife—his "right-head" mate assigned to him by the kinship system—having done so, he was trying to make it succeed. He said before he married he had contracted gonorrhea from a girl on Thursday Island who used to take money from the sailors on the coastal vessels. His story of this incident also made it seem that the "infection" on that occasion was more feared than factual. Concerning the story of witchcraft by the old mainland man, he himself had never been specially convinced of it—the other people in the village had done all the talking about it.

A Disturbed Social Context:
Clash over Children's Quarrels

Schoolboy Ned Sharley was teasing schoolgirl Lois Nelson one afternoon, possibly about her romance with Eric Watson.[4] The teasing developed into a fight in which she broke his forearm with a cricket bat. Ned was sent off to hospital on the mainland and by the next evening the village was aroused over the incident, due in no small measure to the agitating by Ned's mother. Some of the George girls challenged Lois to a fight. Bad feelings between Lois and Edith George had existed before this, because of their mutual connection with Eric Watson.

---

[4] This case was recorded by Michael Friedman (now M.D.) on his elective from Stanford University medical school.

The father of the George family, Lionel, then went across to Nathaniel Nelson's house to find out what the trouble was and to settle the argument. There were apparently some hard words between him and Nathaniel's wife Fay. Nathaniel later claimed that Lionel hit Fay. Lionel denied it, and the consensus was that Nathaniel was lying. In any event Nathaniel clubbed Lionel from behind, knocking him unconscious. Lionel's daughters, after carrying their father home, went back and assaulted Nathaniel. Both Lionel and Nathaniel were seen that night in the hospital. Lionel appeared mildly disoriented, but insisted on going home, claiming that he would be all right. Nathaniel seemed well except for a lump on his forehead but asked to remain in hospital. He was discharged the following day but refused to leave. He complained of a long period of blackouts (this history was never confirmed) and said that he did not feel well. He went home the following day, but returned each succeeding day to the clinic complaining of sore arms, sore eyebrows, and "funny feelings."

The next week Nathaniel went out with the stock team, but had to be brought back several days later when he fell off his horse and lay apparently unconscious on the ground for half an hour. In the hospital examination nothing abnormal was detected. Later he claimed to have had a memory lapse of about six hours, terminating exactly upon his arrival at hospital. He remained in hospital for three days, was discharged under protest, and came back the same night claiming to have just saved himself from fainting again.

By this time there were rumors in the village that Nathaniel had been hit by sticks that had been *puripuri*'d, sung by a now-deceased man. It was recalled that Lionel George once claimed to own such a stick. The discussion in the village was now in terms of sorcery. Nathaniel asserted that each night Lionel's daughters appeared to him in his dreams, standing near his bed holding sticks which they said were the sticks that made him ill. (Traditionally among the Lardil, dreams were used to determine the cause of sickness, especially sickness due to sorcery.) That evening Lionel George called one of the village policemen to his house saying that he would like to discuss things with Nathaniel. He wanted Nathaniel to come to him, but said that he would reciprocate any first gesture. The village talk had upset him considerably.

In hospital Nathaniel's behavior seemed mock-lethargic. He spoke slowly with a sly half grin. The nursing sister said she saw him sitting up in bed one night but when he realized that he was being observed he lay back and started to moan. A member of the visiting team of doctors made up a nonexistent illness, each of the symptoms for which, upon being asked, Nathaniel claimed to have. Nathaniel figured that, being subject to blackouts as he was, he would no longer be able to work as a stock-team member. He wanted some easier job around the mission, such as painting or helping out in hospital. "I might help sister. She could learn me a few things. I could be her right-hand man."

I observed the patient closely throughout the incident and made certain inferences. Since the patient was raised among people who believed in sorcery his conviction that Mary and Edith used "sung" sticks may have been genuine. But from observations of his interpersonal transactions, I concluded that Nathaniel was well aware of the advantages of his sick role; it could even be said that malingering was a feature of his behavior. He may have been looking for an excuse to retire from stock work. Most probably he felt that his behavior toward Lionel had been underhanded and he sought to deflect criticism and retaliation by showing that he was more sinned against than sinning.

Intervention was inescapable in the case of Nathaniel. By keeping the patient in hospital or by sending him away for neurologic examination—a plan I did not seriously contemplate—I would be putting the medical stamp on what seemed a social manipulation. But by discharging Nathaniel in the face of his protestations of sickness I was in effect saying that I thought the patient was shamming. Whichever alternative was chosen amounted to a form of intervention. Several of the village councillors came to me asking how Nathaniel was doing. I replied that he seemed all right; that I thought that *puripuri* was not responsible for Nathaniel's condition, but that the bad feelings between him and the Georges might have something to do with it. Several of the men were quick to pick up the implications of this statement and elaborated upon how they thought Nathaniel was trying to make Lionel look bad. One man suggested that he try a reconciliation between Lionel and Nathaniel and then see if Nathaniel improved.

I am sometimes asked to comment on the assertion that psychiatric symptoms function in the maintenance of a cultural equilibrium, and that treatment from a Western point of view of these symptoms in preliterate cultures is likely to disturb the equilibrium, with undesirable results. This point of view not only overestimates the instability of a cultural system (it is unlikely that a culture could be radically changed by the selective and discreet treatment of its psychiatric casualties by Western doctors), but assumes that all stabilities are desirable ones. Nor does transcultural treatment necessarily mean the imposition of foreign values upon an unwilling people. Those basic values we call mental health are not really so ethnocentric as some would have us believe. They are exemplified in such an institution as sorcery. It is an ancient or exotic syndrome, but fashioned of the universal stuff of mental health—personal comfort and social efficiency.

THE VICTIM OF SORCERY

What kind of people are victims of sorcery? Experience of sorcery in operation on Mornington Island suggests that people adopt the victim role, or have it thrust upon them, for several reasons. In some cases they are suffering from a somatic illness or injury. A substantial proportion of victims are the psychiatric casualties of the community, sorcery being the process by which the occurrence of these psychiatric disorders is reified. Other victims, overtly possessing neither somatic illness nor psychiatric disorder, are enmeshed in social manipulations in which the accusation of sorcery may be used as a lever. This variety is reminiscent to me of "games people play"—the manipulative transactions described by Berne (1961). In a proportion of these cases, sorcery magic is not directed at an aggressive person to control him, but rather the accusation is leveled against him that he is using sorcery. Then social opinion will control him.

This multidimensional interpretation of sorcery victims is consistent with the modern view of witchcraft in medieval demonic theology. It is recognized that behavioral descriptions, expressed in the conceptual language then available (Bromberg 1954), of women in the Middle Ages accused of being witches, or claiming to be witches, correspond in large part with descriptions of presently recognized psychiatric disorders. The interpretation is also consistent with the account given by Marwick (1966) of sorcery in northern Rhodesia examined in its social setting. Here, an act of sorcery is an indication of a moral wrong in human relationships. The wrong is usually committed not by the sorcerer but by the victim, usually the sorcerer's relative or associate. Marwick's analysis demonstrates that sorcery points to foci of structural tension in society, bearing out a Rhodesian maxim that sorcerers never attack strangers but always relatives.

Evans-Pritchard (1937) in his study of the logic of witchcraft beliefs in the Sudan contrasted witches with sorcerers. African usage suggests that a witch does not know what he is about when he starts killing; it is the use of witchcraft, not its mere possession, which is immoral. A sorcerer is a man who may not have witchcraft in his stomach but who deliberately takes the wicked decision to use poisons, rites, and spells against another person.

Gluckman (1955) points out that in Africa bad feeling sets the power of witchcraft to work, but that custom may exclude accusations of witchcraft from very close relationships where difficulties and friction are greatest, as between father and son. The accusation of witchcraft is guided by a man's own grudges, ambitions, and similar sentiments. The accusations have to appear reasonable before the general public, which will debate the situation. Africans appreciate what is implied in the processes by which witchcraft accusations are made; Gluckman refers to a Barotse king who considered that they are lies fostered by hate and envy.

In Australia, it is hard to make the clear distinction between witchcraft and sorcery on the basis of *malice aforethought*, as suggested by Evans-Pritchard for Africa. However it is appropriate to consider the spatial relationships suggested by Marwick and by Gluckman. If a general spatial rule is sought, it is that Australian sorcery divides into two spatial categories, distant and near: accusations may be directed against distant malefactors ("sing him from long way") to apply to true physical illnesses and misfortune. Psychiatric illness tends to be intermediate in kind ("he broke the law some place"), and interpersonal manipulations to be of the near or "neighborhood" variety. This is an impression, for which more Australian cases need to be collected to provide evidence.

At Kalumburu, two *punmun* men and a boy novice in the doctor's dance the stately *palga*. The heavy headdresses are made of colored string wound upon wooden frames, to represent Ungur, the rainbow serpent. (See chapter 4.)

At Mornington Island, a victim of *malgri* is attended by a Lardil tribal practitioner. The victim's body is connected to the sea by means of a long hair-string running over the stick in the middle ground to the channel in the distance. (See chapter 7.)

At Yuendumu, a Walbiri man demonstrates the extent of the *burra* or subincision. (See chapter 8.)

On Mornington Island, an "armory" of sorcery and medical objects was found. *Top to bottom, left to right:* paperbark parcel of aromatic leaves; doctor's brush for brushing spirits from the body; two bones: a pointing bone made of kangaroo fibula with a banded sheath or cover made from the femur of a wading bird; a dart made from the sting of a stringray; the new moon or *bidibil;* a decorated whirling blade or bull-roarer, connected by a string to a bone handle; a paperbark wrapped roll of pipe clay, for controlling tides; two bundles of string, of plant fiber and human hair respectively, for use in *malgri;* the spear *djiduran,* for jabbing footprints; the *bulda* net containing a *birra* stone. (For further descriptions, see chapter 6.)

THE SORCERER

What kind of people are sorcerers? Since it appears that anybody can practice sorcery in Aboriginal society, those who practice it seriously and persistently may well be those who possess character traits of hostility or inadequacy. Such traits could well be heightened by the frustrations and hostilities of camp life, so that sorcery becomes a frequent practice. There is no way of finding out how many engage in its private employment, or with what degree of earnestness. The concealed arsenal of sorcery artifacts in the village may indicate little more than the need to emphasize the transitive aspects of the sorcery process, reducing the dissonance between the transitive hypothesis of sorcery and the more regularly occurring—but unacknowledged—intransitive sequence. In summary of this Aboriginal society, the role of the victim is more important than that of the sorcerer, and more varied. Victims include the physically ill, the mentally disordered, and the participant in a disturbed social situation in which antagonists deceive, exploit, or persuade by accusations of sorcery.

The social contexts of sorcery observed on Mornington Island share another feature that should not be neglected: a white man is often present not merely as a passive observer but as an unwitting participant. Certainly this is true of the manager or superintendent able to arbitrate in the settlement of disputes and the nurse or doctor able to intervene in the management of symptoms. It is therefore important that European Australians who relate to Aborigines develop an understanding of sorcery in action. In particular it will be useful to understand the social conditions under which the occurrence of sorcery is increased.

Marwick (1966) suggests that the coming of modernity to Rhodesia, by increasing human disturbance, may have increased complaints of sorcery. In the Mornington Island population the cases available for study chiefly concern mainland *puripuri;* Lardil sorcery is obsolescent, yielding not to Western causal belief, but to a more prestigious imported sorcery system. It was maintained to me by several informant groups—European Australians, Mornington islanders, and mainlanders—that the level of concern about sorcery is higher on mainland missions and stations than it is on the island. At the mainland mission nearest to Mornington Island, the incidence of complaints and disturbances associated with sorcery is much higher. Police are regularly called to intervene. One Aboriginal informant considers that the reason for the differential is that on the mainland there are more districts, travelers, strangers, social upheaval—and thus more *puripuri*. The mission staff at Mornington Island considers that over the past few years there is increased talk on the island about mainland sorcery, prompted by islanders returning after work on the mainland. Despite this renewal of sorcery, it should not be forgotten that neither sorcery system exceeds in prominence the concept of the spiritual agent as the cause of illness, as in *malgri*. This is also the situation at another isolated and relatively cohesive community, at Kalumburu in the Kimberleys (chapter 4), where the malevolent spirit *tjimi* predominates over *tjagolo*, the sorcerer's "bullet" object. It is not the situation at Lake Nash (chapter 11) with its stressful culture contact and disintegration of spiritual-totemic belief.

My social hypothesis is that spirit possession and sorcery reflect contrasting aspects of the social order. Where behavior is policed through a spiritual construct such as The Dreaming, possession syndromes predominate. In regions where The Dreaming is less influential, the policing of behavior is more the function of the peer group; there sorcery predominates over possession. Observations in New Guinea support this hypothesis: possession syndromes are not uncommon in the villages but sorcery is usually more common and more talked about. In New Guinea village society, sorcery talk often reflects the policing by the peer group of aggressive or competitive behavior. Success in growing garden vegetables is a common occasion for it; dominance in *bisnis* is becoming another. Sorcery threats prevent a man from becoming "too big." The hypothesis accords with Beatrice Whiting's (1950) account of Paiute sorcery, which indicates that sorcery correlates with systems that emphasize peer-group control rather than with systems policed by a superordinate political structure or by internalized religious control through the concept of an omnipotent god.

My clinical hypothesis is distinct because the clinician's perspective is distinct. It emphasizes the active or precipitating role of the victim. The victim may be physically ill, or psychiatrically ill, or enmeshed in social manipulations by which he seeks to discredit a rival through accusations. One of my colleagues, reflecting upon this clinical perspective of what is usually an ethnographic preoccupation, called it "recent advances in sorcery." If advances in understanding exist, they lie in the recognition that the operational study of sorcery sequences leads to reduced emphasis on the transitive sorcerer-victim transaction. It focuses more attention on the victim's role. The victim is no longer viewed as the passive sufferer from an anxiety state precipitated by an act of sorcery. It furthermore shows that the Westerner who lives among primitive people is not outside the sorcery context. While the people inside the system may fail to recognize that sickness often precedes sorcery, the clinician's failure to accept involvement leads to a comparable and more culpable error—for a clinician—in which opportunities for the relief of sickness are resisted.

CHAPTER SEVEN

Malgri: A Culture-Bound Syndrome

ARE THE MENTAL DISORDERS of preagricultural "primitives" different from those found in modern society, or are they variants of the familiar Western diagnostic categories? This chapter will present an account of a superbly interesting culture-bound syndrome, *malgri*, that sheds light upon this question and upon other questions commonly asked about such syndromes. Some of the issues involved in a study of culture-bound syndromes should be outlined (with reference in this case to *malgri*) at the outset. The reader may consider how far these issues pertain to the well-publicized culture-bound disorders or "ethnic psychoses," including *amok* and *latah* (in Malaysia), *koro* (among Chinese in Malaysia), and *witiko* (in Indian cultures of northeast America).

1. *Malgri* describes a pattern of symptoms and behaviors specially characteristic of the culture of which it is a part.

2. The culture exerts both a causal and a shaping influence in cases of *malgri*.

3. There is no one-to-one correspondence between cases of *malgri* and Western psychiatric categories—*malgri* cases cover a range of Western diagnoses.

4. Not all cases of *malgri* are psychopathological. Some are; others represent culturally acceptable expressions, of anxiety or other discomfort, not amounting to psychiatric disorder.

5. Individual differences in susceptibility to *malgri* are traceable to variations in personality and experience.

6. *Malgri* serves the functional purpose, in the culture, of social regulation (by contributing to the maintenance of territorial boundaries).

Malgri is found only in the Wellesley Islands of the Gulf of Carpentaria. Focal distribution of such sicknesses is to be expected in view of the comparatively restricted diffusion between the various cultural blocs of Australia, probably associated with sharp ecological differences, as discussed in chapter 5. (Details of the Wellesley Islands culture are to be found in *Cruel, Poor and Brutal Nations* [Cawte 1972]). The disorder might even be termed culture-specific rather than merely culture-bound.

This disorder was encountered, in a typical sequence, through children's games. Two of my children, a girl of seven years and her brother six, were visiting Mornington Island with me; they spent much of their time playing with a Lardil girl. During a ramble near "Picnic Place" a mile or more from the settlement, the Aboriginal girl found exuding from a tree some resin that was good to chew. After chewing a while my children ran down toward the beach. The Aboriginal child called out to them to stop: they must wash their hands and mouth in a freshwater hole before going to the sea; otherwise the sea serpent would come out of the sea and make them sick or even kill them. My daughter, impressed with this precaution, complied; her brother was skeptical but washed his hands and mouth just the same. He was not going to be the one who got *malgri* and died. An event of the next day showed how justified the precautions were. A Lardil man carrying his small son in his arms came up to the mission. The boy was very distressed and complained of pains in the legs and stomach. He kept moaning and demanding of his father "Rub me guts." The missionary gave him a sedative and he gradually recovered. The story came out that, despite warnings about poisonous jellyfish, he had been bathing in the sea. But it was not a jellyfish that had stung him; his grandfather Jacob, a tribal practitioner, confirmed that it was *malgri*. The boy was lucky to recover, said grandfather who was irritated that he had not been called on to treat it. He did however demonstrate how he would have treated it, using his grown son for the subject, in a posed demonstration for the camera.

It was ascertained from Jacob and from other Lardil men and women that *malgri* was a prominent disorder in the Lardil medical system at Mornington Island: a spirit-intrusion syndrome linked with the totemic organization of the people and their territory. All seemed agreed on the phenomenology.

The central theme in *malgri* is the mutual antipathy between land and sea. A person who enters the sea without washing his hands after handling land food runs the risk of succumbing to *malgri*. Traces of land food are dangerous in the sea and must first be rubbed off with sand and water; even body paint and grease must be removed. *Malgri* spirits can also operate in the reverse direction—from the land—when, for example, a person who has been fishing in the sea uses a freshwater rock pool or lagoon without first cleansing his hands of traces of saltwater food. If these precautions are neglected the totemic spirit that is guardian of that particular littoral is believed to invade the belly "like a bullet." The *malgri* victim grows sick, tired, and drowsy. His head aches, his belly distends, he writhes and groans in pain and may vomit. He is constipated. The pain is described as constant rather than colicky, though the precise symptoms depend on the nature of the spirit doing the possessing. The finding of the distended abdomen might result from diaphragmatic fixation coupled with air swallowing, as in the pattern of pseudocyesis or false pregnancy; some uncertainty exists as to the accuracy of this description of distension. Most islanders seemed to have at least some anxiety about contracting the illness.

To appreciate this disorder one must know that a feature of Lardil cosmology is the division of the coastline of Mornington Island into upward of thirty littorals, each forming the sea frontage for a particular subsection of the tribe or class of totemites, each with its distinctive totem. In many cases the totems, such as the shark, stingray, coolibah tree, and rock cod, are obvious local natural species; in other instances, such as with the moon and sea serpent, the legendary associations of the site are represented. I spent a good deal of time making, with the aid of several islanders and, later, mapmakers, a chart of Mornington Island as its inhabitants saw it (facing page). The territorial scheme is essential to an accurate appreciation of the disorder.

Malgri is a sickness of intruders. The social group occupying the estate enjoys some immunity in its home range. An elderly Lardil, Gully Peters, described this feature.

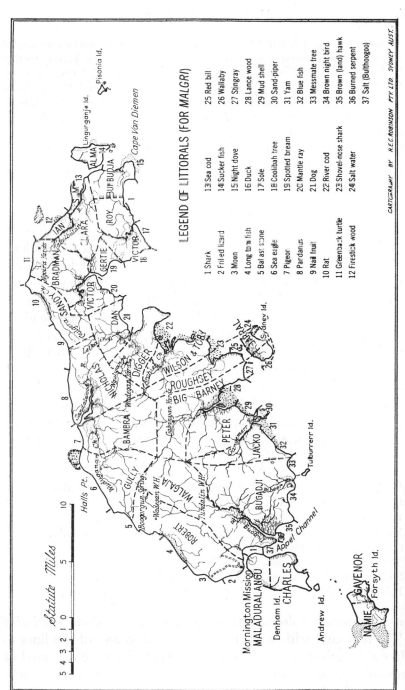

THE LARDIL VIEW OF MORNINGTON ISLAND

Me boss belong that Sandalwood River country. Yarragarra [sea eagle] is boss of the sea around that part. I can eat swamp turtle belong to that land and I can go down to that sea and I can't *malgri*. I say: "It's me, I'm boss of this country, don't *malgri* me, Yarragarra." If somebody doesn't belong to my country, he will *malgri* there. If I go to South Side, Sydney Island way, I can *malgri* there—not my country. If people walk-about a long time at my place, like Fred, they're all right—the sea gets their smell and knows them. It's strangers that *malgri* all the time.

When the cry goes out that somebody has fallen victim to *malgri*, everybody runs to help. A fire is made near the prostrate victim. From the throng emerges a native practitioner or other elder with knowledge. Kneeling, he massages his axillary sweat into the victim's body. A grass or hair belt is unraveled to provide a long cord, which is tied by one end to the victim's foot while the other is run down to the water in order to point the way home for the intruding spirit. The healer commences the song of exorcism; its innumerable verses are sung through the night, while the assembled people scan the sky for a shooting star. The shooting star is the incarnation of *malgri*'s eye, at last diving from the sky to indicate *malgri*'s dispossession and banishment. The string is then snapped. The victim recovers. So runs the procedure for treatment.

For that part of the Appel Channel at the mouth of the Dugong River, where the island's population now congregates, the water front totem is Thuwathu, the sea (rainbow) serpent. A song for his exorcism in cases of *malgri* runs:

Shu! Damudaia, damudma.	Stop biting, unloose your teeth.
Gangulmaia, gangulma.	Unclench your jaws.
Worramaia, worrama.	Open wide your mouth.
Budgerunguru nalma	Move your head from this body.
Gidilingini djuwadju wadju.	Crack, break your backbone.
Mudjinbi djinbi baladma.	Relax your tail and go.
Budjimarana, budjimaran.	Begone you rainbow belly.
Yalkamalara bingula.	Fall back in the hole you come from.

The song goes at a slow rhythmic pace with repetitions. *Djiri djiri* (Make him cold with water) can be added to any of the lines to help the exorcism or to cool the fever. Histories were collected of cases of *malgri* occurring around the time of my visit. Various sickness and behavioral patterns are represented.

MALGRI PATTERNS

A Dissatisfied Woman

A middle-aged woman happened to contract *malgri* shortly after our expedition arrived on the island. She had been on a picnic with two friends and had eaten some dugong meat before washing her hands in the river.[1] A truck had to be sent to fetch her since she insisted she could not move because of *malgri*. On arrival at the mission hospital she complained of prostration and severe abdominal pain. No physical abnormality was detected. She was reassured and after a few hours she recovered and was discharged. Her hospital record showed frequent attendances for complaints of pains in the head and in the chest, probably psychogenic. Medical interviews with her revealed deep dissatisfaction with her family life. Her husband had left her to take a job on the mainland, and she had to look after her boy aged two years and an adopted son of seven years. Her various complaints of headache, "angina," and *malgri* had to be evaluated in this context.

A Children's Stomach Upset and an Envious Matron

A party of five children was taken to nearby Denham Island in the charge of an intelligent and literate Aboriginal matron. *Malgri* spoiled the picnic. She subsequently reported:

> The children ate bread and tinned meat. Then they went swimming in the channel. Two of the children got pain in the stomach in that water. It could not be a jellyfish sting, because only the stomach got sore. It was tight and bulging. I took them to sister. She only given them aspirin, she didn't know what to do. So I took them down to the camp and an old woman said, see Kitchener Steele. He treated those children. He used body sweat and that *malgri* song.

The nursing sister reported:

> Both children were rolling all over the hospital verandah, clutching their stomachs and yelling. I examined them. Maybe their stomachs were distended but they were soft to palpation. They seemed healthy apart from all the screaming, so I didn't admit them. They were better that night.

---

[1] The dugong (sea cow) is once more plentiful in the waters of the Gulf of Carpentaria following its legal protection from non-Aboriginal hunters. Aborigines are permitted to hunt the dugong only for domestic consumption.

Further discussion with the Aboriginal woman in charge of the picnic revealed a transactional situation of possible relevance. She was envious of the mission nursing sister and lost few opportunities of disparaging her in an indirect way. She seemed gratified at being the central figure in an illness context that the nurse was not competent to handle. It is not suggested here that the situation was consciously engineered with this in mind, but, having once arisen, it was exploited in this way.

Four Men Split Up

A middle-aged man reported a hunting trip that was interrupted by *malgri.*

> This morning we got a sea turtle and had it for breakfast. Then we split up and D. B. went along the north side and he went into a freshwater hole. He should know better than that. He should have gone home. You can't take sea turtle into freshwater; this would *malgri.* You should eat it on the beach and then wash your hands. D. B. had to turn back and come to our camp. We helped him in; stomach was all blown up. We got hair string from a belt and put it from a toe to a spear under a tree. We sang him till five in the morning. I saw a star traveling over the sky from the east like a white cloud, very slow. It disappeared at five o'clock and that man got better. People said it was the rat spirit, Dowa—it was rat country —you see these rats at Birri and Rocky Island. We could see light all along the beach, in the water.

It was hard to discover the transactional background of this incident and I was left speculating why the party of four had split up before the isolated member committed his error and contracted *malgri.*

The traditional illnesses of the Kaiadilt group from Bentinck Island were less closely studied than those of the Lardil because of the greater difficulty in communication. From discussions in the village it appeared that Kaiadilt intrusion syndromes were also common and involved the spirits of the soldier crab, reef octopus, and, particularly, the mangrove rat called Wadn't by the Kaiadilt. There was no evidence that these syndromes achieved the complexity of *malgri,* though their generic name, *malgudj,* is similar. They illustrate the confluence between the two cultures and languages that developed in spite of the geographical separation and biological divergence. (See *Cruel, Poor and Brutal Nations* [Cawte 1972]).

A Kaiadilt Childhood

An old Kaiadilt woman was in the habit of talking excitedly to herself a good deal and being generally morose in front of others. Routine physical examination revealed a number of highly cheloidal cicatrices on her chest and back. She said that the scar in the fold under her right breast was made by her mother with a firestick during her childhood on Bentinck Island, as a decoration. The wounds on her back were made by her father, when as a child she was sick, to remove Wadn't, the sea rat, who was making *malgudj* inside her. The old woman volunteered this information separately from my *malgri* enquiry context.

The significance of the *malgri* syndrome was the subject of much discussion by our sociomedical team. In fact it sparked a flurry of conjecture, which—even if it did not arrive at a full understanding of the condition—illustrates the fascination of applying modern interpretations to traditional patterns. Small wonder that exotic culture-bound syndromes provide a happy hunting ground for speculative interpretation! *Malgri* might for example be viewed, from a functionalist perspective, as a part of the total belief structure maintaining social institutions and organization and ultimately adaptation. From the psychiatric viewpoint it is necessary to scrutinize the pathogenic and conflictual elements of the traditional pattern. In doing so, several elements of *malgri* attract comment: the antipathy expressed between land and sea, the handwashing ritual, the violated taboo, the possibility of a corresponding Western diagnosis, and the widespread phobia of the condition.

In classical psychoanalytic idiom, the preoccupation of the islanders with the sea-land antipathy would suggest a displacement of a *family* antipathy, for example that between father and son as emphasized in the Oedipal theorizing of Freud's *Totem and Taboo* (1912) or Roheim's *The Eternal Ones of the Dream* (1945). This would represent a case of the lesser fear displacing the greater terror, as suggested by Freud. In terms of neoanalytic interpersonal theory, the displacement might rather be from the individual's current family and social transactions. Some support for these interpretations could be found in day-to-day observations of the islanders' behavior, in which displacement is a common feature. It has been observed that displacement of hostility is part of the ethos of Mornington Island, an ethos which values the "happy" man, the peacemaker who is consistently generous and congenial, who avoids confrontation and who constantly looks for ways to attribute the village quarrels and fights to forces beyond anyone's control (Cawte 1972).

From the phenomenological viewpoint, the displacement might not represent an antipathy having reference to family tensions, but rather the displacement might refer to the essential difference, for the individual, between the land-sea elements. The conflict between the land and the sea is real and earnest to the Mornington islander. Sometimes the sea yields its food, sometimes the land. A hunting-gathering people exist in a state of sustained competition with nature and with its own members for its survival. From the phenomenological perspective the syndrome is more specifically totem and trespass than totem and taboo. It is part of the network of ecological relationships evolved to prevent trespassing, and to conserve proper distances between human groups. It exemplifies the ethological concept that the "territory" of a social group is a pertinent consideration in discussions of its behavior, indeed often a mainspring of motivation and social interaction. What ethologists call reaction distance has been described in psychiatric patients as the "body buffer zone" (Horowitz 1965). *Malgri* is perhaps the most specific instance in medicine of an illness associated with the concept of territoriality. While it cannot be said to represent simple extrapolation of animal territoriality to human behavior, it offers a striking example of the universal fear of leaving one's own territory and of the danger inherent in breaking the rules on foreign ground.

Some details of the *malgri* syndrome, especially the handwashing and/or contaminatory theme, do not at first sight possess a clear association with the territory theme. The handwashing pattern might be interpreted psychoanalytically as a ritual cleansing of blood after killing the land animal (symbolically father), but phe-

nomenological examination of the situation suggests another interpretation. The injunction underlying the *malgri* taboo is not directed against killing and eating land food, but reflects the need to
propitiate the sea, by refraining from mixing spirits from land and
sea. The sea, like the mother, is the main food-giving element for
the Lardil. Offending it could lead to engulfment, failure of the
food supply or attack by its contained objects. This interpretation
does not deny a possible historical origin of the handwashing precaution in terms of an actual event; the sea does periodically enter
these islands in the form of an exceptionally high spring tide.
Where might the contaminatory theme come from? Enquiries revealed that the traditional Lardil toilet training schedule differs
from the pattern in Western culture where weaning precedes
bowel control. On Mornington Island the child is taught to hide
his excreta around the age of weaning, roughly when he is four
years old, and he is taught by his peers rather than by his parents.
This coincides with the time of the first major developmental crisis
of the Lardil child: weaning or displacement at the breast by the
newborn sibling, a time of tantrums and distress. It may be inferred
that oral-dependent needs are frustrated and aggressive drives pro-
voked at the same time as control of anal drives is developing.[2]
Under these circumstances a man's desire to invade the sea to take
fish might symbolize the repressed urge to enter and take food
from mother, an urge that was controlled contemporaneously with
the desire to soil, and might provoke projective fantasies of being
entered in retaliation by the spirit guardian of the sea.

We found that in the discussion of *malgri* among our expedition
members, "wild" psychoanalytic interpretations were heady stuff,
not always palatable to those reared in the more pedantic biological traditions. The latter observers pointed out that the act of handwashing itself contains biological advantages that possibly operate
outside of conscious awareness to reinforce it. The advantages of
handwashing might for example reside in more successful fishing
with clean hands from which the smell has been removed, or in
better health from removal of hand-borne pathogens of conditions

---

[2] These observations arose in discussion with the child psychiatrist, Dr. Barry
Nurcombe, whose account of Lardil childrearing is found in *Cruel, Poor and Brutal Nations* (Cawte 1972).

such as dysentery. But it has to be conceded that if biological advantage underlies the ritual of handwashing, it does so at an unconscious level; the explanation is one that would occur to a biologically trained team of doctors rather than to primitive people.

Functional explanations of culture-bound syndromes, of whatever doctrinal origin, are not completely satisfying. Room must be reserved to account for the finding that some individuals are susceptible to *malgri* while others are not, a difference traceable to individual variations in personality and to individual experience of interpersonal or ecological transactions. Because of these individual variations, exact correlations need not be expected between modern medical syndromes and culture-bound disorders. In my casebook, *malgri* corresponds most frequently to a gastrointestinal disturbance (often with constipation) overlaid with a psychogenic culturally determined superstructure. In other cases it corresponds to a conversion reaction, and in yet others to a paranoid development. In most instances, the "spirit intrusion" explanation is applied *post hoc* to various entities by the Lardil. Interpretation has to be made individually in each case in the light of all the circumstances, especially considering the interaction pattern in which the patient is enmeshed.

The implications that an awareness of ethology may have for the *malgri* syndrome call for further comment. Some readers may interpret the syndrome as an extrapolation to man of the phenomenon of territoriality that occurs in the animal kingdom. Territoriality is not universal throughout the animal kingdom, especially among the nonhuman primates. It would be facile to relate the territorial behavior that occurs in some lower animals directly to man, as a biological justification of property rights. Klopfer (1969) points out that territoriality is in fact subject to great diversity and represents not one but many different adaptations serving different purposes for various animals. Thus it would be misleading to extrapolate from birds to men without attempting to account for all relevant evolutionary and ecological factors. Nevertheless, without resorting to the possible analogies with animal behavior, it is likely that *malgri* may have something to teach about the composition of the horde in hunting-gathering societies and about the horde's territorial rights.

The aspect of *malgri* sickness that should not be overlooked in concentrating upon its intricacies is that the Lardil's fear is directed toward the intruding spirits that ring his island rather than toward the illness itself. The fear is thus a policing agent in Lardil society. In the definitions of medicine and the law with which this book began, the limited correspondence between these institutions in primitive and modern society was pointed out. The law of real property was cited as an example, it being assumed that a primitive hunting-gathering society would have no comparable concept. Yet here we find the island home of the Lardil seemingly legally partitioned (by a fear of local spirits able to induce sickness) as distinctly as hereditary estates partition an English county.

Malgri therefore provides a source of material for social anthropology in its task of evaluating the nature of the relationship between the organization of a local group and the geographical territory which it occupies. As described by Hearne (1970) the current debate on this issue concerns several interrelated questions of both social organization and territory, including:

1. The composition and stability of local group membership;

2. The distinctiveness or exclusiveness of the local group's territorial boundaries;

3. The availability and variety, as well as the utilization patterns, of the food and water resources to which the local group has access rights or ownership claims; and

4. The nature of the social, economic, and political ties that may bind local groups to one another.

We are reminded by Hearne that Radcliffe-Brown in the 1930s proposed that the "horde" was the residential unit in the social organization of Australian Aborigines. The horde was composed of males and unmarried females, who were members by birth, and the wives of the male members. It was thus an exogamous unit, patrivirilocal in residence owning and occupying a territorial area containing the horde's totemic sites and the food and water resources necessary for subsistence. Radcliffe-Brown's model has been subject to question. Hiatt (1962) argues that local groups failed to form autonomous, separate, and self-sustaining economic units opposed, in a structural sense, to similar units.

The apparent distinctiveness and exclusiveness of the Lardil estates may be attributable to the fact that the Lardil occupy an island, limited in resources and capable of supporting only a limited population, so that territorial rights might be jealously safeguarded. The *malgri* syndrome itself appears connected with the fact that the territory is an island; it is not encountered among mainland tribes. But there are ways in which the "ideal" territorial scheme elaborated by the Lardil might be modified or relaxed. One is that the littorals are not guarded by spirits all equally dangerous in terms of *malgri*, suggesting that some littorals are better fishing sites and therefore need stronger policing. "'Burned serpent'' and "moon" are reputed to be particularly dangerous spirit-guardians, and even today these littorals are prolific sources of food. Thus ecological factors, as well as structural factors, enter in the determination of the territorial units or estates. The "ideal" scheme is relaxed in another way by the practice of allowing outsiders to live with the local social unit. Gully Peters, boss of the sea-eagle country, had in his social unit Fred, from the other side of the island. This was possible, according to Gully, because the sea-eagle spirit eventually came to know Fred's smell, and accepted him as a resident.

It seems reasonable to infer that ecological or subsistence tensions were factors leading to the modification of the composition of island social units. The composition of the social units, after fifty years of Western contact, is not known with any precision, although my map, made with the help of the islanders, provides an approximation with which to begin. It is in any case more a subject for the social anthropologist than for the clinician. Meanwhile, *malgri* provides a superb example of the interweaving of ecological adaptation, social organization, medicine, and the law. It answers the central question with which this chapter began concerning the correspondence between the culture-bound syndrome and Western diagnostic categories. One should not look for a simple relationship because the social dimensions of illness are different in the two cultures. One would indeed need to hold to a narrow medical model of psychiatric disorder even to contemplate such a relationship.

These are the reflections of a Westerner—of one who, contemplating the ideas of a non-Western people, sometimes feels enslaved by his own analytic style of reflection. For a phenomenological appreciation of *malgri*, we must consult the Aborigines. Dick Roughsey responded to my request for the *malgri* legend. This suggests the origin of the pattern of sickness, as seen by those whom it affects.

THE SUFFERING OF THUWATHU,
THE RAINBOW SERPENT

The Thuwathu is a major dreamtime figure who created many story and places on his travels. Thuwathu is caught in his burning humpy which was set alight by his sister Bulthugu because he refused to shelter her child in his big humpy, his humpy was burning when he was asleep. The noise of the fire woke him up from his sleep. When he tried to crawl out he got burnt and he was burnt and had blisters on his body. The Thuwathu was groaning and suffering with pain. The legend has it that the Thuwathu tried to escape but he couldn't. The Thuwathu created Dugong River on Mornington and finally died at Bugugan on the North side of the Island. The roots and straight sticks which are used for boomerangs and spears today are the remains of Thuwathu's bones and his spirit still remains in all the water holes as Mulgri. The young man has broken a tabu by eating land-food and then going down to the salt water without first washing. This is called Mulgri. They try to revive him by singing away the spirit which causes his illness. The song is: I sing your head you go away—I sing your teeth you go away—I sing your jaw you go away—I sing your backbone you go away. This weakens the spirit so that he can be driven away along the string which leads from the sick man to the water. However the young man dies and the body is lifted up to the burial platform and a string leads from his face toward the east to guide his spirit to the spirit home (Yillyillidnye). The old man sings the spirit away and to ensure that it leaves the body he hits the ground with a club. Finally the departed spirits come back and dance. The old man then tries to find out which of these spirits caused the young man's death.

—DICK ROUGHSEY (Goobalathaldin)
Mornington Island, 1968

CHAPTER EIGHT

Why We Slit the Penis

OF THE VARIOUS SURGICAL INCISIONS practiced by Aboriginal Australians, the genital mutilations are of special interest. The peoples that practice circumcision imbue it with much ritual significance, as Aboriginal Australians, Jews, and probably Arabs exemplify (Abbie 1957a). But the Aboriginal Australian people is unique for its widespread practice of subincision of the urethra as well, carried out for other than therapeutic reasons. In this operation (called, at different levels of culture contact, "artificial hypospadias," "Sturt's terrible rite," and "whistlecock"), a slit is cut through the ventral surface of the penis into the urethra, from its orifice to a position about an inch along the shaft of the penis. The slit is usually extended bit by bit until the full extent of the penile urethra is converted into an open channel. Because the channel tends to heal over at the proximal end, some groups, for example the Pidjandjara of northwest South Australia, extend the mayhem by making transverse cuts in this region.

Elsewhere in the world, subincision of the urethra is employed as a therapeutic measure. Western surgeons employ it in the treatment of local affections of the penis, such as papillomata. In the Amazon basin it is practiced to remove a small parasite (*Cetopsis candiru*) that becomes lodged in the urethra. In Fiji, and possibly Tonga, the operation is viewed as a prophylactic against serious disease. Rivers (1926) noted that in these islands the operation acts as a counterirritant and as a means of evacuating blood and other bad humors that are thought to produce disease. Hogbin (1934) observed a similar practice in the Wogeo of New Guinea, who say that women are cleansed by menstruation, but that men, to guard against illness, periodically must incise the penis and allow some blood to flow; an operation that is often called men's menstruation. One of the very rare reports of its use for nontherapeutic reasons, outside Australia, concerns the Samburu people of Kenya; the psychiatrist Margetts (1960*b*) observed that Samburu boys, before they are circumcised at puberty, carry out the operation on themselves while on their lonely job of herding cattle. There are apparently no ritual involvements in this activity, the significance of which Margetts found obscure.

The custom of subincision among the Australian tribes has been widely debated by anthropologists, psychoanalysts, and others. Answers given to the question of significance seem to depend largely upon the point of view of the person observing the phenomenon. The first thorough account of Australian subincision, provided by ethnographer-physician Basedow in 1927, emphasized hygiene: the operation might aim to relieve or prevent inflammatory reactions caused by the entry of dirt, grit, seeds, or insects into the urethra. A popular lay speculation concerns the contraceptive effect of the operation, arising from the presumed failure of semen to be delivered into the vagina. A theory, held by settlers in the outback who are mindful of the sexual life of Aborigines, emphasizes the broader erection of the subincised penis and suggests that the object of the maneuver is to give greater stimulation during sexual intercourse. Early psychoanalytic theory had seen in circumcision a symbolic castration. Anthropologists influenced by the psychoanalytic interest in the general question of genital mutilation postulate for subincision an unconscious desire to simulate the female, who had been regarded psychoanalytically as castrated male; thus Montagu (1937*a* and *b*) argues that subincision was originally instituted in order to cause the male to resemble the female with respect to the occasional effusion of blood and possibly also with respect to producing some feminization in the appearance of the male organ. Roheim (1949) states that they are offering an artificial vagina as compensation for the real one. Social anthropologists engaged in the study of the ceremonial and communal life of the people, as distinct from its interpretation by psychoanalytic theory, refer to the convenience of the subincision region for drawing blood for use in ritual (Elkin 1965).

Thus the theory of subincision—in common with the theories of other social institutions before and since—is affected by the equation of the observer. While each observer claims significance for his own interpretation, it is fair to say that no single explanation is fully satisfactory. The situation suggests that more remains to be discovered on the subject. Bettelheim (1962: 49) summarized the matter cautiously and judiciously: "when men by subincision make themselves *resemble* women, the obvious reason is that they are trying to *be* women. Only if the data themselves rule out such an interpretation must we search for another."

One source of data remains insufficiently exploited. Our investigation therefore concentrates upon the Aborigines' own views of why they ritually subject the penis to subincision, insofar as these views can be appreciated by an observer in another culture. It employs a phenomenological rather than an analytic approach.

The subjects of the study are the Walbiri of central Australia (also referred to as Wailbri, Walpiri, Ilpirra, Njalia, among others). These people are good subjects for the study of subincision because it is an obligatory practice for them; all the adult males have undergone it. In addition, Walbiri experience of Western culture is recent; less than twenty years before the time of my enquiries the majority of them lived in splendid isolation as "desert myalls," avoiding Western contact and being equally avoided. More recently they relinquished their nomadic life on the spinifex plains to congregate at four government settlements established for them. This has permitted studies of their physical characteristics (Abbie and Adey 1955; Abbie 1957*b*) and at least two descriptions of aspects of their social organization (Meggitt 1962; Munn 1964) revealing a complex culture difficult for Westerners to appreciate. The cultural upheaval has led to serious problems of adjustment associated with various forms of psychiatric and personality disorder (Cawte and Kidson 1964, 1965). The present is an ideal time for the study of Walbiri institutions such as subincision; twenty years ago there would have been insufficient contact or rapport, and twenty years hence these institutions will have become contaminated by the contact, if not lost altogether.

METHOD OF INVESTIGATION

The investigators first reviewed the hypotheses about subincision that had either been advanced in the literature on the subject or that armchair ingenuity might conceivably advance. These hypotheses were grouped together under appropriate headings, together with the topics, concepts, and questions obviously associated with them (Table 1). This preparation was made in order that the investigators should be familiar with the subject and able to anticipate possible responses and perhaps to clarify them.

TABLE 1

"Reasons" Considered for Subincision, Prior to Beginning Investigation

"Reason"	Associated Concepts
1. Custom	Tradition. Law. The Dreaming. "God."
2. Hygiene	Cleanliness. Removal of smell, impurity.
3. Initiation	Coming to manhood. Ordeal. Revelation of secrets. *Rites de passage.*
4. Status	Naked societies, unable to infer rank from regalia, emphasize various body incisions.
5. Blood drawing	Ritual blood region for ceremonies, body decoration.
6. Sexual	Altered shape of erection. Altered sensation. Preference by men? by women?
7. Urinary	Altered volume or shape of stream. Posture adopted for urination.
8. Contraception	Spilling of semen. Appreciation of physical paternity? Knowledge of contraception?
9. Simulation of women	Vulvalike appearance. Association (possibly unconscious) of subincision blood with menstruation.

Next, Walbiri men were selected for questioning who possessed a good knowledge of Walbiri lore, with whom good rapport on secret subjects was obtainable, and who were known to be reliable on such matters. The three investigators were in an advantageous position so far as rapport was concerned. One had previously studied the Walbiri medical system in collaboration with its medicine men and as a psychiatrist had assisted in the return to the tribe of one of its best-known men who had suffered from a psychosis. The second, himself a Walbiri, one of the few reasonably fluent in both English and Walbiri, interpreted the nuances of the language and helped clarify points in the interviews. The third had been intimately associated with the Walbiri in research extending over twelve years and had filmed many aspects of their traditional life (Barrett, Brown, and Fanning 1965).

The interviews, conducted chiefly in Walbiri, were recorded on tapes, now lodged in the library of the Institute of Aboriginal Studies, Canberra, where they are available for further study. The procedure followed the lines of a nondirective (loosely structured) interview: after reasonable rapport had been established, in a private place free from interruption, the topic was broached. A list was made of the Walbiri genital terms. These terms may be conveniently outlined here since some will be used hereafter in the presentation: *burra*, subincision; *wida-burra*, circumcision of young men (that is, little *burra*); *ngindi*, penis; *tjindi*, vagina; *gulurba*, testicles; *bindi-pupu*, foreskin; *ngurumba*, pubic hair; *mudjari*, pubic apron; *djanni*, pubic tassel; *njiri-njiri*, glans; *buru*, semen. After this preliminary the informant was reminded that the investigators wanted to find out about *burra* and he was given free rein to express his thoughts on the subject with minimal interruption.

It was anticipated (correctly, as it turned out) that the informants would adhere closely to the "custom" or The Dreaming category of reasons for *burra*. The Dreaming or *tjugurba* is invariably cited by Walbiri to explain matters whose origin is thought to go back into history to the creative epoch—much as Christians invoke God as the Creator (see chapter 9). Their accounts of *tjugurba* often include a description of a Dreaming site, one of many actual spots in Walbiri territory where an ancestor hero or a totemic animal emerged. They go on to describe the hero's or the totem's subsequent travels and adventures through and beyond Walbiri territory.

In view of these anticipated responses we decided that we should also be free to interpolate into the interview the various hypotheses about subincision that occur to the Western mind. It was recognized that this would introduce the factor of suggestion, and that tribal Aborigines are apt to consider seriously almost any suggestion put forward by a white person, however outrageous it might be. It was recognized, however, that suggestion is a factor that could operate in any type of interviewing, even those apparently nondirective in nature (Greenspoon 1955). Care was taken therefore to control this factor as far as possible by not favoring hypotheses, and by interpolating the Western-culture hypotheses about *burra* in as neutral a way as possible. An example of this technique would be: "Some white men wonder if the *burra* causes the *burra* to spill out before it reaches the *djindl* . . . what do you say to that?"

While discussing this problem of control of suggestion, it is appropriate here to anticipate the findings a little by noting that the determinants that finally emerged for the procedure of subincision were different from any of those that the investigators had anticipated (Table 1). As will be seen, these unexpected determinants have to do with marsupials and the Aboriginal dedication to totemism. While this did nothing for our good opinion of our original perceptiveness, at least it gave an assurance that we did not merely get back our own preconceived ideas.

RESPONSES OF THE INFORMANTS

Before describing the Dreamings propounded in Walbiri lore to account for subincision it will be helpful to indicate the informants' reactions to the Western ideas on the subject, as listed in Table 1. Individual responses of the informants are separated by a leader (...).

1. *Custom.* It is just the law . . . The Dreaming . . . Every boy will one day have a *burra.*

2. *Hygiene.* With a foreskin, it smells too much, little bit stink . . . With a *burra*, wider stream, washes out the tip, keeps it clean . . . With a *burra* only time it gets dirty is sexual intercourse . . . People know because flies settle on it . . . *Burra* cleans it.

3. *Initiation.* It is the way to manhood . . . To go through it you must take the rubbishing and teasing . . . The pain . . . You get more respect . . . For *wida-burra* (circumcision of young men) secrets are revealed. Nothing is revealed for *burra* . . . Some

boys these days run away, avoid it, go to another station. But they are told that if they run away the night before, their mothers and fathers might be killed.

4. *Blood drawing. Burra* blood is easier to get than arm blood if you are in a hurry. Sometimes it comes out too quick . . . Some times it is hard to get arm blood, and more sore afterwards. There is less pain when you prick the *burra* . . . The blood is no different, not more special or sacred . . . Arm blood is better than *burra* blood for drinking during initiation . . . Blood from *burra* might be funny taste because playing with a woman recently. Arm blood is good, more like heart blood or kangaroo blood . . . Can't say blood, *yowalyu*, during ceremonies; have to call it *nhaba*, water—*yowalyu* is taboo.

5. *Sexual.* Women are very keen on the *burra*. They get rather silly about it. They always like to find out who has the best *burra* in the camp . . . Gives them more pleasure . . . Girls tell you straight away: you got big *burra*, I won't go to any other man . . . Sometimes the *burra* goes up too big, maybe 1½ to 2 inches wide. Only a strong woman can take this. Some prefer a half man, *wida-burra* . . . You can't take a wife without a *burra*, that's a firm rule.

6. *Urinary. Burra* sprays all over the ground. That's good. A spray is better than a jet . . . When pissing, you hold by the tip or by the skin on top, it sprays wide, this is better . . . It's quicker to piss, though not so quick as a woman . . . It's a strict rule, no woman can see a man piss once he has a *burra* . . . Since wearing trousers, the people stand. Before that we squatted down.

7. *Contraception.* With a *burra*, you get more children, not less. And quicker. That's a fact . . . The width and spread helps. It doesn't flatten out inside the woman . . . Sometimes the *burra* does spill the *buru* during intercourse . . . Don't know if it stops the woman getting pregnant . . . We use all different positions for intercourse, but mainly woman on her back, same as you.

8. *Simulation of women.* Sometimes we say, for a joke to certain friends, your *burra* is just like a *tjindi* . . . Young lovers compare *burra* and *tjindi*, playing out in the bush. They look a little bit alike . . . *Burra* blood is not connected with women's blood in menstruation. Dreamings do not put these bloods together in the

same story... Only by chance... When the woman takes too much intercourse, it makes the *burra* bleed.

The bulk of the interview time was taken up with stories about *burra* from The Dreaming. Sacred myths about *burra* are plentiful in Walbiri oral literature. What can be learned from this class of information? The significance of the myth in Aboriginal life has been the subject of wide discussion. Resemblances between myths and dreams suggest that some myths represent the dreams of ancestors. Their significance might theoretically be extracted as in the dreams of patients undergoing psychoanalysis (Roheim 1945). In this endeavor the conspicuous difference between myth and dream is that for the myth the dreamer is not present to assist the work of analysis. What is possible for myths is "wild" analysis, influenced by the observer's ideas. Elkin (1965) points out that sacred myths may sometimes enshrine actual historical sequences, though the sequences may be somewhat symbolized and distorted.

Many of the *burra* myths concern marsupials and men. The significance of this for the Walbiri did not dawn on us for some time, possibly because we were too preoccupied with the initial hypotheses (Table 1) with which we approached the enquiry. It was hard to step outside this preconceived framework of reference. However, after hearing a number of these myths it was realized that they represented a naturalistic-phenomenological explanation of *burra*. This explanation was always available, but veiled from the searching of analytic Western eyes rather in the manner that the "purloined letter" was hidden in Poe's story.

Characteristic subincision myths, presented more or less verbatim, are here entitled: "The Kangaroo and the Mouse"; "The Kangaroo Discovers the Knife"; "Kangaroos Exchange with Men"; "The Woman and the Crow"; "Knives Carried in the Eyes."

The Kangaroo and the Mouse

The kangaroo on a journey met a little (marsupial) mouse, Mana Bindandji, who knew nothing of drawing blood. They made a camp and the kangarooo said he'd show the mouse something he hadn't seen before—how to draw blood. The kangaroo sang some lovely tunes that the mouse hadn't heard before, and the mouse became very interested and excited. At last the kangaroo said, "Look away." Then he began to draw blood from his *burra* with a stick and pour it around the mouse's shoulders. The mouse was frightened but asked to learn the song and sing it while the kangaroo danced with his *burra* flashing up and down with the stick in it. The mouse asked the kangaroo to cut a *burra* for him, which the kangaroo did. You can still see the *burra* on the mouse; only a little thing, but you can see it.

The Kangaroo Discovers the Knife

In The Dreamtime two Walbiri kangaroos possessing neither tail nor knife came from Chilla Well to Mount Singleton. There they wandered around and found rocks, anthills, trees, creek, and snake —all in songs too long to sing you now. Then they found a flint, *gandi*, which they wrapped in paperbark when they realized it was knife. They traveled on to Vaughan Springs where they put a spear into their behinds which turned alive into a tail. On their long journey south to Ernabella in South Australia they arrived at last at a big corroboree ring where they met other kangaroo pairs from Aranda way, Laverton way, and far-off places. After much happy singing a boy was brought there for circumcision with a firestick. But the Walbiri kangaroos used instead the flint knife, which was better. It was so much applauded that they went on to use it to make a *burra*.

Kangaroos Exchange with Men

Two young Unmatjeri men were going in The Dreamtime through Gunadjeri (Mount Singleton) and met two kangaroos from the north at Mirrura and showed them the knife *gandi*. There is a well-known song for this. The two pairs exchanged languages, which is why we talk Walbiri now. The two kangaroos continued south, cutting the *burra*. Kangaroos have a *burra*—only a little bit now but it used to be the whole length. They came on a little boy being prepared for initiation and when they saw a firestick was going to be used they said: "Leave that alone." They blew their noses and out flew *gandi*, which cut like a razor blade. When the boy's sores healed quickly, they cut his *burra* for him and then they said: "You're free like us." The boy traveled west very pleased with his *burra* and showed its use. . . . The *burra* is copied from the kangaroo who is father of the peoples of central Australia. All the central tribes are sons of the kangaroo.

The Woman and the Crow

In The Dreaming, at Mount Doreen a woman, Napaltjari, wanted a crow for intercourse. The crow was Tjapannanga, which was the wrong skin anyway. Napaltjari was the crow's mother-in-law. They were making love behind a bush for quite a time and while the crow was in action the woman felt the crow's cock, which was all in one piece. The crow said: "Here's a flint. Cut a *burra* for me." This she did and the crow went back to the camp and tried to make love to a young girl. Then the tribe found on the ground the blood from the cutting of the crow's *burra* and saw the crow trying to hide his cock. They took the crow blindfold to a fire and threw him in and killed the woman.

Knives Carried in the Eyes

At the hill Wokulba, near Yuendumu, there is an important camp in The Dreaming. Two lads, Tjapaljari and Tjungarai, were taken there and their foreskins removed with *gandi* the knife. They traveled to Mount Doreen, Yarungunji, taking the knife, but as they had nothing to carry it in they inserted it in the hollow at the top of their eyeballs. They came to a group preparing a firestick for a circumcision so they stayed their hands, threw away the firestick, and handed over *gandi* to the surgeon, *tjimari nganu*. The happy boy made spears and boomerangs as a gift to the surgeon and received in return two, three, four of his daughters. The two young men went on looking for boys being initiated, using stone knives all the time. They went right over east past Alice Springs, and at length came upon a group of Walbiri people back at Yuendumu and taught them the use of *gandi*.

MARSUPIAL "HYPOSPADIAS"

Impressed by the recurring reference in the totemic myths to animals and their "subincisions," we next checked the anatomy of marsupials. While the reproductive system of the female marsupial has aroused great interest and is represented by scores of papers in the literature, little attention has been paid to the male. The classic account of gross anatomy is that given by Richard Owen in his article "Marsupalia" in *Todd's Cyclopaedia of Anatomy and Physiology*, a massive six-volume text published between 1839 and 1847. This author draws attention to the original observation by Cowper, in 1704, that the male opossum possesses a double or forked glans penis. Owen's own treatise confirms that many marsupials possess a grooved penis and in general his descriptions corroborate the observations of the Walbiri Aborigines on the "subincision" of animals.

Owen's text merits attention, depicting as it does the "opossum and other marsupials which, having a bifid glans, enjoy, as it were, a double coitus. . . . The two bulbous processes of the corpus spongiosum soon unite to surround the urethra, but again bifurcate to form a double glans penis in the multiparous marsupials. . . . In the koala, the glans penis terminates in two semicircular lobes and the urethra is continued by a bifurcated groove along the mesial surface of each lobe. In the wombat, there is a similar expansion of the urethra into two divergent terminal grooves." Line illustrations accompanying the text leave no doubt about the curious "split" appearance that may be presented by the marsupial penis.

At Yuendumu, after hearing the Walbiri subincision myths, we examined a male kangaroo. As the Aboriginal informants had suggested, the grooving of the penis was not so extreme "as it once had been," but the urethral orifice proved to be situated not at the tip but on the ventral surface of the penis proximal to the tip. A euro (a smaller kangaroolike marsupial) examined later showed a somewhat more extensive penile groove.

Thus, within the marsupial family, there is clearly considerable variation on this general pattern, but an awareness of this particular aspect of marsupial anatomy imbues the myths with a fresh literalness. In Walbiri eyes, the animals do have a kind of *burra*. The Walbiri hypothesis about the relationships between this anatomy and their own practice of subincision might be expressed:

1. The reasons we slit the penis lie in The Dreaming and are explained in the stories.

2. Since we are kin with the animals and many of the animals

slit the penis, this is one reason why it is an important thing for us
to have a slit penis.

The line that separates Timor-Moluccas on the one hand from
Australia-New Guinea on the other is known as Weber's line. It
also separates the mammals of Southeast Asia from the marsupials
of Australia. On the assumption that subincision in its ritual form
is predominantly an Australian institution, it is reasonable to ask
what feature of the Australian environment may have promoted the
extreme development of the practice. The possibility that the marsupials may have been this environmental feature received some
support from: (a) the totemic religious outlook of the Australians,
in which the marsupials are kin; (b) the importance of the marsupials as a feature of the Australian environment (marsupials occur
elsewhere, but less importantly); (c) the anatomical formation by
which marsupials have the urethral orifice placed proximal to and
behind the tip of the penis, sometimes with a bifurcated glans; (d)
the frequency with which the kangaroo and his *burra* are emphasized in Walbiri mythology, with the kangaroo demonstrating its
value, the improved technique of the knife, and going about the
countryside making converts such as the marsupial mouse and boys.

There are several ways in which these associations may have become embedded in Walbiri theology until they came to regulate
this segment of Walbiri behavior. First, it is possible that an exceptional individual, an innovator, who would possibly be classified as
psychotic today, carried out this genital mutilation on himself and
then persuaded others to follow. Alternatively, it is well within the
bounds of possibility that this innovator might have had a penile
hypospadias—a not uncommon congenital malformation—and for
various unconscious motives connected with projection and compensation persuaded his confreres to imitate it. This may be called
the *folie communiquée* theory of the development of institutional
belief and practice (see chapter 5). Aware of the marsupial penis
formation, this individual may have rationalized it as the raison
d'être of the procedure, and, with the persuasive power of the
paranoid individual in a closed community, may have succeeded in
getting it generally adopted. Such sequences are not unknown to-

day, particularly in extreme religious sects found in comparatively closed communities—or as in the Third Reich before World War II.

Alternatively, if the view be taken that the totemic religion and its social institutions evolved gradually as a form of adaptation to the physical environment rather than as an expression of psychopathology, it is reasonable to conceive of the marsupials as godlike ancestors whose characteristics men should imitate. The subsequent development and extension of the necessary genital mutilation could well have arisen from the various secondary gains of the procedure. These secondary gains are well recognized, both by Westerners in their hypotheses about subincision and by Aborigines in their reactions to these hypotheses. Some are less convincing than others; for example, in view of the present high Walbiri birthrate, infertility cannot be regarded seriously as a consequence of subincision. The Walbiri themselves do not seem ever to have viewed it as a contraceptive operation—quite the contrary, in fact.

The present investigators' conclusion is that the Walbiri hypothesis should be regarded as a part—possibly an important part— of the causal network on subincision, without proclaiming it in any way as the only correct explanation. Those who wish to claim this honor for the theory of subincision advocated by Montagu (vulvaenvy; denial of castration, and so forth) may choose to do so by criticizing the Walbiri hypothesis, and indeed it must be admitted that it is open to criticism on several points. The most obvious point concerns the freedom of the Walbiri to function as good naturalists. While they correctly attribute a grooved penis to some marsupials, they make the "ludicrous" error of bestowing a penis on the crow in the myth. Any naturalist who is free to observe knows that the male crow effects coition by apposition of his cloaca to that of the female. But this objection to the Walbiri capacity as naturalists need not detain us long: the crow in the myth is the crow-ancestor, partly human, though endowed with the insufferable arrogance and conceit of the crow. A more cogent objection to the Walbiri hypothesis—contrasted with the psychoanalytic hypothesis—is that it seems incredible to Western observers that animals should occupy a position of influence in the development of psychic constructs remotely resembling that of humans. But from the Aboriginal point of view the formative influence of animals should not be underestimated. In addition to animals' totemic significance, much of the everyday play and education of children is devoted to them and at night the sleeping child is as apt to be warmed by his dogs as by his parents.

Certain misconceptions about the nature of totemism in the writings of Frazer and Freud need not be perpetuated. Firsthand observations (Elkin 1933) make it clear that an individual owns not one but a number of totems of varied significance, and that the "totemic meal" accorded such significance in Freud's theory scarcely occurs. The significance of totemic animals may not consist merely in representing a displacement of parental affiliations; they have some significance in their own right. This should not surprise us; the close kinship between men and animals is worldwide. Nature is everywhere anthropomorphized, as Aesop, Mother Goose, and Walt Disney bear witness.

A different class of objections could be leveled at the Walbiri hypothesis by anthropologists who see in the institution of subincision an adaptive device, contributing to the social organization and the solidarity of the group. It could be pointed out for example that ritual subincision occurs in other parts of the world where the animals have no penile groove and are of less importance to the people. Such observations would still have to explain why in these regions subincision never attained Australian proportions. Similarly, it might be argued that the historical origin of subincision in the Kimberley zone of Australia may or may not correspond with the zone of concentration of multiparous marsupials. But the evidence relating to the spread of subincision from any source is inconclusive, and cannot be taken to support any particular hypothesis of the historical origin of the custom.

Observers who accept the likelihood of a linkage between the marsupial penis form and subincision (such as Abbie 1969) are nevertheless puzzled as to why, if this is the case, the actual incision should not be imbued with greater ritual and ceremony. The Walbiri men were not specific on this point, but an answer seems to lie in their rather mundane or unmagical attitude to it. Whatever its origin in mythology, in practice subincision is to them preeminently a matter of convenience ("The wider stream washes out the tip") and domestic necessity ("You can't take a wife without a *burra,* that's a firm rule"). Conversely, once a lad has a *burra* he is no longer eligible for sexual games with children—as the crow in the myth discovered to his cost.

My own assessment of the Walbiri hypothesis is a qualified one. I do not propose it as the linear cause of subincision, any more than the vulva-envy hypothesis can be so regarded. I believe subincision to be complexly overdetermined and I do not maintain that because it became a social institution among Aborigines it was necessarily adaptive. It could have had pathological aspects as well. A discussion of the pathology inherent in some social institutions would take us beyond the scope of this chapter; it is a possibility capably examined by Freeman (1965) in his critique of the doctrine of cultural relativism. But adaptive or pathological, the Walbiri take a phenomenological rather than an analytic view of subincision. Western observers invariably tend to apply analytic theories, because these are objective and more characteristic of Western modes of thought. The more phenomenological native view emphasizes the primacy of the subjective experience, more characteristic of modes of thought of the East, and in this respect the "East" includes the Aboriginal Australians. Indeed it is probable that Western observers fail to "hear" phenomenological statements such as that offered by the Walbiri because they are preoccupied in seeking analytic interpretations. The subjective approach should be regarded as complementing the objective approach rather than opposing it. The evidence suggests that more weight than heretofore should be given to the Aborigines' own assessment of the origins of subincision.

FURTHER COMMENT ON AUSTRALIAN SUBINCISION

Sir:

Correspondents in the U.S.A. and Australia have written to me drawing attention to "The Australian Subincision Ceremony Reconsidered: Vaginal Envy or Kangaroo Bifid Penis Envy" (AA 69:335–358).[1] They have expressed surprise that the authors, Drs. Singer and DeSole,

---

[1] This is a letter to the editor of *American Anthropologist* (October 1968, vol. 70, no. 5, pp. 961–964). The figures are not included here. The letter is reprinted because of its relevance to the question of anthropological authority and "writ"—for which the subincision controversy may serve as a classical illustration.

overlooked recent fieldwork available in an international psychiatric journal at the time they published their article (Cawte, Djagamara, and Barrett 1966). Drs. Singer and DeSole give a good review of subincision theories and correctly deduce that some weight as a determinant should be given to the grooved penis form of marsupials. As it stands, however, their article creates an unfortunate impression of their priority in this matter.

Our article on subincision was not based solely on the "classical" literature and films, but on fresh fieldwork in central Australia. The present is a favorable time for this because with good fortune one may find men (such as our own collaborator Nari Djagamara) who are tribally oriented yet have English and rapport with Europeans. With these advantages it is possible to determine more clearly Aborigines' own views on subjects such as subincision and to remedy some of the misconceptions that have been handed down through the literature.

The subjects of our study are the Walbiri of central Australia, good subjects because subincision is an obligatory practice and contact with Western society is recent, about 20 years. In their eyes, their animals (marsupials) have a kind of subincision, and the relationship between this anatomy and their own practice of subincision might be expressed:
(1) The reasons we split the penis lie in The Dreaming and are explained in the stories.
(2) Since we are kin with the animals and many of the animals split the penis, this is one reason why it is an important thing for us to have a split penis.

This is of course an oversimplified account of the Walbiri thesis, for details of which the reader should consult our original paper (Cawte, Djagamara, and Barrett 1966).

Our field studies incline us to agree with our Walbiri informants in attaching some significance to the "marsupial" origins of subincision. We do so partly in the light of the Dreaming stories, which have a subjective immediacy and literalness in the psychology of this people, and partly in the light of the "coincidence" that Australia, land of subincision, is also the land of marsupials. We agree, however, that other functions suggested for the practice of subincision, or that armchair ingenuity might conceivably suggest (such as the provision of a site for ritual bloodletting; vulva-envy; *folie communiquee* induced by an innovator with penile hypospadias; hygiene; etc.—as considered in our paper) could serve to reinforce the practice. These reinforcements, conscious or otherwise, might be viewed in the light of a causal network in a ritual practice that is evidently overdetermined.

It is distressing to see "classical" sources invoked to perpetuate errors of fact, in a kind of linear descent, as when Spencer and Gillen, Montagu, and Bettelheim are successively cited by Drs. Singer and DeSole to show that Aborigines do not possess myths to explain the origin of the sub-incision. This could mean that Spencer and Gillen did not collect any. Aborigines possess plenty of such myths; we quoted some in our article.

One may sympathize with Drs. Singer and DeSole that fieldwork in central Australia is not readily available and that they had little alternative but to turn to "classical" conjectures. Under these circumstances it is gratifying that they kept their skepticism and worked through to a consideration of the marsupial penis. However, marsupials are available in any zoo and examination of them shows that the exaggerated illustration used by Drs. Singer and DeSole (after Grasse) does little justice to the living undissected kangaroo penis. I offer some photographs[2] taken during our work in central Australia by my collaborator Murray Barrett. I think they illustrate not only the kangaroo penis appearance (Fig. 1) but also the need for eclecticism in theorizing about subincision. Figure 2 shows the position of the urethral orifice in a kangaroo (drop of seminal fluid being expressed) and in a subincised Aborigine. Figure 3 shows one of our Walbiri friends using his subincision site for blood-drawing. The sign language photographs are also interesting (Fig. 4): spread fingers in Walbiri hand language connote a "full man" and twisted fingers a "half-man"; apparently these signs derive from the shape of the urinary stream of subincised and nonsubincised man.

It may seem remarkable that Drs. Singer and DeSole should independently publish their communication at this time, though clearly unaware of our fieldwork. Other American psychiatrists and anthropologists are aware of it, however. In my academic lecture to the American Association of Psychiatrists (Western Division) at the 1965 Annual Meeting in Honolulu, I dwelt on this subincision research at some length. The large gathering seemed to find the marsupial penile groove theory hilarious, if not memorable. I dealt with the subincision subject, amongst others, again in 1965 in lectures given at Stanford University, Langley Porter Clinic, and at a public lecture for the Mental Research Institute, Palo Alto. On these occasions also there were psychiatrists and anthropologists present and the marsupial penis aroused some interest. Although Drs. Singer and DeSole are obviously not personally aware of this work nor of these presentations, it is possible that a ripple reached them on the gossip line from California or Hawaii. I appreciate that their original stimulus was probably the subincision film (? that of Tindale).

My main object in writing is not to claim priority in publishing the "correct" interpretation of the origin of subincision, marsupial or otherwise. In our paper we were more concerned to show that we have long passed a point at which anyone, least of all those of us interested in psychoanalysis, should expect to find a simplistic theory. This is espe-

---

2 These figures do not appear in this work. The reader is referred to the original source given in the previous footnote.

cially true of Aborigines, who are a psychologically complex people, despite Bettelheim's opinion of them [Bettelheim 1962: 47]. I feel sure that Dr. Singer and Dr. DeSole would agree that the real issue is why theories such as Montagu's or Bettelheim's, based as they are on the limited data available at the time, should be treated with reverence. Hypotheses should be used as skittles, and I congratulate Dr. Singer and Dr. DeSole on doing this.

J. E. CAWTE
School of Psychiatry
University of New South Wales

CHAPTER NINE

The Control of Women

STUDENTS OF AUSTRALIAN ABORIGINES have always sought for the proper terms to describe the Aboriginal woman's traditional relationship to the man. Three features seem to stand out in this culture. There is a tendency for men and women to segregate, for example into hunting and food-gathering groups respectively; there is a tendency for men to exploit their superior physical strength to dominate the women; and there is a tendency—or rather more than a tendency—for men to exclude women from men's secret ritual which is concerned with the spiritual life and the realm of the supernatural. These three features of the man-woman relationship are interrelated, as we shall see. In summarizing them here, we overlook for the moment the complexities of the kinship and avoidance relationships, the vast individual variations in family and domestic life, and the lessening of tribal authority and social organization caused by the incursion of white settlers and officials.

A physician is in a favored position to observe relationships between the sexes. As a result, he forms some opinions about the significance of this relationship for the health and mental health of the woman. This, nowadays, is a subject with which he is deeply concerned. Within his limitations, however, it is important to direct attention to it, because the role of women in traditional society is relevant to the medical understanding of what happens when this role is relinquished. We need to appreciate the traditional role of women before we can evaluate how the modern changes in that role have affected their health and adjustment. We may be led to infer, for example, that though the realities of daily life of tribal women were harsh, even enslaving to Western eyes, they were stable and predictable, and this was reflected in the stable personality of the women. Before offering the clinical observations and conclusions which I made of Walbiri women at Yuendumu, it will be helpful to review some inferences that have been drawn by anthropologists upon the battle of the sexes—*chez* Aborigines. The fact that this has attracted a good deal of attention from anthropologists suggests that there is something distinctive about it.

ANTHROPOLOGISTS VIEW THE WOMAN'S ROLE

The assessment of women's position in traditional society is a recovery operation suited for anthropologists, and especially for women anthropologists (Gale 1970; Goodale 1971). Although there is a consensus among observers of Aboriginal society that the women were subject to fairly severe control or domination by the men, the right term for their social position is hard to find. In anthropological literature it has been often described in terms of "status." Aborigines have been called "men without leaders" because they were not organized into political units with chiefs, but status exists within these virtually stateless societies. There is a well-defined order of dominances and submissions. Older men dominate the younger, and the men dominate the women. There have been cycles of opinion in the ethnographic literature concerning the low status of Aboriginal women. The early popular view was the "chattel" theory, but it was questioned when more sympathetic and intimate observation could be made. Dr. Phyllis Kaberry (1939), working with Kimberley Aborigines, found the woman to be a complex social personality having her own prerogatives and a place in the secular and religious observances. Kaberry concluded that the Aboriginal woman was a competent and self-reliant person capable of exercising an influence on the affairs of her group. Although dominated by her men, she was like Molière's woman who always had her revenge ready. For a time ethnographic opinion swung from the "chattel" view to a more "feminist" view. Dr. Isobel White (1970) suggests that the term "junior partner" is more descriptive of women's relationship to men.

Although better appreciation shows that the "chattel" view is exaggerated, it does not negate the impression that the female is subject to severe restrictions by the male, when compared with her counterparts in Western culture. Meggitt (1962: 93) corroborates this observation in the case of the Walbiri: "Although husband and wife have in theory reciprocal claims on each other's economic services, there is often in fact marked inequality. The rights of the wife, both in the satisfaction of her just claims on her husband and in the rejection of his unjust demands may be seriously neglected." It is a male-dominated society, organized around the interests of the men. Women's place is as "feeders, breeders, and follow-the-leaders." It is not implied that they develop any distinct "status personality"; within these roles there is room for the wide variety of temperament and personality types seen in Walbiri women. But they do not aspire to the position of men, nor represent the supernatural, as in other primitive societies, as ritual leaders, shamans, or witches. The man, as White (1970) emphasizes, validates his senior status by claiming for himself the power to create and maintain spiritual life.

It may be profitable to view the social relationship between men and women transactionally, in terms of *control*, rather than in terms of *status*. This situation has psychodynamics that have been variously conceived. One line of thought, of which the psychoanalyst Roheim (1945) is a prominent representative, attributes male dominance to a reversal of the "primeval" dominance of the mother over the little boy. A second line of thought, interpreted by the anthropologist L. R. Hiatt (1970), sees the men's dominance in terms of their attempt to extend their mastery into all areas of function, including the female functions of childbearing and childrearing. A third line of thought, reflecting an emphasis upon ecological factors (B. Hiatt 1970) might see male dominance in terms of the need to control women as the vital suppliers of food in a region of periodical shortages[1]—in addition to he functions of supplying children and sexual pleasure.

Early psychoanalytic libidinal theory provided an explanation for female "inferiority" by viewing women as castrated men. In this "Oedipal" view, penis envy led to an assumption of inferior status and to unrealistic competition with men. The inevitable

[1] For a color film of Walbiri food-gathering, see *So They Did Eat*, filmed at Yuendumu in 1953 by T. D. Campbell and M. J. Barrett of the University of Adelaide; available from the National Film Library, Canberra.

frustration resulted in psychological malaise. The analytic task for the female patient was to discover these strivings and to become reconciled to having no penis. Women analysts working within this framework were not long in retaliating: they pointed out that Freud was a man, ready to subscribe to the theory of male superiority prevalent in his culture, and to the thesis that the female sex organs are inferior to the male's. Karen Horney as early as 1926 pointed out that Freud's theory that little girls believed they had been castrated and that they envied boys their penises is a man's orientation to the subject. Clara Thompson ('1943') stressed that the envy of the penis as such is not as important in the psychology of women as their envy of the position of the male in society.

Roheim (1945), from a consideration of myths and rituals, arrived at a functional explanation of the status of central Australian women. He pointed out that in the myths there is paradoxically some evidence of what might be called a primeval superiority on the part of women. In many of these myths, rites first performed by women ancestors pass into the hands of the men. Roheim does not invoke theories about the supposed original matriarchy of mankind to explain these myths; rather, he indicates that to the little Aboriginal boy the powerful mystery is his own mother, a situation that must be reversed to overcome his separation anxiety. He must leave her, as must all children. To a variable degree, this observation is true of any culture. But for the Aboriginal boy, an unusually indulgent mothering is sharply followed by an unusually severe separation, at the time of his initiation ceremony at the hands of the men. For Roheim, "totemism" as a social institution is a defense organized against this separation anxiety, extending as it does the range of succoring objects beyond the mother into nature at large.

L. R. Hiatt's interpretation of male dominance of women rests upon his appreciation of men's rituals. He points out that much of the men's "secret business," from which women and children are excluded on pain of death, is preoccupied with "pseudo-procreation." This is the typical Australian *rite de passage*, in which men symbolically destroy youths and then "reproduce" them as men. He suggests that Aboriginal men believe they are superior to women, but they have two points of insecurity: women's childbearing ability, and their fond relationship with children. The men therefore carry out ceremonies that are an affirmation of male superiority in these areas of uncertainty. The rites force youths to give up their attachments to their mothers. Men say to women, in effect, "the time has come to kill your sons and reproduce them as ours."

Why do Aboriginal men form secret cults which intimidate the women? Roheim suggests that the secrecy is connected with Oedipal guilt. The youths display their incestuous wishes before older rivals, but these wishes are overcome by strengthening of male bonds. The arm and subincision blood poured onto the sacred objects and onto the ground during the rites is analogous to women's blood. The exclusion of females from the sight of this blood is a reversal of the menstrual taboo on men. L. R. Hiatt suggests a further explanation for the aggressive secrecy of the men's cult lodges. It protects the male cultists from exposure and skepticism. The men can thus reinforce their pseudo-procreative rites, away from the enquiring and potentially skeptical eyes of the women.

A third way of viewing men's dominance considers the environmental factors, in particular the ecology and the consequent division of the sexes into hunting groups and gathering groups. In the Australian ecology, the mainstay of subsistence is not necessarily the large beasts from the men's hunt—the kangaroo, bush turkey, turtle, and wild duck—but the small items that are painstakingly foraged by women—berries, seeds, shellfish, roots. Women are important in securing the survival of the community in regions where gatherable foods are plentiful. Betty Hiatt (1970) in a study of woman the gatherer has examined the relationship between the diet, geographical latitude, and the division of labor. It is imperative in some regions and at some seasons for men to control this regular supplier of gathered food, the woman—not to mention her provision of other goods such as companionship and sexual pleasure. But while the men make their arrangements for the care and control of these valuable servants that provide their mainstay, the women resist complete submission. They have desires and viewpoints that may not coincide with the men's. Their bargaining power lies not in their physical strength, but in their ability to withhold their supplies of food, help, companionship, and sexual pleasure. Thus the tension between the sexes is never resolved, though the balance of power and status positions varies within each community, and indeed within each marriage.

Because of the cultural variation in Australia, it is necessary for consistency in our discussion to concentrate upon one group. The Walbiri of central Australia may be taken as the paradigm. In traditional life in central Australia the women gathered vegetable food, seeds, and small animals such as lizards and frogs over a segment of territory radiating from the camp designated women's country. They scoured this country with their children and dogs, bearing digging sticks and other domestic appliances. But Walbiri women have complained to me that the areas taboo for them were not always clearly defined and that they feared making a mistake about where they might go. The men, with spears and spearthrower, hunted game over the men's country. The rules which existed for the sharing of food that resulted were male rules and probably constituted an ideal. In 1964–1965, while I was at Yuendumu, a comparison of nutrition between the sexes, especially of those coming to the settlement hospital, showed a remarkable contrast between fat men and thin women, indicating that men have first gnaw at the bone.

In looking for the general principles that determine the relationship between men and women, the influence of kinship and domestic systems should not be disregarded. Despite the basic rules governing these matters, there is in practice wide variation in the ways in which individuals are affected. In marriage, the Walbiri are polygynous, 30 to 40 percent of husbands having more than one wife. Walbiri men, complaining of the nagging this entails, deplore polygyny—with tongue in cheek. Walbiri women to whom I have spoken feel differently about it; the custom is accepted by them as necessary under the law, but the complaints are heartfelt. The co-wife at Yuendumu who happens to be currently out of favor may be observed expressing her frustration by open destructiveness (such as spear-breaking), or by passive aggression, or by intense bickering with the other wives. The kinship system of the Walbiri, in which eight "skin" (subsection) groups marry and socially interact according to prescribed rules, has implications not easy to grasp. To my mind, the system appears to favor social solidarity amongst males. For example, the same "skin" recurs in patrilineal descent after two generations, in matrilineal after four. (See chapter 10 for details of the Walbiri kinship system.) After puberty, women leave the territory of their fathers and brothers to live in that of their husbands. The full significance of these sex differences in terms of education of the young and of kinship ties and avoidances is not apparent to the Yuendumu Walbiri, who are not prone to analyze matters of tradition.

The Walbiri system of legal sanctions and disciplines applies a double standard not equaled in Western society, itself by no means devoid of one. Detected in an amorous adventure, a Walbiri man may be challenged and fought by the injured party, but the woman must endure the onslaught, not only of her offended spouse, but of members of her own sex as well. In the quarrels and brawls that follow romantic affairs, real or suspect, the woman comes off second best. It is not unusual for a husband before going away on a trip to administer a prophylactic thrashing to his wife. The Walbiri man seems a comparative stranger to feelings of guilt from internalized sanctions. It is open to question whether the same can be said of the woman. Some Walbiri women volunteered to me complaints involving sexual coldness or disinclination to intercourse. Sex seemed a perfunctory matter for many of them. This is not similar to the Western clinical pattern involving inhibition of bodily contact; the Walbiri are accustomed to close bodily contact between peers from the days of infancy. It seemed rather a partial denial that sexual arousal or excitement is taking place. Meggitt observes that a similar double standard exists with regard to the care of children: "Paternal and maternal neglect should be equally culpable and liable to reprimand by the children's maternal kin. In practice, however, the negligent father (who is indeed rare) receives little more than scoldings from his wife and diffuse censure from the rest of the camp. The negligent mother, on the other hand, is sure to be beaten by her husband and very probably by her own mother as well." (1962: 93)

WALBIRI MEN USURP THE FEMALE MYSTERIES

The first thing that a modern doctor finds, when working among tribally oriented Aborigines, is that if he wishes to learn about the medical system he must learn from the men. The Walbiri do not appoint women as their doctors because the power of medicine, based upon the spiritual beliefs, is the prerogative of males. Women carry out what might be described as domestic or household remedies. I observed at Yuendumu measures such as hot sand applied to painful areas or herbal infusions taken by mouth. Some of the procedures used by Walbiri women are sound enough medically, such as breast milk squirted in the infected eyes of children living in areas where the water could be contaminated or is hard to obtain, or the use of resin from the bloodwood tree as a protective application for skin sores. There is no "medicine," in the sense of magic, involved in these household remedies.

Although a role as a physician affords some access, tribally oriented women are usually extremely shy in conversation with white men. Furthermore, secrecy is so crucial to the men, that if one spends too much time with women, it jeopardizes the confidential relationships established with the men, who fear that their secrets may be divulged. I should have little information about Walbiri women but for the assistance of Mrs. D. A. (Pat) Fleming, the wife of the Reverend T. J. Fleming, of the Yuendumu Baptist Mission. Mrs. Fleming is the first, most constant and trusted white confidante of many Walbiri women who have not long since left their traditional life in order to live at the settlement. At the time of our study in 1964–1965, Walbiri exposure to settled European Australian society was of about twenty years' duration. Mrs. Fleming and I together looked at the aspects of Walbiri medicine and law regulating the life of women, using as informants women with whom she was on close terms.

Though Walbiri women possess some secret ceremonies, these are insignificant by comparison with the elaborate spiritual diet of "men's secret business," in which women either do not participate, or play very restricted parts. In the important circumcision ceremony of boys, older (postmenopausal) women have minor roles, but the secrets revealed to the novices are taboo for women. Initiation of girls, if it takes place at all, is limited and unceremonial; evidence of its occurrence occasionally comes to light at Yuendumu in the form of firestick interference with the vulva, apparently for defloration or possibly for introcision with a limited episiotomy. We could discover very little about this procedure. It is unrelated to the clitoridectomy practiced in other countries. The bulk of knowledge of The Dreamings in song, dance, and painting is the property of men.

In the light of the general assumption of female "junior partner status" to the male, reactions to contact with whites are predictable. Whatever their behavior in the camp, Walbiri women are inhibited toward whites, a behavior reflected in the lack of spontaneity in cross-cultural conversations. At the Yuendumu school, a simple genetic test that we were using—the tasting of phenyl thio-carbi-mide—found its greatest obstacles in the girls, who "froze" when pressed for a response. In school, a problem encountered by teachers is that brighter girls withhold their answers until the boys can produce theirs—presumably because of fear of punishment after school. But the Walbiri men, when pressed about their con-trol of females, do not mention social ideas; they emphasize their Dreamings. Because of this insistence it is necessary to consult this class of explanation for the light it may shed on the phenomenon of female submission. I was particularly impressed to discover, with the help of Mrs. Fleming, that the Dreaming gave men power not only over the spiritual aspects of women's life, but over such es-sentially female functions as menstruation and pregnancy. Since our observations do not appear to have been recorded in the litera-ture, yet are germane to the elucidation of the relationship between the sexes, they should be outlined here.

The Walbiri are highly preoccupied with blood—a preoccupa-tion modern man is also spared because he appoints specialists: the daily thoughts of a good Western doctor are concerned with hemoglobin levels, iron pills, transfusions, postpartum hemorrhage, menses, and menorrhagia. For the Walbiri, blood signifies not merely blood, but hemorrhage and the life force, and the adhesive he draws from his body with which to glue designs on his skin for sacred ceremonies. When a society goes naked, blood and women are naturally associated: menstruation and childbirth are conspicu-ous sex differences, and bleeding is featured in both. Two aspects of woman that The Dreamings emphasize are her menstruation and her childbearing. The chief of the Walbiri women's secret rituals is called *yowalyu*. It was first described by women investigators (Kaberry 1939; C. H. Berndt 1950). The singing in this female ceremony was recorded by Elkin in 1953. In the Yuendumu Walbiri (who are extensively of the southern extraction called Ngalia by their Pintubi neighbors), *yowalyu* is collectively the term for Women's Dreaming, for Blood Dreaming, and for blood. Although the ceremonial portraying the *yowalyu* Dreaming at Yuendumu is in a sense women's business, knowledge of it is in the keeping of a man, Tommy ("Granites") Tjapangarti. This kind of arrangement is traditional; Strehlow (1964) observes of the Aranda that women's sacred songs and myths, associated with their own sacred sites, are held in trust for them by their male kinsmen. Several women referred us to Tommy Tjapangarti for proper details of this female Dreaming. The songs as he detailed them are too extensive for our present purposes, but in effect describe how blood became part of humankind. The Blood Dreaming site is believed by Walbiri to be the most dangerous place on earth. It is on a hill to the west of Mount Singleton on a rock with a complex of "blood holes" crisscrossed by channels, of which Tjapangarti provided an elaborate diagram. Only Walbiri men of Tjapangarti and Tjapannanga "skins" may approach it, and then only if they sing code words to protect themselves from hemorrhage. "I am Tjapangarti; I belong to this place and own it; my father was its boss." If the code words are neglected a vein bleeds inside the body. "Jumbo" Tjakamara, a "working-boy" (design painter) for the bosses of the ceremonial, neglected this precaution and was reputedly sung by blood in the brain, and became paralyzed. He refuses to see a Western doctor about it. The boss of The Dreaming may sing a secret curse—*yowalyu kunna nandal kali* (My blood runs like water)—and, by drawing blood from his subincised penis, perfuse a clod of dirt to throw at a victim. The victim of this incantation is usually a woman who has rebuffed him sexually; when the *yowalyu* catches her body "She piss . . . she bleed in that piss . . . she die." Hence *yowalyu* is not merely blood; it is bleeding.

In the myth of the Blood Dreaming, man and woman ancestors camped near Mount Singleton. The man moved from his camp to dig in the sacred ground; the woman, approaching, was caught on the *yowalyu* ground and bled. For five days the woman ancestor bled, and now *yowalyu* bleeds within her children five days in each month like a spring running and stopping. When a woman bleeds she leaves her husband's camp to live in the old women's camp, where she prepares a trough of burning acacia over which she squats so that the smoke dries the blood. In childbirth she bleeds again, and afterwards dries the lochia with smoke. With a first childbirth, the excessive bleeding may call for further *yowalyu* singing to stem the flow. In Walbiri cosmology, functions of menstruation and childbirth are associated with bleeding, with danger, and with banishment. This is true of the southern Walbiri, or Ngalia, that I know; according to Meggitt (1962) menstrual blood is considered less dangerous in the northern division, several hundred miles away.

Imbued as I was with the literature on subincision and the notion of vulva-envy it conveyed, that men made themselves bleed to simulate women, I anticipated a connection between woman's *yowalyu* and blood ritually taken from the man's *burra*, his penile subincision. It is a connection to which attention was drawn by Montagu (1937a and b) and attributed by him to "vulva-envy"— unconscious male envy of female parts. Roheim (1945) suggests Aboriginal menstruation is a castration threat—the vagina is that in itself (absence of a penis) but the bleeding vagina is even more so. When the men represent their own penises as bleeding vaginas they overcome this threat, saying in effect: "We are not afraid of the bleeding vagina. We have it ourselves." On this connection the Walbiri informants are less specific than this literature might lead one to expect. The informants' explanation of the connection, when it is brought to their attention, is that men's and women's Dreamings are not always as separate as they should be, because a mischievous *guruwalba*, tree child-spirit, flies like a spy from men to women exchanging their ideas in dreams.

Equally revealing about the male arrogation of female functions, we found, were the Walbiri notions concerning conception and contraception. Elkin (1954) writes of sexual intercourse in Aborigines that it is a source of pleasure, a means of expressing or renewing friendship, warding off hostilities, or putting others under an obligation. But this is the man's point of view; it is not concerned with offspring, and implies that woman is but an object to be used in certain socially established ways. A reason sometimes advanced for the lowly status of Aboriginal women is the Aborigines' apparent failure to detect the connection between coitus and conception. Thus Baldwin Spencer (1914: 274) wrote "the child enters the woman in spirit form without any reference whatever to sexual intercourse and . . . the child within the woman is the actual representative of one special individual amongst the old ancestors." Speaking as it were theologically, Walbiri say that the child-spirit *guruwalba* must come down from the trees and pierce the woman's body in order for conception to occur. On a secular level, they are aware of physical paternity and one Walbiri woman expressed it in a conversation on conception to Mrs. Fleming and to me in Aboriginal English (which uses the male pronoun when the female is understood): "Got to fuck him, too." They are not, of course, aware of conception and physical paternity in the way modern medicine sees it, as the penetration of an ovum by a sperm cell.

I found that there are Walbiri songs regulating fertility—owned by the men. A Walbiri may sing a conception song to his wife under his breath while he sleeps with her, or aloud at a distance from the camp so that she does not hear. If he does not wish her to conceive he may sing *sotto voce* a contraceptive song while sleeping with her: *Mara wadji kunna kunbul kurra kurri—mara wadji* referring to a tree that grows solid and strong but solitary. The song invokes the tree to impart its likeness to the woman, to poison the child inside. A similar song to keep the woman slim, young, and infertile runs: *Ngunja wali kunna Yurukulkalunu—ngunja wali* referring to a poisonous fruit given to the man by The Dreaming father to sing into the woman.

Women apparently do not possess contraceptive songs; several women denied knowledge of them to me and to Mrs. Fleming separately. These songs could be another preemption by the male. In either case, the existence of contraceptive songs associated with coitus further illustrates the Walbiri double belief in the roles of coitus and tree child-spirits as the prerequisites for conception.

In summary, if one were asked whether Walbiri male dominance should be attributed to an attempt to reverse the mother's early dominance of the child, or to an attempt to extend male mastery into female functions by invoking spiritual forces, or to ecological-environmental factors, the reply must be equivocal. All three factors seem to be involved. The psychiatric ground rule that complex behavioral sequences are multiply determined by a network of causative factors does not lead us to expect otherwise. The only aspect open to question is where the emphasis should be placed.

WHITES USURP WALBIRI AUTHORITY

We began by observing that one needs to appreciate the traditional role of women before one can evaluate how the modern changes in that role have affected their health and adjustment. The uprooting process that began in 1928 for the Walbiri undoubtedly had a profound effect on their social organization and health. The historical events have been recorded by Strehlow (1963). Up to 1928 there had been virtually no cultural or social changes among Walbiri tribesmen. The "splendid isolation" ended in the Great Drought of 1928–1929, which not only strained the resources of the Walbiri but induced some white cattlemen to move their starving herds into virgin Walbiri territory. Walbiri tribesmen attacked two of these cattlemen and killed a prospector who had arrived only two weeks earlier. Police and white settlers took harsh punitive action, in which at least thirty-two Walbiri were shot. Subsequently, settlers moved into the best-watered Walbiri areas. The Walbiri for their part moved into settlements established by the Northern Territory Administration. According to Strehlow, the inability of the old men to protect their groups from violence, or to save the sacred sites from desecration, weakened the confidence of the young generation in them, and grievously lessened the authority of their pronouncements. The place of the old and important men whose power had extended through society was now usurped by white administration officials.

As a source of authority and legal sanction, The Dreaming served the *status quo ante*. The progressive collapse of The Dreaming since the Walbiri congregated at Yuendumu seriously affects the identity and the adaptation of women. This is no mere passive process of letting go. The assumptive world (to use the concept of Jerome Frank [1961]) of Walbiri children is a stake that is being contested by the elders on one side and on the other by the whites —missionary, schoolteachers, and artisans. Many of the whites at Yuendumu are liberal in their attitudes to traditional culture, yet the conflict is sharp. Both Aborigines and whites are experiencing some despair over their prospects of success, and dissatisfaction over compromises. In addition to the conflict between these two sides there is an internal conflict in the Walbiri themselves, as the women now defy their men and aspire to a new independence. The abandonment of The Dreaming loosens men's control and permits these aspirations.

We are now led to consider a hypothesis that women, previously most bound by stringent controls, have now become least subject to regulation and control, and to enquire whether the resultant *anomie*, the loss of goals and norms, is reflected in their high levels of morbidity. One can begin to examine this hypothesis by adducing simple epidemiological indices of contemporary Aboriginal female adaptation. We do not have a sufficiently extensive set of data concerning the Walbiri women alone, although it is reasonable to suppose them representative in many ways of tribal women encountering white influence. Epidemiology is the science that examines the amount of morbidity in a population, or section of a population, in relationship to the environmental factors. In this case we are investigating a possible relationship between disturbed behavior patterns and symptoms on the one hand and social disorganization (anomie) on the other. Do the indices suggest that the effects of anomie fall most heavily upon the women?

EPIDEMIOLOGICAL INDICES OF FEMALE ADAPTATION

Settlement Sick-Bay Attendances

Attending the morning sick-parades at Aboriginal settlements such as Yuendumu, I observed that women of childbearing age are the most common attenders and most implacable complainers. The clinical impression of a high level of anomie associated with high personal discomfort and sick-role behavior, is confirmed by our statistical study of a community, using the modified Cornell Medical Index health questionnaire (Cawte, Bianchi, and Kiloh 1968).

Mental Hospital Admissions

During the decade 1950 to 1960 in Western Australia, males of Aboriginal and European Australian descent had substantially similar rates of admissions to psychiatric hospitals. However, the proportion of Aboriginal females admitted was *over two and one-*

half times the proportion of European Australian females admitted. The figures are similar for South Australia, but not available for the other states (Cawte 1964; Christophers 1965).

Prison Detentions

During the same period, Aborigines and those of Aboriginal descent who socially identified themselves as Aborigines were estimated at 2 percent of the total population of Western Australia. However, they comprised *over 30 percent* of the male prison population. In the women's prisons, Aborigines made up *over 80 percent* of those detained (Robinson 1968).

Birth Rate

The population bulge in all Aboriginal communities is striking. Visiting Elcho Island in 1968, I found that over the past six years the birth rate averaged five babies per hundred of total population —compared with a birth rate of slightly more than one per hundred for the white population of Australia. Impressed by the difficulties Aboriginal mothers are having in mothering the children they bear, we made a documentary film on the subject entitled "Children of Arnhem Land" (Baglin and Cawte 1968). We hoped to show on film how the children structure their time in peer groups rather than in parent-child learning situations. In a settlement of fringe-dwellers at Bourke, on the Darling River in New South Wales, I was confounded to find that the birth rate during the same six years *averaged over six per hundred.*[2] Human society rarely reproduced itself faster, to my knowledge. Should we consider this extraordinary fertility an expression of social pathology, rather than an adaptive fecundity? The question involves us in a consideration of the quality of mothering, as opposed to the quantity of reproduction.

Infant Mortality

If one makes the assumption that infant mortality rates provide a measure of the adaptation to motherhood, the figures are equally striking. During the same period, eleven Aboriginal communities

[2] The figure is provided by Dr. Max Kamien, research physician for the Human Ecology of the Arid Zone Project, Bourke District Hospital, New South Wales, 1970.

in the Northern Territory showed a minimum average infant mortality rate of *130 per 1,000 live births* (Tatz 1970). It is not known whether this exceeds the traditional rate, but it contrasts with a rate of about 20 per 1,000 for those of European descent in Australia, and indicates a "high output wastage"—a high birthrate coupled with a high deathrate.

These indices of psychosocial morbidity affecting Aboriginal women may be puzzling to visitors to contemporary settlements of fringe-dwellers. What little social integration there is in some of these settlements seems to come from the women. This impression is particularly strong if the men are out of work and are drinking liquor. The women in the settlement are at least occupied with the children and with fulfilling domestic responsibilities as best they can under their yoke of poverty. Evidently, the price of carrying on is high in terms of female morbidity, which is to be defined in terms of personal discomfort as well as in terms of social inefficiency and frank psychiatric disorder. Outside the settlements, women's opportunities are limited. Finding few points of articulation with the Western society, they have unsatisfactory outlets in work and recreation compared with the men and children. Laboring work is available for the men and school for the children, at least some of the time.

It is open to question whether the modern change in the status of women has been associated with an improvement of their mental health. It is my surmise—offered tentatively because measurement before alien contact is not possible—that the mental health of Walbiri women has drastically declined. However stressful men's traditional control may have been to women in this primitive society, it was compensated by other stabilities. The World Health Organization (1960) defines a "case" as one severe enough to cause loss of working or social capacity, or both. This definition is of operational value, though in stressing ability to work and ability to carry on a social life, it neglects the inner comfort and the personal cost to the individual of carrying on. Using such a definition, we should have to say that primitive women "enjoyed" good health. Sanctions imposed upon women seem to us authoritarian, even harsh and enslaving, but they were stable, and one might expect this stability to reflect itself in the daily lives of women. Women's new freedom includes the freedom not to conform or adapt. The ancient system of medicine as the law is suddenly without its power to comfort them or to control them. *Cases*—in the World Health Organization sense—are becoming common, as the epidemiological indices reveal.

With these considerations we perforce move from the domain of psychiatric anthropology into that of transcultural psychiatry, which has the added dimensions of epidemiology, treatment and prevention, and which is the focus of the remainder of this book.

CHAPTER TEN

The Exceptional Family

SMALL PRIMITIVE SOCIETIES, especially when viewed from a distance, are often thought to exhibit a shared national character, or modal personality structure. From closer association, a diversity of personalities becomes more apparent. Primitive man, as we have seen, shows a broad range of personality types. Moreover, we find that there are exceptional families, in which most of the members seem to stand out in various ways from the rank and file. This has been termed the "Kennedy Phenomenon" of primitive society, after its counterpart in the political life of the United States. Since the sociocultural and ecological background in primitive society is a shared one, we must look for the origins of exceptional families in such factors as peculiarities of temperament, childrearing, and family dynamics. In clinical medicine, the family history has long been important for the study of the familial incidence of inherited disease, but the direct study of the family group as a social system and/or as a source of pathology did not begin until as late as the 1940s. In this chapter I shall direct this innovation to our study of primitive society by focusing upon a selected family or "descent group." It is of considerable theoretical interest to ask whether Aboriginal society, with its distinctive family structure, illustrates family dynamics that have been so recently emphasized by modern medicine.

In the southern Walbiri, both Aboriginal and white informants pointed out to me a family that is exceptional in respect of a high incidence of outstanding personalities.[1] Also, much of the path-

[1] The family under consideration is exceptional in its status and achievements, as well as in the nonconformity of some of its members in the face of cultural

ology in this whole tribal group—pathology by Aboriginal definition as well as by Western—is concentrated in this one lineage, a
descent group based upon consanguinity. The family is here called
Mawindjia Nangala's lineage, after the common maternal progenitor.[2] Finding the three succeeding generations of the lineage, I
compiled a genealogy, in a clinical rather than an ethnographic
manner, identifying in it those individuals known to be deviant in
some way. Mawindjia's own four children, Generation I, are
elderly (one is since deceased) and all are outstanding characters
in the tribe. If there is one phrase that characterizes them it is "high
arousal." They are active, with unusual initiative, assertiveness,
dominance, and attempted mastery. In this society they are regarded as exceptional, a judgment shared by whites and Walbiri.
Their children, Generation II, and their children's children, Generation III, are also regarded as exceptional, or at least as having
many exceptional individuals among their numbers. Their deviations, however, take a different form from those of Mawindjia's
own brood.

Nearly all members of the descent group are located at the settlement of Walbiri people at Yuendumu. This is the group whose
medical system is described in chapter 3 and who are also the reference group in chapters 8 (subincision) and 9 (women's adjustment). In order to make the presentation meaningful, we need
some background history to indicate the amount of Western contact experienced in the three successive generations, and some
knowledge of the kinship system to show how the family itself is
composed.

We have seen how "frontier" killings led to mistrust and avoidance of white people until recent times when, after the end of
World War II, four settlements were established by the govern-

---

change. Since this family's record is of special value to the understanding of the
medical problems of Aborigines, no disparagement is intended in this record nor
should be understood. To preserve confidentiality, the use of English or usual
"camp" names is avoided and tribal names have been code numbered. The genealogy, which should be continued when the elapse of time permits, may be identified by reference to mission records. The assistance of Dr. Malcolm A. Kidson in
corroborating the diagnoses is gratefully acknowledged.

[2] It has recently become a convention among the Walbiri to use the subsection
name as an English surname, preceding it by some personal or given name.

ment around their original territory and the assimilation of the "desert Myalls" into Western culture began. Thought to be a dying race fifteen years ago, they are today sharing in the population explosion that is one of the striking features of the Aboriginal people. Problems of subsistence and employment caused by the expanding population are made worse for the Walbiri by the lack of local industry of any size. Dependence on government rations is almost complete.

A Walbiri family is not organized on the Western conjugal pattern. The people are polygynous and unions are determined by "skins" (subsections). The eight skins comprising the Walbiri are expected to marry according to a logical system that limits the degree of blood relationship possible between spouses (see Table 2). Wrong-"skin" unions are exceptional.

TABLE 2

PRESCRIBED UNIONS OF MEMBERS OF WALBIRI "SKINS"

		Children	
Husband	Wife	Male	Female
Tjungarai	Nangala	Tjapaltjari	Napaltjari
Tjupurula	Napanangga	Tjakamara	Nakamara
Tjangala	Nungarai	Tjambitjimba	Nambitjimba
Tjakamara	Napaltjari	Tjupurula	Napurula
Tjapaltjari	Nakamara	Tjungarai	Nungarai
Tjambitjimba	Napangarti	Tjangala	Nangala
Tjapanangga	Napurula	Tjapangarti	Napangarti
Tjapangarti	Nambitjimba	Tjapanangga	Napanangga

NOTE: Spelling follows the "Adelaide" convention, which uses *t, p, k* in place of *d, b, g* of the "Sydney" convention.

In the genealogy compiled for Mawindjia's lineage (Table 3) the members are designated by number rather than by name, for purposes of confidentiality. The individuals regarded as disturbed, in the opinion of both the Aboriginal and European Australian community at Yuendumu, are indicated by an asterisk. Little is known of the common progenitor, Mawindjia Nangala. However

TABLE 3
MAWINDJIA'S FAMILY, BY HER TWO HUSBANDS

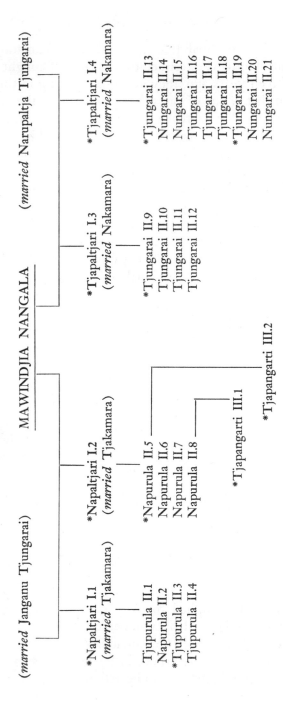

MAWINDJIA NANGALA

(*married* Janganu Tjungarai) (*married* Narupaltja Tjungarai)

*Napaltjari I.1
(*married* Tjakamara)

*Napaltjari I.2
(*married* Tjakamara)

*Tjapaltjari I.3
(*married* Nakamara)

*Tjapaltjari I.4
(*married* Nakamara)

Tjupurula II.1
Napurula II.2
*Tjupurula II.3
Tjupurula II.4

*Napurula II.5
Napurula II.6
Napurula II.7
Napurula II.8

*Tjapangarti III.1

*Tjapangarti III.2

*Tjungarai II.9
Tjungarai II.10
Tjungarai II.11
Tjungarai II.12

*Tjungarai II.13
Nungarai II.14
Nungarai II.15
Tjungarai II.16
Tjungarai II.17
Tjungarai II.18
*Tjungarai II.19
Nungarai II.20
Nungarai II.21

NOTE: Individuals reported by informants as affected by neuropsychiatric illness (they are also cited in the text) are here indicated by asterisks. Roman numerals refer to generations as used in the text; arabic numbers are code numbers assigned for purposes of confidentiality to individual members. The third generation consists largely of children and is not represented here, save for two affected individuals.

it was a simple matter to assemble information about her four children (Generation I) by direct observation, and also about their children (Generation II) by the same means. The third generation is larger and incomplete, consisting mainly of children. It is not represented in Table 3 save for the two children definitely identified as having neuropsychiatric illness. It is proposed to reexamine this generation after time has permitted exposure to risk of developing an illness. Vignettes of the individuals identified as having neuropsychiatric disorders are now given as the necessary basis for in ferences that will be drawn in the commentary and discussion.

Napaltjari I.1 (1890?–1954)

Cheeky is the pidgin sobriquet for Aborigines who are arrogant or openly disobedient. Napaltjari is remembered at the mission as cheeky, as having violent outbursts two or three times a day, for no apparent reason, in which she attacked people verbally and physically. The Walbiri themselves describe her as *wangamara* (gone off, mad) or *warrunga* ("deaf," does not follow instructions, moderately mad).

Napaltjari I.2 (1900?–   )

This thin elderly woman is nearly blind from longstanding trachoma—with perception of light only. Her palate and pharynx are scarred, presumably from yaws. Her head shows many scars, indicating the fights of a cantankerous personality, but including as well regular (self-inflicted) mourning scars. Physical examination is otherwise normal. During the past year she has been called *warrunga*: she is often restless and talkative at night and screams abuse at her daughters who look after her. She wanders around the settlement on her "bad days" muttering to herself and striking at passersby with her billycan. Questioning through her daughters on one of her "good days" revealed to me no signs of dementia, such as memory loss or disorientation. Her daughters cannot account for her behavior; she is a "proper cranky woman."

Tjapaltjari I.3 (1895?–   )

This elderly man has a history of psychosis in middle life, but in earlier days he was a famous and respected native doctor. Even

sophisticated part-Aboriginal cattlemen had great faith in his diagnostic and curative powers. However, fifteen years ago, *wanga-*
mara came on. He had left Mount Doreen to live at Haast Bluff
when his young wife died. Thereafter, he acted strangely, was seclusive, and became violent if approached. He joined tin cans to
lengths of wire, which he strung between trees; he said it was his
wireless and forbade people to talk near it. He chopped up tin lids
with an axe and claimed that he was making money. It was sur-
mised that some evil-wisher had sung his tobacco.

After people started to call him *wangamara* and "Mad" Tjapaltjari he retired from practice as a healer and ceremonial leader. He
now carries out the simple task of sweeping an area of ground outside one of the settlement buildings and seems proud of his efforts.
He flies into rages, but is easily distracted from them by being
given a book. He will chatter eagerly with any white person, without comprehending the conversation. His buffoonlike mimicry of
white ways still earns him the name "Mad," and he needs to be
sedated because of his own irritability and his propensity to irritate
others.

Tjapaltjari I.4 (1896?–   )

This old man has his back and arms covered with a remarkable
array of scars. A notorious fighter, he was evidently able to protect
his front with his shield or by moving in close. His truculent personality is almost legendary with the Walbiri. All his life he has
demanded his way, regardless of the justice of the situation.
He once traded his promised wife to a man in exchange for goods.
When the goods were consumed, he demanded her back and tried
to kill the man when he refused. On ration days he may be seen
consistently contesting his small change, though he does not understand money, and calling the clergyman or any other official dis-
tributing the goods a "robbing bugger." When two men were murdered in 1952, he was suspected by the settlement staff to be the
instigator of the upset. Fights decreased at Yuendumu when he was
extradited to Hooker Creek and increased on his return. He is regarded as a "con man" and "standover man." He often rampages
around the settlement, terrorizing its inhabitants with an iron bar.
He never cooperates by coming to work, never sends his many

children to school or to the infant welfare scheme. His saving social grace appears to be his concern for his own family: he always seems to have more money than anybody else, and he spends it on his family.

Tjupurula II.3 (1915?–   )

This is probably the best remembered *wangamara* man in Walbiri history. A conscientious and reliable young man, he changed in personality in middle life. His truculence became impossible to manage and brought him into contact with the police, but jail failed to curb his outbursts. About ten years ago he suddenly insisted that it was raining on a sunny day and his insanity became obvious to all. He walked about all that night, shouting incomprehensibly. He was taken to an Adelaide psychiatric hospital where cerebral infection was diagnosed; he improved greatly with penicillin. He was well known to me in this context, although not actually under my care at the time.

This might have been the end of the matter had not his camp been over one thousand miles from the Adelaide hospital. Communication was nonexistent. During his absence his countrymen did not know where he had gone and whether he would return and this led, after serious strife and bloodshed in the camp, to a redistribution of his wives. (See Meggitt 1962 for a description of the redistribution process.) When he himself returned briefly to the Walbiri he was not welcomed. He complicated matters by claiming that he had been sung by an evil-wisher and by demanding an enquiry and revenge. A local theory was that a half brother had persuaded the elders to sing a scorpion into his brain. He had to be removed once more and then became institutionalized in the city hospital where he worked in the vegetable garden. His situation is discussed more fully elsewhere (Cawte 1964c) in order to illustrate some problems of Australian transcultural psychiatry and to support a recommendation that a mobile psychiatric service be established in the outback.

Napurula II.5 (1927–1962)

Lim-lim is Aboriginal English for cripple. This *lim-lim* (paraplegic) woman lived for thirty-five years, a survival that would not have been possible in the nomadic life of presettlement times. The story given by some Walbiri women is that she was strong and straight until she was about fourteen, when she fell from a tree; she was silly in the head, with a sore back, becoming *lim-lim* in the legs. Another informant, a man, says that she was spastic from birth. She used to sit on the gound and pull herself along with her hands; later, in the settlement, a trolley was built for her. Her crippled state did not prevent her having three children, only one of whom, Tjapangarti III.2, survived in the present series. In her later years her personality was severely affected; she is described as irritable, domineering in conversations, gossiping and spiteful, swearing at her sisters, creating dissension.

Napurula II.6 (1929–   )

Regarded as normal until she became adult, she has had several self-limiting episodes of severe mental disturbance, in nearly every instance associated with childbirth. Eight years ago while pregnant she complained of noises in her ears and talked to herself in a way that could not be understood. She appeared frightened and vague. The *wangamara* brought her teasing from camp-fellows, who are customarily amused by sickness or emotional instability. She reacted with violence and excitement and late in 1956 the flying doctor recommended transfer to Alice Springs hospital. In 1957 she became "vague and obstinate" and was again sent to Alice Springs hospital for mental illness, but after two months she absconded and walked home. In 1958 she gave birth to a child which subsequently died and there was an episode of irresponsibility and excitement. In 1960 she was again agitated but responded to tranquillizing medication. In 1963, again pregnant, she became disturbed, shouting at society in general and threatening people with a club. After the birth of the baby in the camp she was miserable and could not breast-feed the child. In presettlement days it would not have survived.

Tjungarai II.9 (1936?–   )

Two different histories were given by Walbiri informants of this man's paraplegia. One is that he was a healthy boy until shortly before his initiation (circumcision) ceremony was to be enacted. He was never initiated because his legs became weak and paralyzed.

The other history is that he has been crippled since birth. He was recorded as epileptic fifteen years ago and given phenytoin and phenobarbitone. Unfortunately, shortly before I was to examine him, he was removed from the camp by his uncle Tjapaltjari I.4 (also in this series). From the descriptions available, his back is twisted, and he pulls himself around in a seated position using his strong arms. It can only be presumed that (congenital) spastic diplegia is the most likely cause. He is said to be well adjusted to his infirmity, helped over the past year or two by more considerate treatment from his kinsmen—probably a reflection of the official attitude at the settlement. Formerly he was left much to himself when he could not keep up with the others and in presettlement days he would have perished.

Tjungarai II.13 (1937–1958)

This boy was hemiparetic from birth, with the right arm fixed in flexion and the right leg partially paralyzed, leading to a loping gait. He never learned English and his grasp of Walbiri language was weak. He was well grown as a child and became a big young man. He took frequent epileptic seizures, which are said to have been treated in the conventional Walbiri manner—by banging the head on the ground until the seizure finished. In his seizures he frequently fell into the campfire and his burnt paralyzed arm had eventually to be amputated. As he grew up he was tormented by the other boys and became violent when roused, hitting out with boomerangs and once with an axe. During the last five years of his life he was given severe beatings by his father, Tjapaltjari I.4. In 1954 his father tried to lose him in the bush, following the traditional custom for mentally subnormal individuals, but the superintendent at Hooker Creek organized a search party and recovered the boy. After three more years of being beaten by his father he at last succumbed. Everybody was relieved, although the younger generation of church-going cousins, disturbed by the missionary's absence at the time, asked for an extra burial service on his return.

Tjungarai II.19 (1952–   )

Though only twelve, this boy is regarded both in the camp and in the settlement as wild and undisciplined, showing the traits of his notorious father Tjapaltjari I.4. His attendance at school is irregu-

lar; last year he stayed away a whole term. In consequence he is
two or three years behind the other children in his schooling. He
utterly opposes school discipline, and will not stand in line with the
other children without an argument. The teachers say that he constantly bullies younger children and is at the bottom of many a
schoolyard upset. Yuendumu children coming to school are required to discard their camp clothes, to shower, and to put on
school clothes. When school is dismissed, they resume their camp
clothes, ready for the night on the ground among their dogs and
fires. He does not cooperate. When admonished by a teacher he
threw a stick at him and overturned the desks and chairs in the
schoolroom, bellowing loudly. He is the only child that the missionary remembers to have thrown a stone at him immediately
upon being reproved. His defiance is not limited to whites; he steals
his father's blankets and sells them. His teacher spends much
thought on the strategy of his management and hopefully always
sees some signs of improvement.

Tjapangarti III.1 (1950–   )

This boy was the product of a wrong-"skin" union between a
Napurula and a Tjungarai. The marriage is now dissolved and his
mother has made a proper-"skin" marriage to a Tjapanangga. The
boy was always lethargic, plump, and dull, and is said to be dependent and overmothered—an unusual situation with the Walbiri.
Between 1958 and 1963 his mother took him frequently to the sick
bay. Quiet and timid, he never played much with the other boys
and took little interest in schoolwork. He is not regarded as mentally subnormal, however; on bush walks he is especially clever,
finding and catching lizards in the spinifex with ease.

Prior to his initiation ordeal at Christmas 1963, his usual characteristics became worse. His teacher could not get him to engage in
conversation or to even respond. He walked about with a dazed
appearance, mute, not noticing anybody. He had to be led to the
settlement kitchen to eat, but there sat pushing the food around his
plate and had to be spoon fed. When he would not walk, his
mother carried him to and fro, talking agitatedly. His behavior
caused him to be sent to Alice Springs hospital on suspicion of cerebral tumor, but no physical abnormality was found.

To the surprise of the settlement, when he was initiated by the men the following Christmas his mental state improved substantially. Evidently in recognition that a masculine influence is needed in his life, plans are being made to remove him from school and to place him with his "proper" father at a copper mine in the bush.

Tjapangarti III.2 (1950–   )

This boy was born prematurely and underweight (3 lbs. 2 oz.) from a wrong-"skin" union between Napurula II.5 and a Tjungarai. The union was dissolved shortly afterward and as his mother was mentally ill, he was "growed up" by Tjakamara, his maternal grandfather and the widely known and respected Yuendumu "patriarch." Although fourteen years old, he has the stature of a nine-year-old child and not being pubertal, with no secondary body hair, he has not been initiated.

Though not mentally subnormal, he has always been recognized as abnormal because of mutism and mannerisms. He speaks to nobody, though he hears normally. In the camp he only grunts. Very rarely, when excited, he bursts out with a phrase; on one startling occasion he rushed up to a teacher who thought he could not speak and said "Mr. McClure! The boys are fighting!" and on another he was heard to say to himself "Pictures" when undergoing the expedition's X-ray cephalometry. His mannerisms include private grimacing and smiling, pulling the tail of his shirt over his head, skipping and jumping in private play. In a group of boys playing or bushwalking his position is peripheral, with little or no active participation. His behavior to adults—Aborigines or whites—is polite, smiling, but persistently mute.

THE EVOLUTION OF ILLNESS IN THE LINEAGE

Diagnostic categories were assigned to the illnesses, using psychiatric diagnostic terms in current use in Western medicine. My colleague Dr. Kidson and I achieved agreement as to the presumed clinical diagnosis for each of the cases at the height of the illness (Table 4). The limitations of this procedure in the transcultural situation are recognized, but it enabled us to ask this question: What tendency is there for the diagnoses to cluster in any of the three generations—older, middle, and younger?

TABLE 4
NEUROPSYCHIATRIC DISORDERS IDENTIFIED IN MAWINDJIA'S LINEAGE

Subject	Western Diagnosis
Napaltjari I.1	Personality disorder; aggressive type
Napaltjari I.2	Personality disorder; aggressive type (Brain disease [?] of undetermined origin)
Tjapaltjari I.3	Paranoid state or involutional paraphrenia
Tjapaltjari I.4	Personality disorder; aggressive type
Tjupurula II.3	Brain disease (presumed cerebral treponematosis)
Napurula II.5	Spastic paralysis, congenital; personality disorder
Napurula II.6	Schizophrenia, puerperal; unspecified type
Tjungarai II.9	Spastic paralysis, congenital
Tjungarai II.13	Spastic paralysis, congenital; mental subnormality, epilepsy
Tjungarai II.14	Personality disorder; antisocial type
Tjapangarti III.1	Schizophrenia; catatonic type
Tjapangarti III.2	Schizophrenia, childhood; severe autism

The Older Generation

Generation I (Mawindjia's own children) presents three diagnoses of aggressive personality disorder, one of paranoid state or involutional paraphrenia. Fieldworkers are familiar with the tendency of Aborigines living in camps to stage quick and violent quarrels, often with bloodshed. However, the tendency displayed in the three siblings is excessive and persistent, recognized as abnormal by the other Aborigines in the settlement. These three individuals were all leaders among a people sometimes viewed as "men without leaders," because government rather than being in the hands of a chieftain is evidently conducted by ad hoc councils. In this tradition-directed people, behavior is circumscribed by a powerful network of sanctions associated with the threat of disease and death, as we have seen in chapter 3. Masterful, uninhibited, and assertive behavior is normal when it is transient, but the individuals represented here are considered exceptionally persistent in these regards.

The Middle Generation

There is in Generation II a concentration of congenital spastic paralysis, with two and probably three cases. A familial (genetic) component may be inferred because, although each affected individual is the progeny of different parents, there are no individuals with this condition in the other descent groups comprising the Yuendumu population. Survival of such individuals to an adult age is an artifact of the Western contact situation, in which nomadic life with its active food gathering and foraging gives place to settlement life and subsistence on rations. Another individual was presumed to have cerebral infection; treponematosis is common in this region and a controversy about its cerebral expression is not resolved. The other two diagnoses are of puerperal schizophrenia and personality disorder respectively.

The Younger Generation

With its limited exposure to risk of mental illness, Generation III so far reveals two psychotic illnesses, each diagnosed as schizophrenic, one the progeny of a spastic individual of the previous generation.

In the genealogy commentary briefly presented here, Aboriginal concepts of illness involving sorcery, spirit intrusion, and other aspects of indigenous medical theory with which we were concerned in chapter 3 have been omitted. This does not reflect the state of affairs as seen by the people, but merely that in this instance my enquiries were not directed along those lines. The aim in this instance was to ascertain the Western descriptive psychiatric diagnoses of these cases (Table 4) in order to provide a yardstick of deviance or pathology. From these reference points it was hoped that some inferences might be made about family dynamics and pathogenesis.

The childrearing pattern differs widely from the Western in obvious ways. One is the maternal reluctance to frustrate a young

child. Another is the comparatively late identification of the growing male with adult male figures, an event celebrated by the
dramatic puberty ritual of circumcision. But these patterns are
universals of Walbiri childrearing; we have to ask what were the
peculiarities of Mawindjia's childrearing practices that imparted
excitatory or aroused personalities to each of her four children, male
and female, by two different husbands. We can only conjecture how
much of the arousal of Generation I was on the basis of temperament (hypothetically, inherited) and how much on the basis of a
socially imparted expectancy that members of this family would
manipulate and control others. Whatever the causes, Mawindjia's
four progeny in Generation I became assertive, loosely socialized,
with ensuing degrees of social pathology and disruption.

Developments in Generation II are now very interesting. Those
progeny of the four assertive probands who are identified as sick
cluster around two kinds of diagnosis. One is spastic diplegia, and
as they represent the only three cases in the population this is no
coincidence, but has some basis in biological inheritance. The other
diagnosis is psychosis (one with a probable underlying organic
brain disorder) in which arousal and excitement are again features.
But in Generation II the excitement is different in quality; it tends
to be more intermittent and more extreme, occurring in psychotic
episodes rather than as a continuing expression of the personality.
In Generation III the only two illnesses so far in evidence are autistic and dereistic—clinically, schizophrenic. Time will tell what
became of the original assertiveness of Mawindjia's lineage.

To a psychiatrist, the pattern here is reminiscent of a three-gen-
eration hypothesis of schizophrenia described for modern Western
families. When a grandparent is exceptionally hostile and dominant, the parent may superficially mimic these attitudes and mannerisms without being permitted the appropriate mastery and de-
cision-making. The child in the third generation is confronted by
this mixture of assertiveness and indecision, inducing in him ambivalence, thought disorder, and ultimately autism.

In interpreting the dynamics of an Aboriginal descent group,
however, it must be recalled that the descent group is exposed to
cultural change at a rate faster than that of a similar group in
Western society—fast as the latter rate may be. Whereas the patho-

genetic factors may come primarily from family relations of a particular kind, pathoplastic influences are to be found in the cultural change. This descent group parallels, in microcosm, what is known to be the cultural history of the Aborigines *vis-à-vis* the white intruders. This history may be divided into three adaptational phases. In the initial phase, the reaction to the settler was forthright and assertive, sometimes with opposition, sometimes with interest and friendliness. In the subsequent phase, there ensued gross physical deterioration in response to subnutrition, introduced pathogens, and disruption of habits of life. The disease and death rate in this phase was so high that the extinction of the race was threatened. In the third phase, the characteristic features were shyness, withdrawal, and regression, with failure to become involved in European Australian society. A fourth phase, now beginning, involves efforts by European Australians to promote assimilation, to provide intensive medical care, social welfare, and what is tantamount to rehabilitation—coupled with the emergence of Aboriginal leadership and restoration of social integration.

Thus the possibility must be entertained that whatever evolution in the mental illness pattern occurs in Aboriginal lineages may reflect the historical adaptational process of Aborigines to whites. On this view, evolution in illness patterns is attributable to cultural history. However, it cannot be assumed that the Aborigines' genetic constitution is remaining as before. During their twenty thousand years in Australia, their adaptation to the country has been on the basis of the loss of the handicapped individuals in each generation. When congenital disorders cropped up, natural selection in this rigorous environment eliminated them. Mawindjia's lineage illustrates the emergence of spastic paralysis, from which Aborigines were previously protected by natural selection. How serious the biological effect of the loss of protection by natural selection will be for the Aboriginal stock cannot be estimated. Adherence to traditional mating in small populations would to some extent militate against genetic transmission of disorders by dispersing the gene pool as far as possible.

The rate of natural increase is much higher now for Aborigines than for Australians of European stock, many of whom express a grumbling concern that contraception is not equally available for the black man's family. We shall before long have a larger descent group in which to complete this study, the more clearly to resolve the question of the biological (congenital) basis of disorders in this exceptional family.

CHAPTER ELEVEN

The Sick Society

IF THE TERM *sick society* is ever used, care should be taken to define what is intended. Here, it is used to refer to a society that has a high amount of psychiatric disabilities. Many Aboriginal societies in Australia—or Indian societies in North America—might serve as illustrations. One such is selected to provide the data for this chapter. Communities that have been exposed too long to exceptional stresses from ecological or economic hardships, or from natural or man-made disasters, are apt to have a high proportion of their members subject to mental disorders. The sickness of such a society must be measured by epidemiological means: counting the numbers and types of cases and assessing the stresses.

This concept of sick society is different from the notion that a culture may be abnormal or maladapted in a particular diagnostic sense—for example in respect of some prevailing attitude, usually of a paranoid or sadistic nature. Such a contingency is not unthinkable; claims have often been made that cultural or national groups are psychopathological in respect of some widespread attitude. Such claims should be treated with caution because they may reflect the cultural bias, or the personal yardstick, of the observer. In this chapter we are not concerned with incriminating a dominant mode of mental abnormality, but with examining a society with a high proportion of members disordered in various ways. The case material representing these various disorders will be set out. The theoretical models of the stresses responsible for the sickness of the society will be deferred to the following chapter in the discussion of adjustment to cultural change.

Reports coming from central Australia in 1964 drew my attention to mental instability in the Aborigines who live between the Hart Range and Lake Nash[1] near the Queensland border. Well-informed persons—welfare officers, nursing sisters, an aerial medical officer (flying doctor), and a cattle station manager—were of the opinion that these Aborigines showed an undue amount of instability and frank mental illness. Furthermore, my South Australian hospital records revealed that in recent years Aborigines of this region have been referred to Adelaide for treatment of unusual psychoses. Statistics of the sort available in more settled areas are lacking; there is no local psychiatric service to keep a register of disorders occurring in this population. But the local impression of mental instability among Aborigines is strong and the questions it raises are important.

The region incriminated comprised what the Aborigines who live in it call Yowera (Iliaura)[2] country. Yowera people, an eastern group related to the Aranda tribe, occupy a rectangular tract of land stretching northeast from the Hart Range along the Sandover, Marshall, and Plenty river systems. The margins are open to argument, but most Aborigines whom I questioned regard the country as bounded by four centers—Murray Downs in the northwest, Lake Nash in the northeast, Tobermory in the southeast, and Mac-Donald Downs in the southwest. The population is a small one, probably over seven hundred but certainly not exceeding a thousand at the time of my enquiry. It is cattle country. There are no missions or government settlements and the only population centers are some fifteen cattle stations shown by the pastoral map of the Northern Territory (1955). Of these, the largest is Lake Nash, with a population of about 120. Contact of Aborigines with the stations is of comparatively long standing—in some places, fifty years—so that native culture and social organization are considerably fragmented. Dependency on cattle stations for jobs and subsistence is almost complete. Much movement has taken place in recent years, so that the Yowera people are mingled with neighboring Warramunga, Kaidija, and Walbiri people, as well as with

---

[1] In order to preserve confidentiality for the subjects, coded initials are used instead of names, except in the longer case histories where tribal names—not now generally known in this region—are used.

[2] Recently, probably more correctly, spelled Aljawara (Yallop 1969).

people of the central (Alice Springs) distribution of the Aranda. The population is largely made up of refugees. It could be described as the tattered remnants of tribes, save for the fact that it is now sharing in the population explosion that has shaken central Australia during the past ten years; by ensuring its survival, it is developing a new autonomous identity.

The case histories presented in this series do not represent a survey of the whole Yowera people, but comprise those ascertained by myself at Lake Nash and those previously referred to me for psychiatric care in Adelaide. The chief informants at Lake Nash are the station manager, who is thoroughly familiar with the region and its people, his wife, who is a trained nursing sister, and some of the Aborigines who live there. The cases were examined either at Lake Nash or in the vicinity. They are sketched here in diagnostic brevity, except for some "traditional" illnesses that are presented in more detail because of their ethnographic value. The latter are psychiatric conditions which specially reflect Aboriginal medical belief, and which have been recorded very meagerly in the anthropological or psychiatric literature.

The "thematic" method of grouping cases to be used here calls for comment and some apology. There are several classifications of maladaptation available, each useful for its particular purpose. Chapter 2 suggests a colloquial scheme that dramatizes acculturation problems. Chapter 3 illustrates an indigenous classification according to primitive concepts of disease such as sorcery, spirit intrusion, and the like. Chapter 6 refines sorcery into smaller categories according to the manner of alleged commission. Chapter 7, describing a culture-bound syndrome, and chapter 10, an exceptional family, use the modern clinical classification based on the Standard Nomenclature of Disease. This classification commonly dismays anthropologists because it mixes etiology with appearances and causes with symptoms but medical workers have gotten used to it; it is the best we have! In chapter 12 a review will be given of some models of situational stress supposedly related to mental symptoms.

For the people now under consideration, while conventional diagnoses are not discarded, a simple thematic classification is suggested, relevant to the local situation. It is called a "thematic grouping" because it relates the illness to themes and conflicts in the society; it is not intended to be taken seriously as a "clinical classification." As in all the other classifications, the classes are not mutually exclusive. Class A and Class C, for example, may be found concurrently in the same person. The individual is assigned to his category according to where the emphasis falls. And Class O (organic illness) is in a separate category from the conceptual point of view. Notwithstanding these shortcomings, a thematic grouping has pragmatic value because it draws attention to the psychological stresses acting within a society.

THEMATIC GROUPING OF
PSYCHOLOGICAL DISABILITY IN YOWERA COUNTRY

Class O. Organic illness (1 case)
Class A. Aboriginal identity crises (3 cases)
Class B. Disturbances of refugees (3 cases)
Class C. Disturbances expressing resistance to whites (5 cases)
Class D. Disturbances associated with domestic crises (3 cases)
Class E. Disturbances associated with deprivation (3 cases)

In a small population, a larger and more representative sample of mental disorders may be obtained by considering a period of time rather than a single point of time. Moreover, a "period prevalence" better suits the nature of mental illnesses, many of which characteristically remit and relapse and would be missed if "point prevalence" were used. The term "incidence" usually refers to cases occurring in a year. A period of five years was chosen, up to and including 1964, and eighteen gross cases were collected, using the World Health Organization (1960) criteria that a case not only has to resemble some established psychiatric entity, but has to be of sufficient severity to prevent the individual from working or carrying out his normal social role. Lake Nash, with an average population of 120 during this period, proved to be the home of twelve such cases. Thus the five-year-period prevalence rate for Lake Nash was 12/120 or 10 percent. This affords a basis for comparison with other centers, such as Yuendumu (Kidson 1967), though the rate means little without an evaluation of the setting.

Reasons for Lake Nash's high rate of serious psychological disability become evident when the kinds of illnesses are considered in relationship to their environmental background. This is the purpose behind the adoption of the thematic grouping of cases in place of the usual clinical categories such as "schizophrenia" or "sociopathic personality." The reader may care to suspend judgment, for a time, as to whether this thematic grouping is convincing, or indeed, as to whether the record of psychiatric disorders thrown up by society provides a valid commentary on the society.

Class O. Organic Illness

The epidemiological filter used was too coarse to catch milder psychiatric disorders associated with subnutrition, infection, poor general health, head injury, and alcoholism. Only one case of organic illness was recorded—of severe epilepsy. Interestingly, it appears to have been better diagnosed by the family than by outside observers.

N, age 28

During the past two years N, mother of 14-year-old C (see Class E), has appeared vague, unresponsive, and increasingly withdrawn. She became completely inactive and just sat and stared. It was at first thought this condition might be related to her second marriage, which occurred not long before the illness. She declined to eat and became very thin, so much so that she had to be sent to Alice Springs hospital, where she was referred to Queen Elizabeth Hospital, Adelaide, with a provisional diagnosis of schizophrenia.

Questioned at Lake Nash, her father Wagon Willy told of a history of epileptic seizures, becoming worse during N's pregnancy with C, but improving after C was born. He thought her trouble was "too many fits," but this was not confirmed by other observers. In Queen Elizabeth Hospital, however, neurological investigations, including cerebral angiography and electroencephalography, supported a diagnosis of epilepsy with mental deterioration, proving her father correct.

Some improvement has followed supervised anticonvulsant medication, and she was seen at Amoonguna, near Alice Springs, awaiting a return home (where it may be difficult to supervise the taking of the medicine).

Class A. Aboriginal Identity Crises

Laraga, age 60; Joda, age 37; Digenda, age 35

These three Aborigines are presented together as a family. For purposes of confidentiality in this history, names have been altered. The discharge of Digenda from an Adelaide mental hospital last year marks the end of a sequence of remarkable illness, complicated by official intervention, in a father and his two sons.

Laraga, the father, and Joda, the first son, were central figures of a disturbance among the Aborigines at Lucy Creek station. The welfare officer summoned from Alice Springs by radio found the people at the station upset and exhausted. There had been shouting and commotion because the rainbow serpent was thought to have entered Laraga's body. This required the assistance of a native doctor, but since Laraga himself was a doctor he obtained the assistance of his two sons. The younger son, Digenda, upon ministering to him, found that a fish had entered his own body, rendering him of little further service to his father. The burden of removing both snake and fish fell upon Joda, the elder son. It appeared to the welfare officer that Joda had become a fully fledged medicine man and that the ceremonials were to allow him to demonstrate his powers. Laraga made no improvement however; he said his head was on fire and that smoke was pouring from it. He immersed himself in a water trough to pour water over his body.

The presence of the officer had no effect on the disturbed events at the station. By now Laraga's wife had become disturbed so it was decided to remove the more upset persons—Laraga, his wife, and son Digenda—to Alice Springs for observation. During the trip by Land Rover through the hills to Alice Springs, both father and son were attempting to remove by native-doctor means an internalized animal from the woman's body. In Alice Springs hospital, Digenda appeared to recover and was discharged, but Laraga's excitement continued. He was restless and noisy, made sexual overtures to women patients, tore out photographs from magazines showing a negress and joked that she was his *kwai-ai* (girl). He tried to club his wife and was arrested by the police. Meanwhile back at the station Joda had become violently disturbed and was frightening the residents. He tried to drive the station truck to pursue devils that he said had taken his wife and child—who were in fact standing close by. He, too, was brought to Alice Springs, but was no easier to manage than his father. He struck a nursing sister and would not allow anybody to approach him. He believed he was speaking to God—this surprised the hospital doctors since it was known he had not attended a mission nor received instruction in the Christian religion. Such a teaching could have been known to him through gossip. The disturbance was adjudged unmanageable locally, and it was decided to evacuate both him and his father to Adelaide.

By the time the two Aborigines arrived in my hospital in Adelaide, Laraga was amiable and cooperative, in contrast to Joda who was mute and resistive. Laraga's English was hard to interpret, but it appeared that he thought the rainbow serpent had left him and might now be inside Joda. He was talkative and cheerful. His country was the Plenty and Marshall rivers; his father and grandfather were born there and he wanted to return. He had been a boy and lost his foreskin at Lake Nash. Asked about being a doctor, he replied that others said he was a doctor no longer, and in the future he would not hunt with his people but work on the cattle stations. This was the closest approach that could be made to a conflictual issue in his life. He was flown back to Alice Springs while Joda remained for further hospital observation.

Joda continued to lie mute and motionless in bed, refusing to answer questions or acknowledge attention. His eyes rolled frequently and he appeared to adopt a listening pose. When his limbs were placed in an unusual position, he maintained them there. When obliged to get out of bed, in contrast to his father, he made negligible relationships with others. He sat with averted head, sometimes reaching out to fiddle with another patient's clothing. Soon after, he became excited, shouting and singing in his own language, though he knew some English. He mumbled something about a fish and pointed to his throat. Since tranquillizing medication had little effect, a course of full coma insulin was given. There was considerable insulin resistance. The first coma was reached on 800 units of soluble insulin and the treatment terminated after fifty-two days, reaching a maximum single dose of 1,300 units. At this time, Joda was talking and cooperating. He said the fish and the rainbow serpent were gone. His father having long since departed, arrangements were made to fly him home by himself.

Digenda, the unmarried younger son, was playing a more passive part. Taken to Alice Springs hospital, he appeared to abandon the impression of being the receptacle of internalized small animals. No further administrative attention was paid to him until a year later, when an urgent radio message summoned a police constable to MacDonald Downs station. Digenda was inexplicably threatening the women in the nearby camp. The police officer found him lying on the ground behind a brush windbreak. He was in a peculiar mental state, difficult to arouse and refusing to speak. He had to be assisted to his feet and into the vehicle. When he reached the homestead and was being assisted from the vehicle because of his stuporous condition, he suddenly wrenched free, assumed a threatening stance, and bared his teeth in a snarl, but still did not speak.

The police statement from an Aboriginal stockman at the station, recorded verbatim in the Aboriginal English, gives a vivid account of the events.

> That Digenda started sleeping. Then he get up and walk away, he go down towards that girls' camp. Then I come from my camp, I pick him up and we go back along his camp. He have a drink of tea. When he finish he run away like fun and Joe chase him. He turn that rifle towards Joe. Joe run away. I went back that way along my camp, that Ada sing out for me, then me come round. I heard Amy say, "What you got in your hand?" She was talking to him. I said, "He got rifle in his hand." He sing out to them girls, "Line up." He sing out for me too. I went along him a bit close, he pull the trigger out, he put the gun up along shoulder, like that see (holds arms indicating rifle being held at shoulder level in firing position). I hit him on jaw and grab gun, he hang on to that gun, go off now, along side my head, we hold gun, he bitem me on face, I bitem him on finger. He let go gun now. And we finish, he said, we finish right out. We shook hands, we go back along his camp and I leave him at that camp and I said to him, don't go way, you sleep here. I take gun back to Chalmers. When he point that gun he point at my wife Ada, she stand at my side close up. I never fight with him before, no nothing. He never cause trouble before. When he run towards that girls' camp with rifle they start to walk slow but they come back when he sing out. They were frightened, they were frightened of that gun. This happened just after sundown, real dark. When I fighting with him

he could talk and open his mouth and bit me alright. I reckon he might be silly.

On the return to the Hart Range in the constable's vehicle, Digenda lay in an awkward position with his head bumping the vehicle floor, and remained immobile regardless of the rough road being traversed. His condition had not changed by the time he finally arrived in Alice Springs. He lay on the floor, not responding to commands or answering questions. He allowed himself to be moved without any reaction, with face expressionless. He refused to eat. Previously clean in his personal habits, he paid no attention to the toilet facilities provided and urinated against the wall. His parents were brought to him in an effort to establish contact, but could not get him to speak. His mother, commenting on his single state, said he had shown no interest in the female sex, but she thought he would seek a consort when he aged a bit more. His father considered that it would be best that he should receive treatment as the father himself had done. The doctor diagnosed a state of catatonic schizophrenia and arranged transfer to Adelaide.

In the mental hospital in Adelaide there was no remission of his illness. He was withdrawn, apathetic, and dejected; he would not look anyone in the eye, would not utter a word. At times he gave the appearance of fear. He was examined by Mr. T. G. H. Strehlow, an anthropologist expert in Aranda language and culture, but would not speak to him. Over the course of some months he became less fearful and more cooperative, but persistent mutism prevented an understanding of the thoughts and feelings underlying his condition. He understood spoken instructions well, worked in the garden, and gained weight. An attempt would have been made to repatriate him, despite the mutism and the mystery of his mental processes, but for the caution necessitated by the history of homicidal violence.

After an uneventful ten months in hospital, he had a sudden outburst in which he smashed furniture, attacked the bystanders, and bit off the lobe of a male nurse's ear. Further observation was indicated; another year passed uneventfully. He still declined to talk to white people but had begun to talk a little to other Aboriginal patients. His sociability improved appreciably. He remained occupied at the prescribed hospital activities, played cards with the other patients, was tidy and cooperative. Four years after his admission he was sent home.

Revisited recently, Laraga and Digenda were located at Amoonguna settlement near Alice Springs; Joda and his family were at Jervois station in the Yowera country. The superintendent at Amoonguna thought Laraga and Digenda were both well. Laraga had recently visited Lake Nash. He was genial and loquacious. He was well known as a sociable and excitable person with a higher level of activity than most. He described to me his illness in more detail but did not refer to environmental or personal difficulties that may have preceded it. His description suggested to me that it was a circumscribed manic episode with a content of traditional medical belief, occurring in a personality normally extraverted, during a period of identity crisis.

Digenda, when seen, was working at his regular job of cleaning the ablutions block, at a time when all the other men had gone into the town to shop, visit, and drink. He did not drink or socialize. The superintendent thought him a model, steady worker—an unusual type at the settlement. I found him in fact affectively flat and unemotional. He was a single man with a woman "promised," but little likelihood of marriage. He described his illness at Lucy Creek and at MacDonald Downs as "being silly in the head," and though he gave additional details he was vague about their origin and about any personal difficulties that he may have had. He gave only a hazy account of his mental activity during his long catatonic period in the hospital, saying that his tongue was held so that he could not talk. The reason may have been a dangerous witchetty[3] given him to eat by an old man called Lively, he thought. Despite his long stay in hospital, he had recently visited a native doctor in preference to the settlement sick bay. Shy and solitary, he suggested by his appearance a remitted catatonic illness, again with a content of traditional medical belief, occurring in a personality normally schizoid. The internal conflict over identity will be conjectured shortly.

Joda could not be visited. But the manager of Jervois station, asked about him during the touchdown of the plane I was using,

---

[3] Witchetty: a fat grub infesting the roots of certain native trees, prized as food.

confirmed that he was very well. He was serious and conscientious, in fact one of the best workmen on the station.

It is striking that at Lake Nash, although tribal society is fragmented and the culture diluted after fifty years of Western contact, traditional expressions of psychosis still occur. The reader may feel surprise that in major psychoses that so grossly alter the habits of life, so little explanation is forthcoming from the patients. But this is not only a transcultural difficulty; schizophrenic patients in one's own culture may be equally unforthcoming. The failure of rapport that separates the truly psychotic man from the normal hinders understanding just as it spurs speculation. Speculation, then, is offered about these Aboriginal men, in the certain knowledge that it can reflect only a fragment of the truth. We may comment first on the cultural roles of the patients.

Distinct from the intrusion of solid objects by sorcery, Aborigines commonly complain that spirit animals are lodged in the body and control it—the process called possession. In this instance we seem to be concerned with the personal totems of the medicine man that normally function as familiars—animal servants or genii that leave his body to assist in diagnosis and treatment. These totemic animals are "transfused" by the doctor into a sick man's body and exert a strengthening or curative action. When the time comes for a tribal practitioner to pass on his calling to a successor, the personal totem is "transfused" in the same way to the successor, in many instances the son. It is my conjecture that in Laraga's family, possibly because of the degree of culture change and fragmentation in the world around, the attempted transfusion proved incompatible—unacceptable and confusing—to the totemite sons. The father, bred in tribal culture, reacted to the situation with increased efforts at mastery, derangement of brief duration, and the firm conviction that the trouble was a spirit "inside me" (clinically, mania). The sons, bred in the alien-contact situation, reacted with a withdrawing kind of illness of more prolonged duration and with a splitting in the mental apparatus by which the troubling spirit was judged "outside me" (clinically, schizophrenia). There were for the sons additional stresses, not the least the unavailability of a spouse for the younger son. The change in the psychiatric reaction pattern down this lineage is reminiscent of the sequence described in Mawindjia's family (chapter 10), relating illness to culture history.

Class B. Disturbances of Refugees

B, age 60

This distinguished-looking elderly man is a Warramunga Aborigine from above the Sandover River country but he has lived for many years among the Yowera at Lake Nash, where he has children. He says he became very sick last year and has not recovered. He had camped by himself during the pumping season at a bore (artesian well) in the Tobermory country, as he had often done before in the course of his work at the station. In his own words "Night time I seen him . . . come along me, big mob—animal or devil or *kurdaitcha*[4]—more than twenty. White on em, horns on em, run up close. I been frightened, leave my swag, run away to next bore. At next bore, another blackfellow and his old woman, they been frightened now and run away along me, I leave everything behind but the waterbag." When the station manager found them, all three were not convinced by his reassurance because white men could not see them. They said *kurdaitcha* were building yards around them and they had to break out. Brought back to the station by the manager, B has been unsettled since; he appears aged and is less active and he is unlikely ever to look after a lonely bore again.

W, age 40

This Aborigine says he comes from Hatches' Creek, but his tribal dialect cannot be readily understood by the Yowera natives at Lake Nash. He does only occasional light work around the station because of an illness he had a few years ago; before that he was physically a strong man working on a stock camp. His version of this illness is that an old Warrabri native doctor called Camel Jack caught him with a *djula* (kangaroo fibula). This strained his belly

---

4 *Kurdaitcha:* Aranda term for the party of men appointed by the council of elders to avenge a tribal misdeed by assassination. (See Tjanba avengers described in Chapter 3.) They lie in ambush for their intended victim, made invisible by a special costume that includes boots of emu feathers. The boots disguise their tracks over the ground, normally closely read by Aborigines.

so that he could not work, and he says he lay down in his camp for three years. He went to Mount Isa hospital, where the white doctor operated and said he was all right. But W says he was not all right until Camel Jack relented, came to him and rubbed his belly with bullock fat and extracted a three-inch *djula* from him. He claims that he himself is a native doctor, but his conversation reveals that he is poorly grounded in Aboriginal medical lore and is poorly socially integrated. Rubbing, smacking, and blowing to stop pain comprise his repertoire; he is a physiotherapist rather than a socially sanctioned doctor. Information from the station reveals that his admission to Mount Isa hospital was for a hernia operation.

M, age 26

This young man, an intelligent Walbiri working as a mechanic at Yuendumu settlement, gave an account of a "traditional" illness that afflicted him on his only visit to Lake Nash country. Here is his account:

> I was sick that Queensland way, really sick. I saw Dreaming about animals. Those people reckons animals get into people. I went out droving through Alexandria about three years ago. Through to Lake Nash along the Georgina, camping near Roxborough, along the Georgina. I see old Aboriginal grave. An old man told me, watch out for animal Dreaming. That old man's name Eric. Night time holy animal from Dreaming come. I feel full inside of animal bones, through legs, belly, chest, head. I get very sick. Holy animal from the Dreaming—they didn't tell me what sort. They got different animals. Wild looking thing, white color all over, black front and face. Different from cat or dog. Big head, sharp teeth. He don't eat meat, only people. He get in heart, in belly, in chest, in neck—put in bones of man. Then he get out. All night. They take me to doctor man at Dajarra in car belonging to Aborigine boy. They carry me. Not walk. Not eat. Talk a little. That Eric meet me, bring to camp. Lay me down on tarp. Eric put bushes and branches across his arms, tied on. Then he brushes out bones out of me with branch. I see 'em on tarp. Two big shin bones, old, dry. Big mob little bones. After that, give me blood. Lot of men—about twenty—cut arms with razor blade and string on arm. Get bucket nearly half full of blood. I drink all, slow. I get right straight away, eat, drink all right. I pay them all thirty pounds. I stay two weeks at Lake Nash, school teacher bloke Mr. Benjamin look after me. I won't go away droving anymore. Might get sick. Eric told me common thing here, animals leave bones in people.

At Lake Nash and at other cattle stations in the region, displaced persons tend to congregate, whereas persons with more intact social ties tend to remain at the larger population centers such as missions and government settlements. Displaced persons, dislocated from a supportive social credit network, unfamiliar with local vernacular and usages, show a higher incidence of mental disorders. Common varieties described elsewhere have been given such names as acute culture shock, transitory delusional state, alien's paranoid reaction, and the "*bouffée délirante aigue*" described (in Nigeria) by Collomb (1965). The refugee Aborigines of this region exemplify these syndromes, expressed however in terms of the medical system of the culture.

Only the old men at Lake Nash have a clear idea of the medical belief system and "world view" underlying these illnesses. Important in this system is *wilaiba*, a devil animal that lives in a tree, in size like a kangaroo rat and furred like a dingo. *Wilaiba* makes people sick by putting its paw on the victim's mouth while he sleeps. Or it may enter a victim's body to fill it with bones. Lake Nash itself is the kangaroo rat Dreaming. The native doctor owns a wormlike servant, *lokwokwa*, which lives in his body and may be used in therapy. But the medical system that may be gleaned from the Yowera people is sketchy; it is not the complex and elaborate body that is held by more tribally oriented people such as the Walbiri. It may be that the ideas of animal internalization prevalent in this region lend themselves to disturbances of special intensity. In combination with the ubiquitous singing (sorcery) this makes for a substantial content of traditional belief in illness.

Class C. Disturbances Expressing Resistance to Whites

M, age 28

This Aborigine has been overactive, unpredictable, and violent, to a degree requiring hospital admissions, for ten years. When working at the station he habitually tries to take charge of equipment and vehicles, though he lacks the ability and permission to use them. He tries to joy ride in any available car and consistently steals car keys (and any other key he finds) when he can. He tried to shoot "head noises" with a rifle and singed his scalp. He cannot be managed at the station because of the risk and stays at Amoonguna settlement near Alice Springs, where he is overactive and rebellious. He is attracted to cars, machinery, and the appurtenances of Western culture in what appears a buffoonlike way; for example, he climbs the water tower and sits on top "driving" it, making noises like a motor car. He behaves similarly with the lawn mower.

K, age 18

A step-brother to M, age 28, whose case was just discussed, K resembles M in his failure to establish a cooperative or even a working relationship with white people. He attended school at Lake Nash intermittently for several years, but was uncooperative—refusing to sit down, frequently kicking the walls and furniture. Little is known of his present condition, because although he lives with his relatives in the camp at Lake Nash station and eats the station food he hides in the bushes by the river whenever a white person approaches. He is completely unoccupied. Attempts to show him to the aerial medical officer are unsuccessful because he cannot be found. He is regarded as frightened of whites but harmless to them.

M, age 15

This young man seemed bright and normal as a boy; he worked in the stockyard and was friendly and cooperative. After his initiation at about twelve he appeared to change and had violent episodes. Two years ago one of his violent and unreasonable outbursts caused him to be admitted to Alice Springs hospital. He sat on the wood heap and said he would kill the station manager, with whom he had previously had a good relationship and who was at a loss to understand the change.

T, age 28

After an apparently normal boyhood, T became sulky, unreasonable, and violent. He became actively opposed to authority without ever making clear his reason. On one occasion on a neighboring station he went into a house with a gun; he has had other violent episodes. He is somewhat helped by chlorpromazine tranquillizer but is on the whole morose, especially when with white people.

M, age 45

M is fat and lethargic and has a complaining manner. He says he is sick, that he strained himself in the guts through hard work and though he is still able to move around he is unable to work. He says he worked too hard as a young man, yard building, wood carting, butchering, making windmills and bores. Now he claims that when he works hard he takes a fit, in which he feels his blood run cold and his teeth clench. Because of these complaints he was investigated in Alice Springs hospital five years ago on suspicion of cerebral tumor. Investigations were negative, but he has adopted the sick role since. On the station he is regarded as aggressive in a concealed way; he is a subversive influence on the younger working men and discourages the women from attending the sick bay with their babies.

Resistance to European Australian society is a common theme, a legacy of the past exploitation of Aborigines by whites, and more recently, of the resigned indifference of whites toward what was thought a dying race. Better policies and better intentions of whites in the present era do not erase this ingrained mistrust. Some of the men described here show aggressive outbursts toward whites, others complete avoidance. Still others express hostility in devious ways by complaining, idleness, or sabotage of white endeavors. Still others, after initial contact with Western society, attempt to return to traditional Aboriginal beliefs and behaviors. This pattern among the Yowera at Lake Nash produces a social conflict that may be focused as *progression* versus *regression*. Each side has its spokesman and the issue forms a constant undercurrent to life in the station (or ranch as it would be termed in the American West).

At the time of my visit the chief spokesman for progression at Lake Nash was the elderly man and tribal rainmaker called Wagon Willy. He could not read and caused amusement at the station by proclaiming a small official form, his "Acknowledgement of Electoral Claim," as an authority from the Big Man in Canberra to tell the Aborigines what to do. His advocacy of Western ways had a pathetic ring: "I tell everybody, no more spear, no more bone. All gone. All gone. If you want to fight, just knuckle up like white man. Then you don't do no harm. If girl go to man, got to marry, just like white man. I with white man all the way, now I send my rain stones away to Walgiri George in Queensland. Black man got to be same as white man."

Other influential old men, such as Warramunga Beasley, though not openly spokesmen for regression, are conservative and make things hard for progressive Aborigines. Indeed, most of the Aborigines are not at all sure that they want to adopt white ways. When Beasley's daughter Irene got her sums right in school, the teacher rewarded her by having her write them on the blackboard. Such was her father's ridicule that Irene sneaked back after school and altered them to make them wrong.

On cattle station properties the demand upon Aborigines for some contribution to the general work in hand, though by no means excessive, is always present; there is less tolerance of conservatism or regression than on a government settlement or mission. Pressures from the management, in the face of complete absence of bargaining power by Aborigines, inevitably stimulate direct or devious aggressive responses by individuals unable or unwilling to make their contribution. These responses comprise part of the cause and content of the hostile personality disorders described in this series.

Class D. Disturbances Associated with Domestic Crisis

D, age 30

This normally healthy woman, the wife of M, age 45, had a severe illness two years ago. She became suddenly sick and frightened, could not stand up, and was convinced she was dying. No physical illness was apparent to the nurse at the station nor to the aerial medical officer who was called to see her. For six weeks she pined away, losing twenty pounds to the alarm of the nurse trying to look after her. Her husband asked for a native doctor to be brought in to treat her. That night there was an "operation" and ceremony, and the next morning she was better and doing the washing. The story emerged that husband and wife had disobeyed tribal custom about their son's initiation, and the old men had "boned" her.

N, age 28

This mother of three young children is the niece of N, age 28 (see Class O). She has always been a vague person, but has become very disturbed during and after her last two pregnancies. She was required (by the welfare officer) to marry her husband, although her mother opposed it because of the closeness of the tribal kinship. A year ago she became intensely agitated for six months, especially at times when her husband was away. She was unmanageable, hiding in the bushes with torn clothes and matted hair; at other times she ran around the camp threatening everybody with a stick. After this period of agitation, she became vague and withdrawn. Chlorpromazine is now being given, but its administering cannot be supervised regularly; at present she is clean and looks after her children.

A, age 30

This woman, abandoned by her husband two years previously, with three children to support, became thin and exhausted. She seemed disinterested and miserable, neglecting herself, not doing her hair, and contracting sores. She received no support from the others in the camp; an enquiry to the social services department about a pension for her as a deserted wife received no action. Given food, encouragement, and an indoor job by the station manager's wife, she improved rapidly and is now very well.

Anxiety has a social context, including a work context and—especially for young married women—a domestic context. The case histories of the three young mothers recorded here are not peculiar to Aboriginal society; Western readers may feel they have a familiar ring. It may be, however, that establishing a domestic ménage along Western conjugal lines has special frustrations for serious and ambitious Aboriginal mothers—frustrations of opportunity, of poverty, of education, and of cultural exclusion—lured by the unattainable model of the affluent white household at the station. (See the discussion of the theme of cultural exclusion in chapter 12.)

Class E. Disturbances Associated with Deprivation

M, age 35

This man, of good intelligence, comprehension, and work habits, has been completely mute since childhood. There is no deafness. It is said that a taboo on talking was placed on him by the old men when he was a boy of six or seven, so that he did not have the chance to practice speech.

B, W, and C—children

These young Aborigines, ranging in age from 5 to 17, are subnormal in intelligence, in comparison with the older children in the camp. They are dull, show poor comprehension, and cannot be trained to simple duties or housework. C is the daughter of N, age 28 (see Class O). Physically they seem healthy.

The developmental hazards facing Aboriginal children have been sketched in chapter 2. They are formidable. Central Australia has an exceptionally high infant mortality rate and the morbidity is also substantial. In camp conditions, young children are subject to intermittent subnutrition coupled with recurrent infection of the intestinal tract and upper and lower respiratory tracts. Their growth rate is significantly inferior to that of European Australian children. In the homes there is lack of stimulus for cognitive and verbal development, with little reinforcement afforded of what is learned in school. The personality development is impaired in a household in which arrangements for eating, sleeping, and toileting are unreliable, and the reward-punishment system arbitrary and often chaotic. Deprivations of this kind are so striking that we later directed special attention to the medical and psychiatric problems of childrearing in Aboriginal settlements (Nurcombe 1970).

From the epidemiological point of view, it hardly seems open to question that a sick society may display not so much a dominant mode of mental abnormality as a large proportion of members disordered in various ways. Medicine, a healing profession as well as a science, is interested in the factors responsible for such high incidences and these will be explored in chapter 12. We carry forward in our minds some impression of suffering experienced by hunting-gathering folk who have become refugees in the cattle country of white Australian settlers. In parallel, we have an impression of some of the dominant themes of these illnesses: the crisis of Aboriginal identity, the resistance to whites, the disturbance of domesticity associated with poverty, the social fragmentation, and the pervasive deprivation.

CHAPTER TWELVE

Casualties of Change

WHEN CONCEPTS such as "maladjustment" or "sick society" are
applied to Australian Aborigines, there is some danger that an unfavorable impression may be created of their constitutional temperament and stability. In a pluralistic society, those on the top
socioeconomically are often psychologically prepared to credit
this impression, so that it would be doubly unfortunate if medical
studies designed to assist those on the bottom should contribute to
this sort of misunderstanding. In fact it is equally true that one may
marvel at the quality of the adaptation to cultural change being
made by some individuals. It is not the object of our work to study
these individuals, blessed with remarkable personal attributes and
good fortune; they are mentioned here merely to offset the sweeping imputation to which psychopathological studies sometimes give
rise, even among apparently sophisticated people. The imputation
is that the personality disorders, the neurotic and psychotic patterns, reflect racial instability arising from some biologically determined defect in concept formation. It is true that some biological
(genetic) factors are operant and that these may have effects on
temperament, as the family history in chapter 10 suggests. But it is
not known how important they are. They appear insignificant by
comparison with the environmental stresses, producing anxiety as a
common denominator of Aboriginal malaise.

Environmental stress is a complex concept because it is regulated
both by the objective trauma and the subjective perception of the
recipient. Several useful models of environmental stress are available from current psychiatric research into adaptation in contexts of
cultural change. I have kept these models before me in this book,

thinking of them as complementary to each other rather than as competing. I have been indebted in particular to the work of Eitinger (1964) on gross stress; of Leighton (1959) on interference with vital strivings; of Brody (1966) on cultural exclusion; and an approach that is emphasized in my own material, on the collapse of the social institutions of medicine and the law. Though the latter model has predominated in this book the other three should be outlined in the interests of conceptual balance.

The response to gross stress is exemplified by the research of Eitinger (1964) who studied the sequelae of painful and unrelieved trauma in concentration camps, including fear, semistarvation, and physical brutality. Gross stress came into vogue in World War II as a medical category to accommodate the psychiatric reactions of combat personnel that could not be described in terms of the conventional categories used in ordinary civilian medicine. In peacetime, it became convenient to apply the "reaction to gross stress" to community disasters such as fire, flood, earthquake, or tornado. Four overlapping phases of the response of individuals are described (Tyhurst 1951; Weiss and Payson 1967). An anticipatory or threat phase may last hours, or persist for years. The impact phase may be as brief as a few minutes or hours. The recoil phase may last for days, or weeks. But the posttraumatic phase, if severe, may endure for life. As studied by Eitinger, there are two common outcomes to painful trauma of this kind. There may be a successful outcome, with spontaneous recovery and integration within the group, sometimes with increased self-confidence. Or there may be unsuccessful outcomes, with chronic anxiety expressed in a variety of ways. Some of the syndromes identified by Eitinger include catastrophic behavior in which traumas are painfully reexperienced, with nightmares; chronic anxiety states with fatigue and indifference; personality change with unfavorable concepts of the self, the group, and the world; "survivor guilt"—obsessed by feelings that "others died so I could live"; hostility and aggression expressed passively against authority. Although the concept has not been applied transculturally by Eitinger, the situation in Aboriginal communities is often adverse enough to suggest that gross stress is an appropriate model. Because of the chronicity, the refugee camp comes to mind rather than the concentration camp, as the analogy.

Interference with vital strivings is emphasized by A. H. Leighton (1959) who has developed this concept to refer to the fundamental personality processes such as the quest for physical security, opportunities for creativity, a sense of identity, and a sense of moral order. In the case of women, opportunities for satisfactory mothering is an important aspect of "vital strivings." As we have seen in chapter 9 concerning the position of women, it is an appropriate model for the stresses of detribalizing women. Inasmuch as interference with vital strivings itself constitutes gross stress, or may be associated with gross stress, Leighton's model overlaps with Eitinger's. But it casts its net more widely to include more of the contingencies of human life. And it suggests more strongly than does the concept of gross stress a certain reciprocity between the environment and the individual's behavior.

Cultural exclusion is a concept proposed by Brody (1966) to refer to the state of uncomfortable equilibrium that is reached when a disadvantaged and subordinate ethnic group exists in a wider community. It focuses attention on the exclusion of sectors of the population, or social subsystems, from complete participation in the culture of the larger societies to which they belong. Brody notes that the elements of culture in which affected individuals are denied full participation may be divided into at least four categories: First, experience of free choice, self-determination, and equality. Second, individual gain through collective behavior. Third, the shared symbols and experiences important to the development of incentive. Fourth, the richness, continuity, and integration of experience. Using a concept of the ego as colored and shaped by a man's participation in the social matrix of his experience, Brody's model studies the impact of cultural exclusion on character and illness. It is particularly applicable to the study of Aboriginal women, a further excluded section of the already excluded community.

In this book, the psychiatric malaise with which we are concerned has been approached from the direction of medicine and the law, the social institutions designed to alleviate suffering and to safeguard social security. If these social institutions collapse without replacement, individuals express their loss and bewilderment in emotional and behavioral disorder. In the alien-contact situation in which the Aborigines live, we have been concerned with the shattering impact of the collapse of this traditional machinery that provides the individual's orientation. Durkheim (1930) described as anomie the abandonment of community goals and of the social rules for reaching them, a situation in which the individual is underregulated by his social group. This book has described an example of this process. The cultural gulf to be bridged was perhaps the widest ever in a situation of cultural change so that the traditional institutions of medicine and law were peculiarly unadaptable. This gave rise to a widespread belief that the Aborigine, as a "Stone Age man," is perforce unsuccessful in adapting to Western society. Many Aboriginal communities today, especially those on the dusty fringes of outback towns, appear to support such a conclusion. Generally in Australia, a country that modern technology has transformed into a land of affluence and opportunity, Aborigines are at the bottom of the socioeconomic scale. Poorly represented in trade, industry, commerce, and the professions, they live in inferior and often squalid conditions. It cannot be said that they are "on the march" in the manner of, say, New Guineans. New Guineans are in an entirely different situation; they have never been dispossessed of their lands to the same degree, and in a gardening economy the means of subsistence has always been available to them.

European Australians are trying to adjust to the idea that Aboriginal Australians are not a dying race after all—the latest vagary of an unpredictable people that has always baffled white Australians. Aboriginal character is particularly elusive, unless one has the opportunity and capacity of anthropologists A. P. Elkin (1954), T. G. H. Strehlow (1947), or R. M. Berndt (1951) to spend long periods in intimate association with them. Most European Australians fall back on stereotypes of Aborigines: shy and retiring; spontaneous and carefree; irritable and quarrelsome; lacking in foresight and stamina. Few whites have ever perceived the range of Aboriginal psychological adjustments to cultural change, including pathological manifestations. Few have seen the enervating anxiety that pervades Aborigines. This chapter will review material intended to correct this misapprehension, drawing attention to the signs, symptoms, and behavioral expressions of Aboriginal anxiety. Before doing so, however, it is necessary to indicate briefly what a psychiatrist understands by "anxiety," and to outline significant features of the social setting in which it occurs in this instance.

For medical validity the concept of anxiety must be broader than the mere idea of manifest or visible anxiety. Its definition and measurement should include three aspects: the characteristic unpleasant subjective feeling; the bodily signs and symptoms; and the behavioral manifestations associated with it. The first two aspects can be calibrated by interviews, questionnaires, and objective tests of involuntary functions. This we have done elsewhere for Aborigines (Cawte 1972). The linkage between anxiety and behavior is harder to test. Opposing views are held of its nature. One school of learning theorists holds that anxiety is the main drive to action. A contrasting psychoanalytic view, that anxiety disorganizes effective action, may be more heuristically useful in studying a people whose effective action is considerably disorganized. Whence does it spring? In our work its source is viewed not so much as a biologically based instinct as environmental stress—from the risks, even the risk of failing, inherent in the culture contact.

Any theory of adaptation that emphasizes anxiety as a central concept around which behavioral phenomena may be ordered should be treated with caution. However in transcultural work the opposite mistake is more likely: Western observers tend to be unaware that indigenous peoples are anxious because the expressions of anxiety differ from Western ones. The evidence suggests that Aboriginal anxiety is overlooked because it is expressed differently and is experienced at an intensity more disintegrating to adaptive behavior.

The gathering perturbation of European Australians about Aborigines tends to polarize them into two quasi-political movements. The radical movement attributes Aboriginal difficulties to oppression by the white colonist—by plunder, murder, and denial of human rights. The reactionary movement attributes difficulties to Aboriginal "primitiveness," to biological and social shortcomings, and to the cultural gulf between Aborigines and European Australians. Both views are simplifications and carry the overtones of racial conflict. Both views ignore questions raised by ecological, sociological, and psychodynamic studies. For reformers, the diversity and complexity of these problems seem to throw a kind of pall over straightforward remedial social action.

The resurrection of Aborigines is itself a factor that vitally affects adaptation. Demographically, Aborigines have been subject to severe fluctuations. Around three hundred thousand are thought to have been in Australia when European colonization began in 1788, though how this estimate is formed is obscure. As we have observed, the response to early white contact was not to decline but to plummet toward extinction. All were soon dead in Tasmania. Elsewhere in Australia the effect of introduced pathogens, bullets, and subnutrition consequent upon dispossession of lands and disruption of social organization was such that before World War II the Aborigines were considered a dying race. The main task for Australians was to "smooth the dying pillow."[1] But advances in public health measures—chief among several influences—reversed the decline until today a phase of rapid population growth amounts to a population bulge in some places and an explosion in others. Censuses lead to a present estimate of 120,000 Aborigines, one third full blood, one third mixed blood, one third of recognizable Aboriginal origins and social orientation, though not so identified in the censuses. This represents only 1 percent of the total Australian population but a natural increase rate several times higher. Today's Aboriginal birthrate is about 40 per 100 per year, becoming higher than 60 in some groups—as high a birthrate as ever reported for human society.

In the center and north of the subcontinent, the subordinate and disadvantaged Aboriginal population is not a minority one. These are the regions of the minerals industries that are pouring new wealth into Australia's economy, but offering little work or wealth for the indigenous populations. Though the Aborigines' poverty is not increasing, they are not sharing equally in the economic growth, so that the relative inequality is increasing. These demographic and economic changes have further overthrown the family as a social system responsible for the training and emotional security of children and as a social system articulating with society at large.

Aboriginal congregations articulate with Western society at four

[1] The phrase popularized by Mrs. Daisy Bates in *The Passing of the Aborigines* (1941).

levels of culture contact, termed bush, outback, fringe, and city. Bush Aborigines live in detribalizing, multitribal clusters at Christian missions and government settlements in the continent's north and center; a few of them live at more remote outstations and still fewer remain seminomadic at least for part of the year. Outback Aborigines live in a relationship with the cattle industry as stockmen or housegirls. Fringe Aborigines, usually of mixed descent, live in shanty settlements on the outskirts of country towns, a few "passing" into the town to assimilate with the whites. In general they have lost their traditional culture, though a few try to reconstruct the lost culture, using cues from books, gossip, and fantasy. Purveyors of this pseudoculture are sometimes sarcastically dubbed "professional Aborigines," in a characteristically unkind discrimination. City Aborigines usually congregate in a few streets of the older slum suburbs of the capitals, having come from the country to look for work.

Although these different assemblages identify themselves as Aboriginal it follows that there is not one Aboriginal social problem but many, not one Aboriginal social character but many, not one pathology but many. They share some themes such as Brody's cultural exclusion, but the universality of such themes among Aborigines has been exaggerated by the stereotypers.

In the discussion of one of my case histories (chapter 1), we saw that a typical stereotype trait is "walkabout"—an Aboriginal English term to describe the movements of a foraging horde around the countryside. Bush and outback Aborigines still "walkabout," but for vacations and to visit relatives. In fringe Aborigines "walkabout" reflects the changing location of the labor market for seasonal and unskilled workers. In some individuals it represents the vagabondage of the socially isolated man, reared in poverty, relieving tension by alcoholism and petty crime. Despite all these themes, the portmanteau word "walkabout" survives in many an employer's mind as a characteristic of all manner of Aborigines and one that diminishes their industrial capacity.

In this book attention has been directed chiefly to "bush" (the more traditionally oriented) Aborigines. Since it is reasonable to suppose that there were adaptive difficulties before European colonization, it is unwarranted to relate all their difficulties to the culture contact. The role of the natural environment, especially the aspect of "fluctuating abundance," should not be neglected. Comparative studies that match one Aboriginal group with another reveal how human adjustment is influenced by ecology.

In the book *Cruel, Poor and Brutal Nations* (Cawte 1972), a striking illustration of the importance of ecological factors in adjustment is afforded by the Kaiadilt, the little nation of Bentinck Islanders in the Gulf of Carpentaria first reported by the navigator Flinders in 1803. Separated for millennia from the mainstreams of mankind, Australian Aborigines are reckoned to have been one of the world's isolated peoples, but the Kaiadilt appear to have been isolated even from other Aborigines. Their island is a natural prison situated over the horizon from other islands, making purposeful navigation difficult for a rafting people. The occurrence of microevolution in this natural prison is corroborated biologically not only by the absence of the dog in their community but by the entire absence of blood Group A, which has a common occurrence in the other tribes of the Gulf. The Kaiadilt are characterized by having blood Group B, unusual in Aborigines though common in Asia. When contact was finally established twenty-five years ago, the Kaiadilt were a sick nation. By comparison with other tribes in the region there was a high incidence of depressed, paranoid, and suicidal conditions, with a high incidence of physical disease also. Reconstruction of their recent history suggests that in a series of good years the Kaiadilt population would build up, but if bad seasons ensued the population would exceed the food resources available at the existing low level of technology. People then killed to survive, until vendetta, social disintegration, mental and physical decline engulfed their overcrowded existence. Thus an unsatisfactory human ecology is capable of producing social fragmentation that begets mental disturbance that begets more social fragmentation in a downward spiral of malfunctioning. The broader question concerns the extent to which the adaptation of Aboriginal groups was always affected by the fluctuating abundance that is so conspicuous a feature of Australia.

Sorcery and possession syndromes provide one index of anxiety and mental disturbance. In chapter 6 I addressed attention to actual cases of sorcery as they occurred in relation to the observable drama, to the social context, and to the personality, but the question was deferred. Is sorcery a stress disorder? The series of complaints of sorcery reveals that the effective agent is usually the victim and not the sorcerer, but it cannot be too much emphasized that about a third of the victims prove to be suffering from physical disease, such as tuberculosis, which they and their confreres interpret as sorcery. In another third the victims are suffering from psychiatric conditions, their complaints of sorcery again serving as the culturally regulated rationalization. In most of the other cases there is an interpersonal conflict in which the accusation of sorcery had been leveled by the victim at an antagonist in order to manipulate the climate of opinion of the group—one of the "games people play." Clinical study of complaints of sorcery also reveals that they become more prevalent in situations of culture contact—rather than less prevalent as might have been expected. For example they appear more common in outback Aborigines, chiefly multitribal aggregations, rather than in single-tribe cohesive communities. This suggests that social fragmentation is part of the gross stress that affects levels of anxiety in a community and so affects the complaints of sorcery.

As a castaway clings to his overturned boat rather than swim for the distant shore, traditional Aborigines cling to folkways that give rise to socially divisive strains today. One such "inappropriate" retention of a cultural norm is polygamy in Arnhem Land. Baby girls are bestowed to a "promise man" of the correct marriage subsection. The system gives older men several wives of varied ages but leaves wifeless perhaps half of the young men. Two factors made the system workable in former times: the surplus of women associated with high mortality in men and the outlet of ritual sexual sharing as in the Kunapipi ceremony. Male mortality and ritual sexual sharing have succumbed to European Australian law and order, but polygamy survives in what is now an unbalanced state. The resulting conflict between peers, between families, and especially between the older generation and the younger is well depicted in a recent work entitled *Kinship and Conflict* (Hiatt 1965). Splits and coalitions associated with retention of inappropriate cultural norms are the more troublesome to Aborigines inasmuch as they offset their chances of local political union to achieve common ends.

Fringe Aborigines are noted for their strong identity as Aborigines—even when they are part white—and for their cohesiveness as an outgroup to European Australian society. This cohesiveness is further strengthened by the existence of the caste barrier and by the strong Aboriginal pressures toward maintaining group obligations and loyalties (Fink 1957). However valuable this cohesiveness may be, it should not be assumed that Aboriginal families are necessarily cohesive or that they provide a supportive and integrated system for the raising of children. The Aboriginal family as a childrearing system has undergone drastic alterations (Beckett 1965) and the impact of these changes on character formation in children has been insufficiently studied. Inevitably many of the observations are of an impressionistic kind.

The unprecedentedly high fertility recently bestowed by medicine and welfare on Aboriginal women has been a veritable gift of the Magi. The pathos of their situation was evident on sociomedical expeditions to Arnhem Land from my school, not as yet reported. Thirty women of childbearing age were interviewed in one village, one at a time, using a vernacular language and under relationships of reasonable rapport—unusual conditions for such an enquiry. Sixteen were not aware that white women used techniques of preventing pregnancy. Fourteen said they knew this, but several of them had only learned it from the expedition members during this visit. Asked if they would like to use these techniques, twenty-six said yes and four said no. Of the twenty-six who said yes, many were desperately eager to have some form of family planning and asked further questions.

Some of the women interviewed were trying to stop having babies by sexual abstinence, others by magical methods, traditional or idiosyncratic. Their methods give an indication of cultural beliefs likely to affect the introduction of planned parenthood: "Spread the milk of the Narrawu tree on your menstrual rag . . . put your menstrual rag in a crabhole . . . stop eating fish and honey . . . eat hot stones with your meat . . . cut up your placenta and throw it in the salt water . . . heat the wax from the Mayping tree and sit on it during menstruation . . . to get rid of the baby tie cords tightly around your belly and pummel it furiously. . . ."

Because good rapport is usually lacking, whites who contact Aborigines fail to perceive the extent of their problems and fail to appreciate that Aborigines in general do not regard themselves as fit and healthy. Aborigines communicate their complaints in a stereotyped fashion that invites underdiagnosis. The study in northern Queensland that went to the very considerable trouble of administering in the vernacular a modified Cornell Medical Index health questionnaire to a tribally oriented population produced striking results (Cawte 1972). Ninety-one percent of the adult population was tested. There were five high peaks of complaints, concerned respectively with musculoskeletal pains such as backaches, respiratory troubles, insomnia, lassitude, and anger. Musculoskeletal complaints were no surprise: possibly the Aborigines' build is better evolved for long-distance walking than for labor with heavy loads. Respiratory complaints were predictable from the atmospheric conditions of high dust and smoke levels and extreme diurnal temperature variations. The insomnia—surprising to observers who see Aborigines sleep during the day—reflects a crowded and disturbed sleeping environment and in many cases poor health, anxiety, or depression. Fatigue came as no surprise either since it was known that this population is subject to hookworm infestation and to dietary uncertainty. Suppressed anger was understandable in a people little experienced in high density group living. What is perhaps surprising is the remarkable consistency of the complaint pattern in all the groups, though the highest levels of complaints are found in the older age groups, the women, and the more socially disadvantaged people.

In outback and fringe Aborigines, a set of symptoms not adequately recorded by questionnaire methods and not complained of by the subjects themselves is the tendency to alcoholism and gambling. These tension-reducing devices give rise to further difficulties that contribute to the downward spiral of malfunctioning. Where alcohol is not available in more protected Aboriginal communities, petrol sniffing is resorted to by stimulus-hungry youths. Patterns of drinking have been described among fringe Aborigines (Beckett 1964). Although alcoholism is found in a number of Aboriginal people it is open to question whether it is more prevalent than in European Australians. What is clear is that Aborigines are less protected against its severe effects by their economy, by their social network, and by the availability of medical services. In the crowded environment of slum, fringe, or settlement even a small number of alcoholics have a disintegrative effect on the community in general.

Indeed of all the stresses imposed upon Aborigines by the cultural change, perhaps none is more disruptive than high density camp life, especially in people that traditionally spent only a small part of the year congregated together. Many of the traits attributed to Aborigines may in fact be artifacts of camp life. Camps erupt in periodic brawls that often become riots involving most of the community until the police intervene to carry off combatants to the lockup. That these riots are not due merely to drunkenness is obvious because they also occur on "dry" missions and settlements. There they are put down to disputes over women. Whatever their origins, the riots are disastrous for harmony in the camp, as they are for the blackfellow's social image before the whitefellow.

Characteristically the spark that ignites the riot may be a child. A child beats another, the defeated child's mother protests to the victor's mother and receives a blow with the fist, the husband retaliates with a stick, the relations and in-laws join in. Coalitions crystallize around old grievances. Soon there is a melee of fifty people. Equally characteristically, between riots the ethos of the community is one of tolerance and—especially—of evasion of confrontation. The "ideal man" tends to be a restrained, generous, peacemaker who never confronts another with his grievances until these become serious. Thus he becomes the victim of the carping wife, the dependent relation, the forgetful borrower, and the stealthy manipulator. Whites see Aborigines as indecisive and lacking initiative. Observations of riots suggest that this is related to evasion of confrontation and to the necessity to consult group opinion rather than take an individual stand and so run the risk of group conflict. It is an ethos that puts Aborigines at a disadvantage with whites, who expect communication of a more direct kind, with irritability expressed but controlled.

The other important affliction of the culture contact upon Aborigines is impoverishment, associated with poor education and employability. Oscar Lewis' (1959) observations on poverty as a culture that perpetuates certain character traits has an obvious attractiveness for observers of Aborigines. Reared in poverty, it is comprehensible that their limited concept formation and present-time orientation to life might prohibit mastery of the world of regular work, technology, education, and affluence.

A warning is in order. The "culture of poverty" theory is itself in danger of becoming a rationalization that can inhibit social action directed against poverty. It is possible to apply the theory that poverty shapes personality in childhood more strongly than Lewis himself intended. Middle-class observers fail to appreciate that unsatisfiable want is also gross stress in the here-and-now. It is gross stress that cannot be evaded when times are hard and resources few. The head of the family, however sturdy his personality may be, cannot feed, clothe, or educate his family. Eventually he ceases to strive.

So we leave him. His place in the world is that of the modern primitive who has been relatively unsuccessful in adapting to Western society. I undertook in this book to view him, his medicine, and his law through the eyes of modern medicine and psychiatry. His medicine is his law no longer. Neither is it much help to him. The modern clinician may sometimes feel that he has little better success with him, but there is something more he can do. He can argue his case as might an advocate. Through case histories, personal histories, and biographies, I have tried, however imperfectly, to depict how it is to be a modern primitive—to indicate something of the anxiety, discomfort, frustration of the person, and of the defects in the medicine and law intended to safeguard him.

Taking the medical and legal perspective of man's adaptation that has been propounded in this book, what may be projected for the future? Many observers do not expect any deep involvement by medicine and law while these professions are mainly absorbed in their fee-for-service relationship with affluent society. Others point to the signs of change. In Sydney, for example, there is an Aboriginal Legal Service, led by the dean of law at the University of New South Wales, J. H. Wootten, and with a council consisting mostly of Aborigines. It provides a volunteer band of lawyers for the defense at law of Aborigines. Movements of this kind are doubly important if they indicate that the powerful societal professions of Westerners are becoming more attuned to the needs of the dispossessed.

One of the medical solutions, most relevant to the theme of this book, should be mentioned here. We have seen that Aborigines lose their ability to adapt when they lose their social integration—of which the traditional practitioner was the pivotal figure and tangible symbol. This observation led us, in a further research study,[2] to replace this pivotal figure with a modern medical practitioner. In this research, the practitioner in the community concerned fills a role broader than that of a dispenser of medical advice and first aid. In addition to this well-understood medical role, he is trained in the methods of community development and social change. Operating as he does within the context of sickness, he enjoys the advantages universally conferred by this role. In the community being studied he has become a nucleus for social integration. It is fair to indicate that in this "research" community, some success is attending these efforts, but their reporting here would take us beyond the scope of the present volume.

[2] This study is being conducted in the far west of New South Wales by Dr. Max Kamien, under the general title of "The Human Ecology of the Arid Zone: The Doctor as Social Change Agent" (publication forthcoming).

CHAPTER THIRTEEN

The Visions of the White Man

HE SEES THE VISION SPLENDID
OF THE SUNLIT PLAINS EXTENDED
—*A. B. Paterson (1895)*

A HIDDEN REALITY obstructs the delivery of health services across a cultural barrier. It is rarely if ever referred to in the literature of psychological anthropology, but I have yet to meet a transcultural psychiatrist who does not concede its existence in practice. This reality is simply the presence of the white man.

Essential services which are set up to serve a disadvantaged ethnic group at some perimeter of Western society may not reach their intended goals because Westerners place themselves in the way. These "consumers" cannot be evaded, for they are demanding as well as deserving. Because of their greater education and sophistication, they make stronger claims on the services than do indigenous people who may have the greater need. Despite the best intentions of the transcultural psychiatrist he may find that much of his time and energy is absorbed by attending to his own ethnic group.

This problem has always been in evidence in the field researches conducted from the University of New South Wales, although the researches were not designed to study it. For example, during a three-year survey of ethnopsychiatry in New Britain, the psychiatrist appointed to this region, Dr. John Hoskin, found that a good deal of his time was claimed by the nonindigenous population, both European and Chinese. Dr. Hoskin saw compelling reasons for assisting these groups: he did not wish to conduct a medical practice on apartheid lines, restricted to one ethnic group; he needed the backing of the expatriate group for his daily subsistence; and these patients were in genuine need, and brought this need to the only specialist in the region. Despite these distractions, Dr. Hoskin and his colleagues produced some useful indigenous studies, to which the interested reader may care to refer (Hoskin 1969 *a, b;* Cawte, Cuthbertson, and Hoskin 1967; Hoskin, Friedman, and Cawte 1969; Hoskin, Kiloh, and Cawte 1969; Pulsford and Cawte 1972).

Similarly the two psychiatrists presently stationed at Darwin, in the Northern Territory of Australia, Dr. Don Eastwell and Dr. Pat Cowdy, find that much of their time is preempted by the white population. Many of their cases also have a forensic or legal aspect, onerous but inescapable. While it is natural to deplore this situation, it is better to accept its reality and try to learn more about the behavior and motivation of "perimeter whites."

In an extensive sociological and historical study of Aborigines (Rowley 1970) there is much emphasis placed upon the collective behavior of the white man. This literature documents how Aborigines suffered from destructiveness of white settlers, and instances of spectacular injustice and inhumanity by officials. The suffering of Aborigines at the hands of white men is surely a cause for indignation, though it should be pointed out that it was much less in extent than that which resulted from semistarvation and infectious diseases inadvertently introduced. Insofar as white settlers and officials are being incriminated for their behavior, it is important to study the psychiatry of the frontier. In the behavioral repertoire of the frontier, psychotic and sociopathic behaviors form a considerable part, and in these extremes something may be discerned of the vision, or the world view, of the white man who assumes this burden.

Most full-blood Aborigines today are found in the central and northern expanses of Australia, remote from the main centers of white population. In these remote regions, full-bloods are a socially disadvantaged, but not a minority, population. Their numbers are approximately matched by white Australians who live under conditions loosely described as "frontier." In fact, the terms *frontier* and *wilderness* have never been much used in Australia, having connotations for Australians that romanticize the reality; *outback* or *bush* are the terms in common usage. Outback Australians are contributing to developments of utmost significance for the future of the country as a whole. Indeed the mineral developments in these regions are likely to prove the major source of the country's income. The social and economic balance of these numerically matched ethnic sections of the community is a matter of equal significance for the future of the country.

Much has been documented concerning the sturdily adaptive white people who pioneered these regions. It need not be emphasized here, except to marvel that so many of them had the reserves of energy and altruism to support the native populations. Missionary, medical, and welfare groups have carried out their work amid disheartening difficulties. Less is known about those who may have had personality disturbances of various kinds, reflected in their personal lives and in their dealings with the indigenous inhabitants. The European Australian side of the alien contact has had little close or sympathetic attention from anthropologists, with a notable exception in R. M. Berndt's *From Black to White in South Australia* (1951) describing the failure and abandonment of an outback mission station.

Is it possible for men of diverse ethnic and cultural origins to live together without exploitation or humiliation? Can they make cooperative use of these zones where the environment is especially difficult? These are large questions, beyond my capacity to answer. In this chapter I want merely to bestow a glance on some aspects of the psychodynamics of whites who go to work in these zones. I would like it to be understood that I have selected case material concerning persons who go into the outback in an attempt to solve their personal problems. No disparagement is intended, especially of the fine people who make a good and constructive adaptation. The case histories presented here represent failures in coping, for these are the ones relevant to our discussion. Success, like mental disorder, is a matter of degree; each person, at a given moment, occupies some point on a continuum with respect to both. I hope that case histories of coping failures will have something to teach those who, by good fortune, find success.

My records of frontier patients show that the stresses of the outback have not been solely responsible for the serious psychiatric breakdowns. Nor are these breakdowns necessarily the outcome of flight by persons escaping the consequences of social depredations and failures in more settled areas. The syndrome can perhaps best be understood by referring to the concept of ecology, or, more precisely, human ecology, man's interaction with his natural as well as with his social environment. When man intrudes into the wild, he takes a place in the complex interrelations that exist between the people, plants, and animals already living there together. He adds his uncertain transactions, regulated according to his personality traits, to the exigencies of mining, prospecting, ranching, or some other activity appropriate to the frontier regions. In some instances he is ecologically successful: a "predator"; in others he is less successful: the "prey."

This account is intended to illustrate one conspicuous form of interaction between certain personality types and the frontier environment, an interaction that suggests some mutuality in the transactions involved. This is a concept familiar to plant and animal ecologists. The idea of "ecological niches" suggests that a creature often occupies a special position in a community to which it is adapted by its structure or physiology. The zebra of the veldt has a special niche because his vivid stripes make him less, not more, conspicuous in the grass of his natural habitat, which helps to conceal him from his enemies. The giraffe has a niche in respect of his ability to utilize the topfeed. The human ecology of the frontier raises the question of whether human ecological niches occur by virtue of psychological peculiarities. Medicine may need to depart from its traditional concentration on the individual, or even from its newer transactional preoccupation, in order to apply concepts of animal ecology—such as niches, dominance, zonation, and succession—to the study of human beings. In human ecology, dominance appears to have some correspondence with mastery, zonation with social class, and succession with change in time. Although ecological concepts are undoubtedly applicable to man, the theories involved must, of course, be elaborated and refined in order to provide insights concerning the complex human community. The clinical material presented here demonstrates how ecological concepts can be used as a basis for expanding one's understanding of the dynamics of frontier breakdowns.

The illustrations of "flight into the wilderness" as a psychiatric syndrome come from a group of about a hundred patients referred to me for care, during the period 1950 to 1960, after a disturbed experience in the outback. Of these, it happens that twelve reported visions of distant objects. More frequently, the emotional and ideational attachment to the outback is in the nature of an overvalued idea, falling short of delusional intensity, but exceeding a passing fascination. Flight into the wilderness may be variously associated with such psychological maneuvers as an attempted solution of severe psychic conflict, an escape from delusional persecutors, or a quest for solace and bountiful protection. Individuals who escape society by roving in the back country are popularly described in Australia as going "bush" from the cities, and going "troppo" in the bush—phenomena considered to be far from rare in the outback. "Troppo" is argot for tropical eccentricity or insanity, popularly believed to be due to close association with native people, with loss of white identity. These conditions are not well documented in medical literature, for information is hard to obtain and there is no way of checking on those who fail to survive. In the overtly psychotic flights, the more fortunate ones are recovered by the remarkable tracking skills of Aborigines employed by the police. Those who recover quickly after return to a population center are probably not referred to hospitals, so that information about their experiences is also limited. The chief group available for study comprises those who recover more slowly and are referred for psychiatric care. In many instances these are psychotic or psychopathic people who have experienced in the bush a further development of a preexisting psychic disturbance. Frequently it is this disturbance that led them into the bush in the first place. Thus they provide a different "experiment in nature" than do shipwrecked sailors, who develop disturbances such as a hallucinosis for the first time in personalities that presumably had been well integrated previously.

Nosologically, my frontier patients were classified as having severe character disorders, including "psychopathic depression" in Hamilton and White's sense (1959); catatonic, paranoid, and manic psychoses; schizophreniform disorders in Langfeldt's sense (1959); and anxiety-ecstasy disorders in Leonhard's (1961). A statistical presentation of my small series is not contemplated. Nor is it possible to relate in full detail the premorbid and intramorbid histories. The case histories are presented briefly, condensed in order to focus on the climacteric experience of life in a wilderness.

In the commentary on the cases, the concept of human ecology will be kept in the foreground and special attention will be directed to an obvious feature of the frontier—distance. Some cases will show, for example, how distances characteristic of the frontier environment may be for the patient a symbolic representation of an aspect of his relationships with people. Other cases will show a striking feature of frontier psychiatry—the placement of the hallucinated object in the far distance, at the extremity of perceived space. It should be borne in mind that individuals selected for presentation here are extreme cases; while their own psychopathology is in itself nothing remarkable, its interaction with outback culture and environment is of considerable interest.

HUMAN ECOLOGICAL BREAKDOWN

The first case history exemplifies the occurrence of "psychopathic depression" as a clinical syndrome, as delineated by Hamilton and White. This case illustrates not merely that psychopathic individuals react to frustration with self-destructive behavior without conscious guilt or self-accusation, as these authors indicate, but that their level of frustration may be regulated by ecological factors.

A Station Overseer

A thirty-two-year-old married man with a suicide note in his pocket was found comatose on a city beach. On recovery from coma he gave an account of the difficulties that had caused him to take an overdose of sleeping tablets. He said that life had always gone well in the bush but that the city had brought him nothing but troubles. He had left the bush only because of his wife's loneliness. As overseer of a cattle station in northern Australia, he had frequently been away from home for a month at a time droving cattle. This had been no hardship for him but his wife had resented it. They had been married only two years and had no children. He said he was deeply attached to the outback and had spent most of his life there since running away from home at the age of twelve.

Since arriving in the city he and his wife had had financial troubles. He had leased a shop in a suburban shopping area and had set himself up in business as a maker of leather goods, borrowing money for leather, warehouse goods, sewing machine, carpet, and showcases. Tooled leather work had been his hobby on the stations, where he was able to sell more than he could make. However, the city had shown little interest in handtooled handbags depicting horses; business had been bad and he had found himself heavily in debt. He had tried to sell the business, and his wife had gone to work.

The crisis suddenly took a new direction when a policeman queried the wife about a year-old complaint, which had followed them from state to state, that the husband might be a bigamist. When the husband came home and found his wife in distress about it, he rushed back to the police station and brawled with the larger and stronger policeman. The fight was stopped by another policeman before the patient had a chance to get hurt. He was charged with assault and required to appear in court.

Before he could appear he had an accident in his car. He woke up in the hospital, claimed not to know whom or what he had hit, and was diagnosed as having had concussion. The insurance company refused to pay for the damage to the car, since in moving from state to state he had neglected to pay the premium. After a still further disappointment when a prospective buyer for the shop failed to arrive to inspect it, he went to the beach and swallowed all his sleeping tablets. The note found in his pocket is interesting diagnostically:

To whom it may concern:

This is to state that I have taken my own life because I see no way to carry on. But I should like to state that the charge of assaulting the officer had nothing to do with it although I was actually assaulted by him. I only wish to humbly apologise to those that I have hurt, particularly my wife, who has been the only person I have ever loved. And thank any that have tried to help me.

[Signed]

P.S. Because I am a coward I shall attempt it with sleeping tablets. I pray to God I am successful.

He was successful only in having a boy find him on the beach.

His early years reveal something of the origin of his adjustments and affiliations. He lived in a country town with his mother, stepfather, four brothers, two sisters, and two stepsisters. He felt unwanted, the odd one out. Wandering about in a lonely way he formed a comforting image of the bush, daydreamed about it as the place where he would be happy, and ran away to it at the age of twelve. In psychotherapy he analyzed the significance that the outback held for him. Work with big animals and wide spaces seemed to have a compensatory function for his feelings of inadequacy; it made him feel that he was a strong male who could master such objects. At the same time he perceived in the bush a nurturing, succoring function normally supplied by a mother. The increased interpersonal distances represented some security from retaliation by people whom he habitually discomforted. Since the outback environment was so valuable in one way or another for his adjustment it is reasonable to describe him as having found in it an "ecological niche." To some of the observers in the hospital he gave the impression of a grown man playing a game of cowboys and Indians. He delighted in showing a large collection of color transparencies of himself at work in the outback. He apologized at length when one slide showed him sitting awkwardly on his horse, saying the camera happened to catch him momentarily off balance.

The city, on the other hand, appeared to elicit unconscious atonement; here he regularly inflicted on himself injury and failure. The division between the succoring frontier and the punishing city illuminates the importance of cultural factors in his adjustment, with the imposition of internal preoccupations upon the available range of outside realities.

The following case illustrates a common sequence involving departure from the city to a remote region, progressive social alienation, depressive and paranoid developments culminating in a suicidal attempt, and finally, expulsion back to the city.

A Railway Repairman

A thirty-seven-year-old repairman on a railway in central Australia fired a bullet into his chest, narrowly missing his heart. The wound was treated at the hospital, where the doctor noted that the patient suspected that the other patients and staff were laughing at him and talking about him. Given tranquillizing medication, he became more trustful and revealed that he was worried about going mad. He thought he heard voices at night urging him "Go on! Go on!" in response to his suicidal thoughts.

Transferred to psychiatric care in the city, he described his progressive alienation from society for some fifteen years. He had gradually become convinced that society was hypocritical and hostile, pretending to be helpful but inclined to act deliberately to his disadvantage. This idea had induced him, some five years previously, to take his wife and six children to live at a remote siding in central Australia. According to the wife, life in the repairman's hut was at first bearable, but soon he complained of interference from and hypocrisy on the part of his workmates. He refused to allow his family to accept social invitations. His wife was forbidden female company. Stockmen from a nearby cattle station were for a time allowed to call, but he erected a barbed-wire fence around the hut and refused visitors after sunset. He attached padlocks to gates and doors and even hid the food.

The children, deprived of varied food and worried by the persistent heat, began to lose weight. One suffered from asthma. Nothing they could do pleased their father; whatever they suggested drew a negative response. His wife described some of his rages as bizarre, including episodes of yelling and thumping on walls during which he did not seem to register what was happening. Sometimes she went without sleep at night trying to calm him. A workmate whom he had threatened took his knife away and advised the wife to dismantle the gun and hide the bullets.

His wife reported that his sexual life, always perverse, became sadistic. She said that he sometimes lay upon her, sticking pins into her arms and pinching her body. He refused to consider contraception, maintaining that it was the wife's duty to become pregnant as often as possible. If she dressed up, curled her hair, and made up her face, he made jealous accusations; when she did not dress up, he called her a "black gin" and abused her. Eventually she deserted, taking the children with her. Making no attempt to follow, he continued at his work, living alone and evidently drinking alcohol to excess. After several months of living alone he shot himself and survived only because of the unusual path of the bullet through his chest.

Under enforced surveillance in the city he was at first opinionated and resentful, but eventually became more cooperative. During a physical examination an electroencephalogram recorded a focal discharge in the left temporal region. There was no clear-cut history of epileptic seizures, but a suggestive account of angry outbursts during states of altered consciousness was obtained, and he was given antiepileptic medication. During the prolonged period of supervision in the psychiatric hospital there was improvement in his opinionated, self-righteous, and defensive attitudes.

He was the fourth of five children and had experienced a rejected and frustrated childhood in a broken home. His school record was fair but he left as soon as the law allowed, at fourteen, to work in a market garden. At work he was apparently seclusive but not disliked, and at the time he married four years later there was no real evidence of the pathological developments that were later expressed in his personality. Over a number of years his emotional distance from other people changed to feelings of suspicion, injustice, and persecution. These feelings were reciprocated by workmates and family, culminating in his "frontier" solution. For him, the significant aspect of the outback was its lack of habitation. But even in the remote railway siding, fortification had seemed necessary against a hostile world, and this defense had in turn led the outback inhabitants to repudiate his need at its height.

Frontiers have a subculture like an underworld, producing individuals whose asocial conduct elicits from the city's authoritarian subculture pressures toward banishment. The next case illustrates a sequence in which an individual returns each time he or she is banished. These returns to the arid zone represent not so much flight to the wilderness as unsuccessful attempts to return to a home culture that does not possess a psychiatrically trained social agency to manage crises of this kind.

An Outback Female Vagrant

A nineteen-year-old unmarried woman was rushed to town from a remote cattle station where she had tried to kill her mother and then to hang herself. This was just one incident in a life of roving and delinquency in the outback punctuated by periods of enforced care by welfare agencies in the city. The policeman who escorted her to the psychiatric service stated that he doubted if the homicidal attempt was genuine, but the suicidal behavior was serious enough: when found she had a cord tightly tied around her neck. She had swallowed an open safety pin as well, she said. An X-ray film confirmed the presence of the pin and she was transferred to the surgical service for an open operation to remove it.

The day after her return from the surgical service she told the psychiatrist that she had swallowed another open safety pin but an X-ray picture happily proved otherwise. She continued to harass the nurses with suicidal gestures—such as threatening to jump from the stairs—usually if they appeared to take insufficient interest in her.

She had tried to kill herself, she said, because she had been separated from her boyfriend, who was somewhere in the Northern Territory, and because she was tired of arguments with her mother, a station cook who moved freely about the outback. She also said that she had not recovered from a recent upset—the birth of her baby four months previously in the city, where it had been adopted. When she had returned to the Northern Territory after the birth, she could not trace the father. She had become vagrant, picking up men or sleeping in the open. Sometimes she charged two pounds for herself, at other times she was grateful for what she got. She said she had had six convictions in police courts in Northern Territory, two in New South Wales, and two in South Australia. When the Territory police had last arrested her for vagrancy they had insisted that she live with her mother, but the constant quarrels made her think of suicide. She had made several attempts to kill herself, and two weeks before the hanging incident she had swallowed all the tablets given to her for depression and had been admitted to the hospital.

Inquiry revealed that her *de facto* husband, the father of the baby, was serving a twelve-month imprisonment. He was a habitual criminal, with a record in most states, who had finally settled in the Northern Territory. The patient herself belonged to the relatively exclusive group of second-generation European immigrants of the Territory. She was accustomed to roving freely around this region, identifying with a fringe element or the underworld associated with petty crime, prostitution, and alcoholism.

Her childhood was one of serious emotional and cultural deprivation. She never knew her father, who was reputedly an American serviceman. Her mother had three children by various fathers. The patient had traveled with her mother until she was fifteen, when the growing violence of their quarrels forced them to part. Her first police conviction at about this time was for drunkenness; on her mother's refusal to pay the fine she had been sent to a reformatory. Since then she had had convictions on a variety of charges and had become adept at manipulating prison staffs by what she called "playing up," which included suicidal gestures. From time to time her personality disorder was recognized and she spent brief periods in mental hospitals. Under supervision she was by no means a totally affectionless or shiftless character. She had considerable energy and industry and gave glimpses of the possibility that she might relate better to society if she was placed in the right emotional atmosphere. The mother could not come to the hospital for an interview but her letter indicated that although she was literate and intelligent she undoubtedly suffered from a paranoid personality.

Schizophrenic persons who "go bush" in Australia sometimes report the placement of hallucinatory and delusional objects in the far distance. These reports amplify and confirm the observations of Havens (1962) on the placement and movement of hallucinations in space and on the association of movement with changes in affect. Some of the changes in affect are remarkably specific. The patient who reports hallucinations in the far distance displays special characteristics, not the least important being an effort to approach and to be engulfed by a hallucinated nonhuman environment. In a similar way, delusions and overvalued ideas may be placed at specific points along a spatial continuum. Psychodynamic features of the placement of hallucinations by some of these persons suggest that changes in the position of the hallucinated object in space reflect conflicts in relationships with other persons. The first schizophrenic history selected for presentation concerns a patient who effected a sequential placement of hallucinatory objects outward from within, the movements being associated with well-defined changes in affect. The following two histories will illustrate patterns that diverge from this "classical" sequence.

A Traffic Light in the Sky

A thirty-seven-year-old unmarried migrant from Indonesia was found ten miles from an isolated station by a police constable and an Aboriginal tracker. A week earlier his car had been discovered, abandoned in perfect working order, near the transcontinental railway. Since then the man had covered fifty miles on foot, without food, into the saltbush plain. He was exhausted when found and probably would not have lasted the night. Rain had hampered the search by obliterating tracks but had helped him survive by providing surface water.

Under psychiatric observation he explained that he had been drawn into the plain toward a red light rising into the sky like a column. He had been searching for this light because he had seen something similar several years previously when in the bush. When he found it, he tried to walk into it, but it faded and he was lost in the plain. He attempted suicide by gashing his arms but he had nothing sharp enough to make a deep cut.

Questioning, while he was in the hospital, revealed a progressive hallucinating of objects into space. At first, several years previously, he had merely felt a "heavy burden" inside himself; he had felt the burden in a physical way, but he described it as "my sins, I suppose; sins and iniquities; I hope they are forgiven." He next heard his thoughts spoken and was unsure if they came from his head or elsewhere. Shortly afterward they definitely moved outside him and appeared to be spoken by a companion, in English and in the Dutch language of his childhood; they contained words and phrases such as "rhythm" or "I love you." These snatches of conversation were well disposed toward him, or neutral, rather than hostile or critical. He felt depressed and tired, found it hard to go to work. After this period he started changing his job frequently because he believed that people knew his thoughts. He noticed that when he was speaking hesitantly, groping for a word, people were apt to supply exactly the one that he was going to use. From being depressed he became annoyed. The companion's commentary faded out and his attention focused on the tormentors in his vicinity. One day he was given a menial job to do in the electrical factory where he worked and was offended at what seemed a deliberate insult. He went home that night and tried to fight one of his fellow boarders, who scarcely knew him and declined the invitation. As though guided and drawn, he then drove his car six hundred miles into the plain until he found the light on the horizon. Recollecting this vision in the hospital, he startled his doctor (who was prepared for some association with a biblical miracle, such as the pillar of fire that led the Israelites through the desert) by a concrete comparison with a large traffic stoplight.

In terms of Havens' scheme of hallucinatory positions, this seems to illustrate the "classical" progression of hallucinatory objects—in this case from initial recognition as an introjected object to the position of the constant companion to the position of the hostile vicinity and finally to a visual nonhuman form in the far distance. In the distant stage, the patient wishes to approach and be engulfed by the object. Visual hallucinations are traditionally associated with acute rather than chronic psychosis and especially with toxic illness. Here the visual hallucinosis is not of toxic origin and can perhaps be described as an acute manifestation in a chronic psychosis. It represents the end of the line in a progressive distancing of hallucinatory objects in space. The change from auditory to visual modality must be appreciated in this context.

Placement of hallucinations in the far distance has not been studied much by psychiatry but is familiar in two conditions: the acute religious hallucinosis and the survival-isolation hallucinosis. Rarely, experiences outside the normal field of the sensation—so-called extracampine hallucinations—are also encountered in temporal lobe epilepsies and related affections of brain substance. In religious psychosis, the individual may suddenly hear "The Voice" or see "The Light" after a period of troubled brooding and depersonalization. In such cases, the distant placement is evidently determined by the convention that God, Jesus, and the angels are up in the sky.

In the survival-isolation illusion, travelers lost in the desert see an oasis of cool water or shady trees; survivors at sea see terra firma. In contrast to the distance experience of the schizophrenic, such visions may be a shared experience, an anticipatory phenomenon in which the group situation is relevant, and they may also result from physiological influences, such as water depletion and acidosis (Anderson 1942).

But as Havens suggested, the outback patients' reports of the placement of hallucinations in subjective space indicate a connection between the placement, the affect, and the degree of psychotic alienation. Havens describes the psychological significance of the placement by means of a scheme that is both clinically and conceptually attractive. His spatial classification provides a useful alternative to more usual classifications of hallucinations based on sensory modality, content, symbolism, or presence of insight.

Havens postulates four positions in which hallucinatory objects may be placed in space:
1. The position of Extreme Distance
2. The position of the Constant Companion
3. The position of the Introjected Object
4. The Hypochondriacal position

Commonly, a position is associated with a prevailing affect. Thus, a hallucination in the first position may be acknowledged by anger and abuse if the subject has a conviction that it is not safely anchored there and is impinging closer upon him. On the other hand, it may be treated with flat indifference if he thinks it is staying "out there." With movement inward, the hallucinatory object is more regularly and constantly experienced and the patient may be observed to go from flatness, through anger, to depression. Thus there appears to be a spatial gradient for hallucinatory objects, running from far to near or near to far, with each step on the gradient characterized by a different psychological function. The case material presented here to illustrate this movement shows that it can take place in either direction.

Since Havens defines extreme distance as meaning hallucinations in the ceiling or behind the wall—close enough to be "within earshot"—an obvious emendation is necessary in order for me to use his scheme with my cases. In my material, the term extreme distance—or "far distance"—will be reserved for hallucinations placed out in the bush, at the horizon, in the sky, or even beyond, as in the "outer space" of the astronauts. It is probable that Havens omitted this position because he observed hospitalized cases rather than because of actual space differences in the respective American and Australian ecologies. Havens' first position might appropriately be redesignated "middle distance" or "within earshot."

Rearranging the Constellations

A thirty-eight-year-old unmarried man was reported missing from a ghost town near the border of South and Western Australia, where he had arrived only a few weeks before. A police constable found him some days later wandering in the sandhills, heedless of his state or safety. He told the constable that he had heard voices that told him to test his faith by walking into the desert. In the psychiatric hospital he gave details of his experience in the sandhill wilderness. He believed he had merged with the distance and was simultaneously here and in outer space. Manifesting what has been called "cosmic identification," he spoke of being on top of the sun rather than on the earth. He believed he could change the patterns of the stars and that the voices he had previously heard were now in the stars and the sky. His excited hallucinosis persisted and became an annoyance to the other patients in the hospital. During group meetings he talked continuously, regardless of interruption by doctor or patients, and was annoyed if patients challenged his starry fantasies. He was ecstatic and blissful and sometimes had visions of Jesus.

The psychosis did not quickly abate and a reason soon became apparent. It emerged that he was distracted and desperate at the closeness of people, restlessly going out of the door and coming in again. He could not sit in company because he was experiencing a genital "pressure," which caused an "eruption" from which he could get relief only by leaving the company. He felt "corrupted" at being in the hospital since he thought of himself as having a moral and spiritual complaint, not a mental one.

After some months in ecstasy and excitement, cosmic preoccupation subsided and his activity in the group became appropriate though guardedly distant. The doctor noted that he seemed to respond to a "nonhuman activity"—golf. In retrospect he described how he had been depressed before his hallucinatory illness, living alone in a trailer on a vacant block. The control of his sexual impulse had absorbed his attention. He turned for help to the Bible, taking as a text, "Carry your vessel in honour,"[1] and applying himself to tasks and privations for spiritual and physical uplift. These strictures were eventually experienced as voiced and finally as the instructions that took him toward the far desert and cosmic objects.

The revisions of the spatial placement of hallucinatory objects in different phases of this psychosis are less striking. A genital sensation of hallucinatory quality is superseded by spoken instructions, as though from companions and taskmasters. There is agitation and depression. The accomplishment of the cosmic placement of the hallucinatory object is associated with renewal of hope proceeding to ecstasy. The apparent need for the stimulus of distance to evoke this placement lends plausibility to Riss' (1959) suggestion that hallucinations may be based on illusions, such as mirages.

The emphasis given by Searles (1960) to the nonhuman environment in personality development is also relevant. Searles holds that the schizophrenic may fear a "phylogenetic" regression to an undifferentiated nonhuman state. This ingredient in human existence must be seen in an ecological as well as in an individual context. The frontier, harsh and above all nonhuman, is available for Australian schizophrenic persons in search of a nonhuman environment. Outback case histories show how some individuals, in a maneuver to bypass an externalized and hallucinated bad object, find a nonhuman environment in the far distance. In general terms, the schizophrenic quest is for relief from the enemy within, from disillusionment, guilt, and despair—all of which may be represented in transactions with the semidesert in the outback ecology.

The next example adds support for these views.

Fishing in a Mirage

A twenty-four-year-old unmarried European migrant hired a room in a hotel at Alice Springs and periodically set off on foot into the hills, taking fishing gear with him. Since the hills were dry, this "stunt" caused some amusement.

Denial by humor is a cultural defense in central Australia. Be-

---

[1] This Biblical reference is undoubtedly the patient's distortion of Paul's words to Timothy, "He shall be a vessel unto honor." (2 Timothy 2:21)

havior that would be "troppo" in an individual is sustaining and
hilarious when it is part of a shared cooperative effort, as the Hen-
ley-on-Todd regatta held in Alice Springs testifies. In this annual
event, sweating yachtsmen engage in a contest by hauling boats
along the dry river bed.

When questioned, the "fisherman" became agitated and said
there were too many noises at night in Alice Springs and that he
went to the mountains where cars could not follow him and he
could get a good rest. He was eventually taken to the town hospital for observation, but his evasiveness hid the presence of psychosis and he was permitted to leave on the southbound train. He
left the train on the edge of the Simpson desert, the most formidable in Australia, without food or water. When found, he said he
got off because the train was uncomfortable and he wanted to catch
the next one. Later he said that he had overheard Russians on the
train and that they had changed the handles on his luggage and had
tried to take his money. He also thought the other passengers were
afraid of him.

Inquiry in the psychiatric hospital disclosed a progressive psychotic development since he had been a displaced person in Switzerland. At that time he had continued his trade as an electrician
for a while, but had felt tired and unable to get up in the morning.
Discontented, he consulted the Australian consul and was flown
to Australia. Here the structure of his life further disintegrated.
He tried many jobs in several cities but, without friends or job,
mostly lived from social service and Red Cross benefits. While
eating in a cafe, he saw that his skin was turning red and concluded
that he was being poisoned. He fled to the country with the firm
idea that assailants were after him. He achieved relief in Alice
Springs while going off into the deserted hills as a tourist with fishing gear. The relative calm was short-lived and was replaced by
panic when the police cut it short, hospitalized him, and then
evacuated him on the train.

In the psychiatric hospital the response to therapeutic efforts was
feeble. No trust or rapport developed. Twice he absconded, returning of his own accord but complaining that he was being un-
justly detained. Before arrangements could be completed for his

return to his brother's care in Switzerland, he absconded a third time and did not return. Searches revealed no trace, leaving the question of his survival open to serious doubt.

In this case, the hallucinatory object, at first inferred hypochrondriacally in the body and on the skin, was soon displaced by spies and enemies in the vicinity. This is a commonplace shift and is often accompanied by an alteration in affect toward resentment, with fear in lieu of anxiety. In turn this gives way to placement in the far distance, which affords the sufferer temporary respite and relief and concomitantly enables him to evade a society perceived as hostile.

Is the omnipresent mirage of central Australia a stimulus for the placement? In the patient described here there was no thirst, water depletion, acidosis, heat exhaustion, or other cause of desert delirium. It is unlikely that he was deceived by his ignorance of the mirage illusion; rather, he structured it to meet his needs. His behavior tells us, in effect, that he was impelled to evade the hallucinatory object threatening in his vicinity; he was, in addition, attracted by a new object placed afar, one offering the prospect of peace, quiet, and comfort. The procurement of fishing gear was a psychotic tour de force, in which fear gave way to comparative calm. In clinical terms, there was a shift from paranoid to heboid symptoms.

In the next example, resort to the wilderness assumed a clinically manic form, lending itself to the concept of regression conjectured by Lewin (1959).

Mania in the Wilderness

A forty-year-old lone prospector, with a degree in geology, was taken to the psychiatric hospital for management of intense excitement, assaultiveness, and refusal of food. For two months he had harangued people in town about massive mineral deposits that he believed existed in the desert. His expansive monologue included pronouncements about the development of the Northern Territory and Australian science, art, and literature. He admitted that the bush made him a little queer and said he was writing a better story than *We of the Never-Never* (Gunn 1907), and that for a hoax he had included an elaborate fabrication about Mars, space travel, and distant galaxies.

He said that his eleven years as a lone prospector had been preferable to a life of clashes with colleagues. He knew that his failure to share in cooperative geological exploration detracted from his chances of success but it spared him the criticism of the experts. A letter written while he was in the hospital is revealing:

Dear Dr. C.:

Ten days ago I smuggled out of the lockup a letter to Dr. Schweitzer and another to Aldous Huxley. Supposing the two and Bertrand Russell reckon that I am not a lunatic and write to the Prime Minister? Suppose I worked out something new, rather stumbled on it, am all exalted and worried, too, about it: say, since invention of Infinitesimal Calculus by Newton and Leibnitz, since Hypervariants standing over Determinants like Det. are above Algebra and Alg. above Arithmetic? Now: via Mass/ Light//Space//Time//Interference//analyze the crazily speeding shiny utility with Mankind as passenger, prior to a cosmic accident. . . . Parallel I am spinning a long yarn about N.T.: horse-plants, black-fellas, prospecting for minerals and womenfolk, rows all the time, individualist no-hopers out in the scrub. . . .

In the hospital, the manic element subsided, but since he persisted in returning to prospecting and was disinclined to take tranquillizing drugs it was no surprise when he was returned within eighteen months. He had been found "in a sleepwalking condition" in the bush by the police. He remained drawn to his distantly placed objects in his conviction of mineral deposits and his references to cyclotrons, shifting sands, radio telescopes, rockets around Venus, astronomy, and the Eureka experience described by Sir John Eccles.

The legend of Lasseter's lost gold reef in the dead heart of the continent is perhaps the best-known expression of the imposition of internal objects on distant reality. In 1893 an Afghan camel driver found the apparently insane Harold Lasseter wandering in the central Australian desert. Lasseter claimed he found a gold reef to surpass all reefs, somewhere about six hundred miles west of Alice Springs. In 1930, he led an expedition in search of his El Dorado. The seventy-two camels in the expedition all died of thirst, and the aircraft and the truck broke down. Impatiently Lasseter pushed ahead of the party and perished. His body was eventually found in the Petermann Range country southwest of Alice Springs near the Western Australian border. Far from being unpopulated today, this area because of the Aboriginal population explosion is now the scene of a mushrooming settlement of Pitjantjara. Called Docker River settlement, it is housed largely in caravans and brush shelters set in the grandest desert scenery in Australia. There is no gold. The historical incident has been dramatized in *Lasseter's Last Ride* (Idriess 1931). It may be profitable to extend the concept of projected, introjected objects to cover the related phenomena of delusions and overvalued ideas. Indeed, these have a vivid, almost hallucinatory quality and, buried out of sight in the desert, elicit the same approach behavior from the subject. How much exploratory or pioneering activity is performed on the basis of distant placement of internal objects?

What does the quest for an El Dorado represent? A useful conjecture is suggested by Lewin's proposal for a psychology of elation. For Lewin, mania is a regression, just as depression is a regression. But the elation is regression to a much earlier stage. Lewin believes that the model of elation felt by the psychotic was the satiety from union with the mother's breast in earliest infancy. This enjoyable state before the reality principle was established signified supreme pleasure at a time when the child did not know about death. Lewin considers that the elation in mania is analogous to a happy dream at the mother's breast. The subject is not necessarily denying a depression. He is "denying death and the fear of dying by a declaration of invulnerability and immortality." The manic-paranoid person who goes bush, heedless of danger and death, elated in his conviction of an El Dorado, may be viewed as having recreated the "happy dream."

The final case is selected for presentation to illustrate the Australian ambivalence toward the outback. In this case, a masochistic and intermittently psychotic woman resorted to the desert fastness even though there appeared no absolute social or domestic necessity for her to do so. The case also illustrates the phenomenon of the hallucinated close companion.

A Hallucinatory Lover in the Bush

A thirty-seven-year-old housewife who lived with her husband and only child on a lonely station in the northwest part of South Australia had several admissions to mental hospitals for psychosis. During these episodes her imaginary lover, a city doctor, was at her side. She hallucinated his conversation and erotic attention, imagined that she was made pregnant by him, and believed that he was quarreling with her husband. At these times she lost interest in her housework and spent most of the time in bed. When her husband came in from work she would lock herself in her room. She imagined that he was poisoning her and cooked her own food separately.

In the hospital these ideas usually persisted for a few weeks, though she was disinclined to discuss them. She was domineering and sarcastic with staff and patients; she put on makeup but neglected personal cleanliness and was unoccupied. Recovery was heralded by willingness to work, considerateness, and depression. With the hallucination abandoned, she would miserably blame her frequent mental illnesses for the family's isolation and lack of prosperity. This contrasted with her previous peevish attitude of blaming her husband for the isolated life. When not psychotic but depressed, she saw the loneliness and hardship of frontier life as something she inflicted upon herself through her own actions. She seemed to demand further self-denial and self-punishment in the outback, and therefore insisted upon returning, despite medical advice to the contrary, and despite her husband's professed willingness to consider a change.

This martyred outback wife may view distance and isolation as punishment and, characteristically, her masochism makes her reluctant to leave loneliness. She therefore needs no specific hallucinatory object in the period of depressive adjustment. In episodes of psychosis, the depression is relieved and the punishing object retires, deposed by a hallucinatory object in the form of a constant companion supplying erotic satisfaction. Here is an instance where removal to distant places and preoccupation with a hallucinated object, though sick behavior, is apparently successful in removing depression. Though not adaptive, it is adjustive in the manner of the "Walden Pond maneuver" of H. D. Thoreau.

"Flight into the wilderness," considered as a clinical syndrome of the frontier, encompasses a variety of psychological phenomena. From the viewpoint of the human ecology of the frontier, in which personality types possessing certain psychic conflicts tend to interact with the natural and social environmental features, the syndrome is often found in a person who believes that his personality traits are best accommodated by certain aspects of lonely regions. In many instances such persons achieve an ecological niche with reasonable success. Psychotics who flee into the wilderness may project internal objects onto the distance, leading to the phenomenon of placement of a hallucinated object in the far distance, associated with characteristic changes in affect.

It is recognized that psychopathic individuals, poorly socialized in their subculture, tend to be uprooted and to move from place to place. They cover a wider range of territory than do most people, partly to gratify a need for new experience, new sexual contacts, and new activities, partly to avoid retaliatory action by society. Inevitably, a proportion of such people radiate farther out from the metropolis toward the frontier. Sometimes they achieve in this environment what may be considered as ecological niches. The less fortunate continue social depredations at a rate that exceeds the normally high tolerance of the frontier, so that a social crisis is created. Not infrequently, during the crisis, there is an impulsive bid for suicide, a denouement that confirms the opinion of instability held by frontier authority, including the medical profession. This opinion usually leads not to an attempt at management but to expulsion back toward the metropolis.

One of the tragedies of this kind of sequence emerges from the fact that some social institutions of the outback are heavily indebted to persons possessing moderate personality disturbances. This is an example of the "psychopath's bounty": In the ecological niche that may be achieved by the mentally disordered person, some contribution to society is possible. He is sometimes found fulfilling necessary roles shunned by more conforming citizens and at the very least he represents a pair of hands where hands are needed. Some recognition of this niche is implicit in the unusual tolerance of social deviation encountered in the outback. "Eccentricity," "robust individualism," "troppo," "no-hoper," "grog-artist," are local concepts for this class of behavior—almost any terminology may be employed in the argot except "mental illness," which is taboo. The deviation needs to be highly disruptive before evacuation to a city is arranged through medical and legal channels. With even minimal psychiatric attention, there is little doubt that in many cases the disruption would not reach these proportions. The contribution of such persons might thus be retained and safeguarded. The provision of psychiatric first aid may indeed be a more realistic policy for the outback than the personnel selection envisaged by the large industrial and mining companies. Viewed in this way, psychiatry is a technology, part of the "human engineering" necessary for the modern frontier.

Desert symbols are universal, but Australia is particularly well endowed. The symbolic choice of the desert as a site for the solution of life's problems—or at least for retirement from the fray to contemplate them—is illustrated by *The Rubaiyat of Omar Khayyam*, in Edward FitzGerald's translation, first version. In his efforts "to grasp this sorry scheme of things entire" (Quatrain 73), Omar chose some "strip of herbage strown, that just divides the desert from the sown" (Quatrain 10). This "strip" comes very close to the geographical definition of a frontier. Iran's dependence on exotic rivers causes such frontiers to be of utmost significance to its culture and ecology. Visitors from North America to Australia are quick to diagnose ironic humor displayed by Australians toward their own country as a reaction to disappointment that the heart of the land is not a fertile Mississippi valley. In Australia the call of the West is a cry of hope cut short by despair.

The cultural ambivalence is reflected by the traditional Australian poets. The basic view is expressed in Henry Lawson's story, "His Country—After All" (from *While the Billy Boils*, 1896). Lawson, born in 1867 in a tent in outback New South Wales, identified with the harshness of this region in disillusioned writings that became the best-known, if not the best, depiction of the Australian outback. His vignette describes a disgruntled Australian traveling in New Zealand, contrasting the lush landscape he sees with his own tough country. The sight of some imported Australian gum trees momentarily silences him by bringing his past before him. After a spell of reverie he castigates an English tourist who has been imperceptive enough to echo his previous criticisms of Australia. Henry Lawson died in Sydney in 1922, alcoholic and in poverty. His persistent appeal to the Australian imagination is shown by the appearance of his portrait on the Australian ten-dollar note, along with sketches of Gulgong, then a shanty town, where he spent his childhood. A more sanguine but still ambivalent view is "Banjo" Paterson's reaction, in the lines: "We followed where our fortunes led, with fortune always on ahead—and always further out." Andrew Paterson ("The Banjo"), Lawson's rival as the popular versifier of his day, conducted with Lawson a literary controversy about the merits of the bush. Paterson more than Lawson identified with the managerial and landowning viewpoint and was thus in a better position to appreciate "the vision splendid of the sunlit plains extended" (from *The Man from Snowy River*, 1895). Sturdy human mateship is stressed as making a harsh landscape tolerable. But the bush-style popular songs of today reveal the sardonic ambivalence: "Tan me hide when I'm dead, Fred" (Harris 1960).

If modern medicine and justice should accept their place as part of the technology necessary for adaptation to the difficult frontiers that remain in the twentieth century, improved delivery of services is a necessity. A twentieth-century frontier should not have to await population growth in competition with a city for its services. A mobile unit, based on psychiatric first aid and undertaking the training of local community caretakers to act to psychiatric advantage in the problem situations, would do much to safeguard people who live in these zones. The very nature of their individualism can mean that such people have a special contribution to make to the region in which they choose to live and to the people they find already living there.

We have depicted psychiatrically in this chapter extremes of the human condition. Integrated society asks that such deviant individuals have some access to medicine and to justice. The individual's security is at stake, as well as the security of the public. These extremes of behavior also pose a challenge that should be increasingly accepted by schools of anthropology. The skills of anthropologists trained to work in concert with medicine and the law are needed to assist the delivery of social security in plural societies. We began this chapter by noting that in Australia the presence of white people tends to obstruct essential services from reaching Aborigines, and we proceeded to give examples of some of these obstructions. We conclude with a plea for anthropologists to be trained to assist the service professions.

The invitation to anthropology is intended not merely to ensure disadvantaged peoples a better access to social security. Anthropologists who are engaged in clinical duties will also bring fresh and lively theoretical interests to their science. The work of Henry (1972) may be taken as an example. It is therefore appropriate to conclude this discussion of our "white" data not with answers, but with questions that seem of special moment for anthropology.

Are the grosser inflictions of white society upon Aborigines (or other disadvantaged ethnic groups) made by normal people? Or are they in some instances made by whites who suffer from a psychiatric disturbance? For several reasons, chiefly involving problems of access, I have not directed attention to situations of this kind, and my own information is largely anecdotal. Until this question is better studied it must remain unanswered. This is the individual factor that is missing from the sociological study of the destruction of Aboriginal society (Rowley 1970). Indeed the retroflexive effect of the disturbed individual upon his group is a subject that is only now coming to the attention of psychiatric research (Leighton 1971). Until now, research emphasis has been on the effect of the group upon the individual; we should examine the other side of the coin.

How representative of white society are those who actually make contact with indigenous people? In speaking about the alien culture contact we customarily use broad and general terms such as Western culture or modern society. Is this generality justified? The material which we have been considering suggests the likelihood that the contacting whites may be unrepresentative, firstly in respect of personality traits that led them to separate themselves from more settled society, secondly in the behavioral responses elicited by the special stresses and privations of the frontier, and thirdly in the new social organization that they evolve.

At the frontier, are individual and group behaviors and attitudes toward indigenous people more aggressive than those characteristic of the culture as a whole? A good deal of historical evidence would appear to support this hypothesis. Many of the liberal and philanthropic attitudes of the London founders of the South Australian Company were abandoned in the colony, to be resumed fully a century later (Dunstan 1966). In a recent referendum on the question of voting rights for Aborigines, the regional distribution of "yes" votes was pointed out by Mitchell (1968): Whites who live in the same regions as Aborigines gave a substantially higher "no" vote. We need to explore the origins of the apparently heightened aggression in the culture contact, if we are to be concerned with its mitigation.

Finally, are the visions and fantasies of those frontier whites whom we have called psychiatrically disturbed peculiar to them and alien to their culture? In this chapter we have been examining the histories of people who discerned the fulfillment of their deep-felt needs in the far distance, and who pursued it there. To what extent are they expressing, with their concrete logic, a psychological complex held by Western man—to the consternation of the distant peoples whom he oppresses as he salvages? When do the visions of the white man become the torments of the black?

Envoi: Psychological Anthropology and Transcultural Psychiatry

IMPLICIT IN THE TITLE AND SUBTITLE of this work is the notion that psychological (psychiatric) anthropology and transcultural psychiatry are closely related disciplines and indeed form a kind of continuum. This notion is made explicit in the Introduction, and the remainder of the book further develops the idea that these two disciplines represent different perspectives of basically related sets of data.

True as this idea may be in theory, in practice it is premature to the point of being misleading. In most parts of the world, and in most universities, integration between these two disciplines has yet to begin. Few countries are further from achieving an academic rapprochement than Australia. Psychological anthropology follows its traditional pathways and its own internal logic; transcultural psychiatry, insofar as it is active at all, does likewise. Their appearance together in this book is probably only due to the circumstance that it is the work of a single author. Sharing of the data here may not represent any real trend toward integration.

This divergence can only be deplored as a deficiency, to be remedied if possible. It is worth examining its historical origin. The major failure to communicate undoubtedly arises on the psychiatric side of the axis.

Psychiatry in Australia, as elsewhere, has been busy serving mental hospitals and in providing private care for the more affluent sector. Transcultural psychiatry emerged after World War II, when there was a sudden upsurge in psychiatric training by our universities and a new awareness that the indigenous peoples of Australia, Melanesia, and Oceania had problems in adjustment. Wedded, these two social factors gave birth to transcultural psychiatry; but nobody can boast that the offspring is vigorous. Frankly, the most relevant barrier to ethnopsychiatric activity in this part of the world is not the inherent linguistic and cultural barriers, but the lack of financial resources and of trained professional manpower.

Cultural and linguistic diversity is vast both in Australia and Melanesia. At the time of European contact, Australia had about 500 distinct cultural-linguistic groups. Papua New Guinea had about 700. While this diversity is a barrier to the delivery of modern health care, for ethnopsychiatric research it is not so much a barrier as a stimulus and an opportunity. It affords a rich opportunity of comparative studies. For example, by comparing the theories of disease causation held by the various Aboriginal or Melanesian cultures we can determine what are the shared features of these theories and what are the variables. By joining together epidemiology and ethnography in our study we can substantially advance the formulations offered by the anthropologists of that era, who operated without epidemiology. We have attempted to exploit this opportunity for comparative studies in this book.

One of the guiding principles of work from our School of Psychiatry at the University of New South Wales is that we are more likely to make an advance through multidisciplinary research. Clinicians alone, anthropologists alone, psychiatrists alone, psychologists alone are less likely to make a critical contribution to transcultural psychiatry. Their combined activity is needed—with that of the linguist, educationalist, geneticist, epidemiologist, lawyer and—should one say?—bureaucrat. Our greatest barrier may be communication between these social and behavioral disciplines. Our school's experience of interdisciplinary collaboration shows many examples of studies in which the contribution of another discipline was a factor in the success or failure of the study.

During the ten years of its existence, our school has organized psychiatric expeditions to survey remote indigenous communities. These expeditions have gone out once a year, sometimes twice, for about one month each (usually the annual vacation of the participants). In addition, there have been two research stations maintained over several years, each with a resident psychiatrist and other researchers and visiting consultants. One site was the Gazelle Peninsula of New Britain and the other is in the far west region of New South Wales. We have published findings in some forty papers in the psychiatric and anthropological literature, and my book *Cruel, Poor and Brutal Nations* describes the methodology of economical psychiatric surveys (Cawte 1972).

For the past five years we have invited social and behavioral scientists from other disciplines to accompany the expeditions. We recognize that psychiatrists, however experienced they may be in transcultural situations, are incompetent to handle all the data with which they must work. We have been directly associated with workers in psychology, education, the law, social work, social anthropology, physical anthropology, sociology, internal medicine, pediatrics, genetics, dentistry. Our ethnopsychiatric expeditions follow no fixed theoretical framework, unless *psychiatric pluralism* is a theoretical framework. Our guiding principle is the operational indivisibility of the social and behavioral sciences; we consider that the interaction between indigenous and Western culture is not properly appreciated unless adequate data are simultaneously available from the biological, personality, social, and politico-economic systems.

THE CLINICIAN

On our expeditions the clinical psychiatrists are primarily concerned with symptoms. They conduct censuses and surveys of the target populations; they compile case histories and conduct examinations designed to record the symptoms of mental illness, of personal discomfort, of social incompetence. They have to establish an epidemiology by the sweat of their brow, because in these populations few if any data exist from hospital admissions, court lists, or other institutional records. Quantitative psychiatric data then have to be matched against social and cultural variables.

Our doctors in these expeditions also *treat* symptoms, by pharmacological means, or by consultations with the community caretakers. This psychiatric first aid is our passport to cooperation in the local community, which is often profoundly grateful for the relief of symptoms.

In this connection, one should allude to the research opportunity that this process opens up. We have been deeply interested in the reminder by Leighton (1971) that we should not rest content with the notion that society and culture produce symptoms. Symptoms also have a *retroflexive* effect on the level of social integration. A few mentally ill individuals can effectively disrupt a whole group. In future research, we shall be looking for ways to assess the social effect of our actions in reducing individual symptoms.

The following instances of interdisciplinary collaboration with psychiatry concern only our short-stay expeditions. Our continuing project involves a psychiatrist stationed for several years in an Aboriginal community, permitting a study of his efficacy as a social change agent. We are watching the results with interest and excitement, but it is not discussed here.

THE PSYCHOLOGIST

The closest and most comfortable collaboration is with the psychologist. Psychiatry and psychology are used to working together. Professor D. W. McElwain has accompanied our teams to assist with the construction of tests and rating scales, and with the handling of data. These are skills psychiatrists do not possess. In addition, he has been developing the Queensland Test, actually a battery of tests of cognitive capacity designed for conditions of reduced communication. This is an individually administered nonverbal performance test; if not culture-free, it has a "culture-low" loading.

There are many transcultural situations where one needs an estimate of the intelligence of the subject. In Aboriginal Australia where infant mortality is high from endemic infection and subnutrition, one must be alert to morbidity in the form of minimal brain damage. In an Arnhem Land community, we met another group of people habitually attending the nurse's clinic, with convictions of bodily disease. If these frequenters of the sick bay are contrasted with a matched control group, one can determine the characteristics of these "neurotic" members of the community. It was found that their mean score on the Queensland Test was significantly lower, that is, there was a covariation of sick role behavior with lower intelligence. There were, of course, other covariations, but this one would have been overlooked without our psychologist.

THE GENETICIST

Another straightforward interdisciplinary collaborator is the physical anthropologist and geneticist. In 1968 in the Wellesley Islands, we had Dr. Sardool Singh, who was very interesting to the people of the islands because he is a Sikh, a delectable curry cook, and a fine performer on the sarode. In his spare time he put us in possession of genetic (blood group and fingerprint) data that completely separated the *genotype* of the population of one island from that of the next island. Our psychiatric data showed that the *phenotypes* of these two groups also separated them on the basis of emotional instability, easy arousal, and a tendency toward quarreling, depression, and suicide. We had now to ask if the genotype led to the phenotype. The question could have been answered if we were confident that the environmental experiences of the two groups were comparable. Unfortunately they were not. But the distinctive gene frequencies of these neighbor tribes are a reminder—to those seeking to understand personality wholly in terms of culture—that genetic factors should never be overlooked.

THE ANTHROPOLOGIST

We find collaborating with social anthropologists is like a stormy romance. In Australia, few are used to working in a medical setting. In view of the rich ethnography still available, it is not surprising if there is little tendency for anthropology departments to turn their attention seriously to medical anthropology. And medical faculties have held out little inducement to them.

The potential contribution of the medical anthropologist is illustrated by the book *Health in a Developing Country*, relating delivery of health care to social and cultural factors (Pulsford and Cawte 1972). Anthropologists working in government administration are important potential contributors, particularly if the research has a component of social action. At present such an anthropologist, I. S. Mitchell, participates in our study of family resettlement and adjustment among Aborigines in New South Wales. If ethnographic literature exists for the area being studied, the psychiatric team should be thoroughly familiar with it. We have been helped, for example, by the record of Arnhem Land life compiled by R. M. and C. H. Berndt (1954).

The stormy romance arises in the areas of research design and field participation. It is characterized by the anthropologist's ambivalence about medical objectives. A great deal depends upon his previous exposure to health departments and doctors. Some anthropologists stereotype psychiatry as psychoanalysis. Others identify it as the descriptive-classificatory psychiatry of the hospitals. Others approach it like the fearful magic of primitive medicine. In addition to these misconceptions, there is sometimes a sheer territorial problem involving seignorial rights to the data, or to the people.

Ambivalence is disastrously time-wasting if it has to be resolved on the job. One example will be enough. A social anthropologist employed to assist the fieldwork of a rather untheoretical clinician set up an academic dialogue—or was it a duel? He held the conviction that no research worthy of the name was possible without mastering the language, living in the village for a seasonal cycle, and appreciating the nuances of cultural relativism and structuralism. The more he reduced the doctor to a faltering medical identification, the more he was subjected to medical authoritarianism by the doctor. They systematically destroyed each other. They should have resolved this conflict before working together in the field, but because of administrative difficulties arising from shortage of trained workers this was not possible.

Here, if you like, are cultural and linguistic barriers to research —between two Westerners of diverse culture and language! The task for the future will be to improve communication between these two basic disciplines. It will only be done by coming closer. Contemporary problems are too pressing for psychiatrist and anthropologists to spend energy trying to evict the other from what he regards as his territory.

THE FUTURE OF INTERDISCIPLINARY COLLABORATION

In few research centers around the world are the social sciences concerned with mental health coming together with the behavioral. A noteworthy leader in this convergence is the East-West Center, where at the Social Science Research Institute of the University of Hawaii, a dozen workers from the "culture and mental health" disciplines come together from different countries. They meet regularly around a table, and they work together in the same building. Out of such mutual exposure should grow an awareness of the advantages of interdisciplinary collaboration for mental health in the developing countries. There also grows a sensitivity to the barriers that oppose collaboration. In my experience these barriers are not only cultural and linguistic, but perhaps more importantly barriers of a professional, doctrinal, and personal nature.

What is now needed is a research program, or a series of research programs, designed to bring together these basic disciplines in the field rather than around the conference table. We need experience of ways of working together in the field on actual clinical and epidemiological problems. And we need to concentrate our efforts on short surveys, and on the economic and efficient delivery of health care. Elaborate and long-term programs, though they have their place in research, are simply not feasible for the vast majority of populations in the developing countries.

When the final data on a target population come in, integration will call for systems thinking. We shall have to integrate data from the four basic systems—biological, psychological, social, politico-economic—cognizant of the fact that the future of the individual is influenced by factors in each of these systems.

As transcultural psychiatrists, none of us is yet experienced in the use of systems analysis. We have in mind that each of our participants will define the ends to which planned action in his field should be directed. We might ask him, for example, to project his information to predict the outcome in the years 1980, 1990, and 2000. An effort will be made—no doubt intellectually strenuous for us—to predict the effect of several lines of simultaneous action on one another.

This is one reason why it is essential for this research to involve both local leaders and distant bureaucrats. We should offer our findings and our conference selves to the people of the region, and to those having authority for them, so that specific responsibilities can be assigned to the points of greatest competence. In this way, we should aim to achieve our two objectives. One is to show how to relieve the symptoms caused by social conditions. The other is to show how to relieve the social conditions that cause symptoms.

Bibliography

Abbie, A. A.
  1957a. Anthropology and the Medicine of Moses. *Medical Journal of Australia* 2:925–930.
  1957b. Metrical Characters of a Central Australian Tribe. *Oceania* 27: 220–243.
  1969.   *The Original Australians*. Wellington, N. Z.: Reed.
Abbie, A. A., and Adey, W. R.
  1955.   The Non-Metrical Characteristics of a Central Australian Tribe. *Oceania* 25:198–207.
Ackerknecht, E.
  1942a. Problems of Primitive Medicine. *Bulletin of the History of Medicine* 11:503–521.
  1942b. Primitive Medicine and Culture Pattern. *Bulletin of the History of Medicine* 12:545–574.
  1943.   Psychopathology, Primitive Medicine and Primitive Culture. *Bulletin of the History of Medicine* 14:30–67.
Adler, L. L.
  1965.   Cross-cultural Study of Children's Drawings of Fruit Trees. Paper presented at First New York City Psi Chi Psychological Convention, New York University, N.Y.
Anderson, E. W.
  1942.   Abnormal Mental States in Survivors, with Special Reference to Collective Hallucinations. *Journal of the Royal Naval Medical Service* 28:361–377.
Arieti, S., and Meth, J. M.
  1959.   Rare, Unclassifiable, Collective and Exotic Psychotic Syndromes. In *The American Handbook of Psychiatry*, edited by S. Arieti. New York: Basic Books.
Baglin, D., and Cawte, J. E.
  1968.   *Children of Arnhem Land*. Color-sound documentary film, 16

mm, 22 minutes. Available from Douglass Baglin Pty. Ltd., Crows Nest, N.S.W., Australia.

Barrett, M. J., Brown, T., and Fanning, E. A.
1965. Outline of a Long-term Study of the Dental and Cranio-facial Characteristics of a Tribe of Central Australian Aborigines. *Australian Dental Journal* 10:63–68.

Bartels, M.
1893. *Die Medicin der Naturvölker*. Quoted in *Primitive Concepts of Disease* by F. E. Clements, 1932.

Basedow, H.
1927. Subincision and Kindred Rites of the Australian Aboriginal. *Journal of the Royal Anthropological Institute* 57:123–156.

Bates, D.
1941. *The Passing of the Aborigines*. London: Murray.

Bateson, G., et al.
1956. Toward a Theory of Schizophrenia. *Behavioral Science* 1:251–264.

Beckett, J.
1964. Aborigines, Alcohol and Assimilation. In *Aborigines Now*, edited by Marie Reay. Sydney: Angus and Robertson.
1965. Kinship, Mobility and Community among Part-Aborigines in Rural Australia. *International Journal of Comparative Sociology*. 6 (1):2–23.

Benedict, R.
1934. *Patterns of Culture*. Boston: Houghton Mifflin Co.

Berndt, C. H.
1950. Women's Changing Ceremonies in Northern Australia. *L'Homme*, vol. 1.
1964. The Role of Native Doctors in Aboriginal Australia. In *Magic, Faith and Healing*, edited by A. Kiev. New York: The Free Press.

Berndt, R. M.
1951a. The Influence of European Culture on Australian Aborigines. *Oceania* 21:229–235.
1951b. *Kunapipi*. Melbourne: Cheshire.

Berndt, R. M., and Berndt, C. H.
1951. *From Black to White in South Australia*. Melbourne: Cheshire.
1954. *Arnhem Land: Its History and Its People*. Melbourne: Cheshire.
1964. *The World of the First Australians*. Sydney: Ure Smith.

Berne, E.
1961. *Transactional Analysis in Psychotherapy*. New York: Grove Press.

Bettelheim, B.
1962. *Symbolic Wounds: Puberty Rites and the Envious Male*. New York: Collier Books.

Breuer, J., and Freud, S.
    1895.   *Studies on Hysteria.* Standard edition, vol. 2. London: Hogarth
            Press.

Brody, E. B.
    1966.   Cultural Exclusion, Character and Illness. *American Journal of
            Psychiatry* 122:852–858.

Bromberg, W.
    1954.   *Man above Humanity: A History of Psychotherapy.* Philadel-
            phia: J.B. Lippincott.

Burton-Bradley, B. G.
    1960.   The Amok Syndrome in Papua and New Guinea. *Medical
            Journal of Australia* 1:252–256.

Campbell, T. D., and Barrett, M. J.
    1953.   Dental Observations on Australian Aborigines: A Changing En-
            vironment and Food Pattern. *Australian Journal of Dentistry* 57:
            1–6.

Campbell, T. D., Simpson, J. M., Cornell, J. G., and Barrett, M. J.
    1954.   *So They Did Eat.* Documentary film. Adelaide: University of
            Adelaide, South Australia.

Cannon, W. B.
    1942.   Voodoo Death. *American Anthropologist* 44:169–181.

Capell, A.
    1952.   The Walbiri through Their Own Eyes. *Oceania* 23:110–131.

Capellman, A. P.
    1901.   *Medicina Pastoralis.* In Latin. Bruxelles: Société Belge de
            Librairie.

Cawte, J. E.
    1964*a*.   Tjimi and Tjagolo: Ethnopsychiatry in the Kalumburu People
            of North Western Australia. *Oceania* 34 (3):170–190, plates.

    1964*b*.   Australian Ethnopsychiatry in the Field: A Sampling in North
            Kimberley. *Medical Journal of Australia* 1:467–472.

    1964*c*.   A Psychiatric Service in the North? *Australian Journal of Social
            Issues* June: 20–32

    1965.   Ethnopsychiatry in Central Australia: Traditional Illnesses in
            the Eastern Aranda People. *British Journal of Psychiatry* 111:1069–
            1077.

    1966.   Australian Aborigines in Mental Hospitals. Part I: Statistics
            1954–1963. Part II: Patterns of "Transitional" Psychosis. *Oceania*
            36 (4):264–282.

    1967.   Flight into the Wilderness as a Psychiatric Syndrome: Some
            Aspects of the Human Ecology of the Arid Zone. *Psychiatry:*
            30:149–161.

    1968.   Further Comment on the Australian Subincision Ceremony.

American Anthropologist 70 (5):961–964, with 6 photographs by M. J. Barrett.

1972. *Cruel, Poor and Brutal Nations.* Honolulu: The University Press of Hawaii.

1973. Multidisciplinary Teamwork in Ethnopsychiatry Research. In *Proceedings of V World Congress of Psychiatry*, Mexico, D.F., 28 November–4 December 1971. Edited by R. de la Fuente and M. N. Weisman. Amsterdam: Excerpta Medica.

Cawte, J. E., Bianchi, G. N., and Kiloh, L. G.
1968. Personal Discomfort in Australian Aborigines. *The Australian and New Zealand Journal of Psychiatry* 2:69–79.

Cawte, J. E., Cuthbertson, G., and Hoskin, J. O.
1967. The New Guinea Islands Psychiatric Research Project—A Preliminary Report. *Papua and New Guinea Medical Journal* 10 (3):71–75.

Cawte, J. E., Djagamara, N., and Barrett, M. J.
1966. The Meaning of Subincision of the Urethra to Aboriginal Australians. *British Journal of Medical Psychology* 39:245–253.

Cawte, J. E., and Kidson, M. A.
1964. Australian Ethnopsychiatry: The Walbiri Doctor. *Medical Journal of Australia* 2:977–983.

1965. Ethnopsychiatry in Central Australia: The Evolution of Illness in a Walbiri Lineage. *British Journal of Psychiatry* 111:1079–1085.

Cawte, J. E., and Kiloh, L. G.
1967. Language and Pictorial Representation in Aboriginal Children: Implications for Transcultural Psychiatry. *Social Science and Medicine* 1:67–76.

Christophers, B.
1965. Aboriginal and White Prevalence Rates of Mental Illness in Western Australia. Ph.D. dissertation, University of Western Australia.

Cleland, J. B.
1936. Australia—Ethnobotany. *Mankind* 2:6–9.

Clements, F.E.
1932. *Primitive Concepts of Disease.* University of California Publications in American Archaeology and Ethnology 32, no. 2. Berkeley and Los Angeles: University of California Press.

Collomb, H.
1965. Bouffées Délirantes en Psychiatrie Africaine. Mimeograph in French. Abstracted in *Transcultural Psychiatric Research Review* 1966, 3:29–34.

Cook, C. E.
1966. Medicine and the Australian Aboriginal: A Century of Contact

in the Northern Territory. *Medical Journal of Australia* 1:559–565.

Coolican, R. E.
1969. An Ecological Handicap: To Be Born an Aborigine. Address to Psychiatry School, University of New South Wales, Sydney.
1973. *Morbidity in an Australian Rural Practice*. Archdall Memorial Monograph No. 9. Glebe, New South Wales: The Printing House.

Devereux, G., and Opler, M. K.
1961. Discussion of the Stability of Shamans. *American Anthropologist* 63:1088–1093.

Dunstan, D. A.
1966. Aboriginal Land Title and Employment in South Australia. In *Aborigines in the Economy*, edited by I.G. Sharp and C.M. Tatz. Brisbane: Jacaranda Press.

Durkheim, E.
1930. *Suicide*. New York: The Free Press.

Eitinger, L.
1964. *Concentration Camp Survivors in Norway and Israel*. London: Allen and Unwin.

Elkin, A. P.
1933. Australian Totemism. *Oceania Monographs* 2.
1945. *Aboriginal Men of High Degree*. Sydney: Australasian Medical Publishing.
1954. *The Australian Aborigines: How to Understand Them*. 3rd ed. Sydney: Angus and Robertson.
1965. *The Australian Aborigines*. 4th ed. Sydney: Angus and Robertson.

Engel, C.
1970. Personal communication and unpublished lecture to the College of Psychiatrists in Sydney, on "Sudden Unexplained Death."

Erikson, E. H.
1950. *Childhood and Society*. New York: Norton.

Evans-Pritchard, E. E.
1937. *Witchcraft, Magic and Oracles among the Azande of the Anglo-Egyptian Sudan*. Oxford: Clarendon Press.

Festinger, L.
1957. *A Theory of Cognitive Dissonance*. New York: Row, Peterson.

Field, M. J.
1955. Witchcraft as a Primitive Interpretation of Mental Disorder. *Journal of Mental Science* 101:826–833.
1958. Mental Disorder in Rural Ghana. *Journal of Mental Service* 104:1043–1051.

Fink, R. A.
1957. The Caste-Barrier: An Obstacle to the Assimilation of Part-

Aborigines in North West New South Wales. *Oceania* 28 (2): 100–110.

Flinders, M.
1814.   *A Voyage to Terra Australia, undertaken for the purpose of completing the discovery of that Vast Country.* London: W. Bulmer. Our copy in Australiana Facsimile Editions No. 37 by the Libraries Board of South Australia, 1966. Original: G. and W. Nicol, Pall-Mall.

Fortune, R. F.
1932.   *Sorcerers of Dobu.* London: E. P. Dutton.

Frank, J. D.
1961.   *Persuasion and Healing.* Baltimore: Johns Hopkins Press.
1966.   Galloping Technology, a New Social Disease. *Journal of Social Issues* 22 (4):1–14.

Freeman, D.
1965.   Anthropology, Psychiatry and the Doctrine of Cultural Relativism. *Man* 59:65–67.

Freud, S.
1912.   *Totem and Taboo: Resemblances between the Psychic Lives of Savages and Neurotics.* Translated by A. A. Brill. London: Routledge.
1930.   *Civilisation and its Discontents.* Standard Edition XXI, London: The Hogarth Press.

Fry, H. K.
1953.   Anthropology and Psychology. *Medical Journal of Australia* 1: 549–552.

Gale, F. (ed.)
1970.   *Women's Role in Aboriginal Society.* Australian Aboriginal Studies No. 36. Canberra: The Australian Institute of Aboriginal Studies.

Gil, R.
1934a. *A Short Catholic Catechism.* Tract typewritten in the Pela language; copy seen at Kalumburu Mission, North Kimberley, 1963.
1934b. *The Life of Our Lord.* Tract typewritten in the Pela language; copy seen at Kalumburu Mission, North Kimberley, 1963.

Gilbert, W. S.
1885.   *The Mikado.* The Savoy Operas. Our edition 1959, London: Macmillan and Co.

Glass, A. J.
1955.   Principles of Combat Psychiatry. *Military Medicine* 117 (1): 27–33.

Glick, L. B.
1967.   Medicine as an Ethnographic Category: The Gimi of the New Guinea Highlands. *Ethnology* 6:31–56.

Gluckman, M.
1955.   *Custom and Conflict in Africa.* Oxford: Blackwell.

Goodale, J.
1971.   *Tiwi Wives.* Seattle: University of Washington Press.

Greenspoon, J.
1955.   The Reinforcing Effect of Two Spoken Sounds on the Frequency of Two Responses. *American Journal of Psychology* 68: 409–416.

Gunn, J.
1907.   *We of the Never-Never.* Melbourne: Robertson and Mullens.

Halliday, J.
1948.   *Psychosocial Medicine.* New York: Norton.

Hallowell, A. I.
1935.   Primitive Concepts of Disease. *American Anthropologist* 37: 365–368.

Hamburg, D. A.
1971.   Crowding, Stranger Contact, and Aggressive Behavior. In *Society, Stress and Disease,* edited by Lennart Levi. London: Oxford University Press.

Hamilton, M., and White, J. M.
1959.   Clinical Syndromes in Depressive States. *Journal of Mental Science* 105:985–998.

Harris, R.
1960.   *Tie Me Kangaroo Down, Sport.* Popular song. Sydney: Castle Music.

Havens, L. L.
1962.   The Placement and Movement of Hallucinations in Space: Phenomenology and Theory. *International Journal of Psycho-Analysis* 43:426–435.

Hearne, T.
1970.   Ecology and Affinal Ties among Kung Bushmen and Coast Salish. *Mankind* 7:199–204.

Henry, J.
1963.   *Culture against Man.* New York: Random House.
1972.   *Pathways to Madness.* London: Jonathan Cape.

Hernandez, T.
1940.   Social Organization of the Drysdale River Tribes, North West Australia. *Oceania* 11:211–232.
1941.   Children among the Drysdale River Tribes. *Oceania* 12:122–133.
1961.   Myths and Symbols of the Drysdale River Aborigines. *Oceania* 32: 113–127.

Hiatt, B.
1970.   Woman the Gatherer. In *Woman's Role in Aboriginal Society,*

edited by Fay Gale. Canberra: The Australian Institute of Aboriginal Studies.

Hiatt, L. R.
1962. Local Organization among the Australian Aborigines. *Oceania* 32:267–286.
1965. *Kinship and Conflict: A Study of an Aboriginal Community in Northern Arnhem Land.* Canberra: Australian National University Press.
1969. Totemism Tomorrow: The Future of an Illusion. *Mankind* 7:83–93.
1971. Secret Pseudo-Procreation Rites among the Australian Aborigines. In *Anthropology in Oceania*, edited by L. R. Hiatt and C. Jayawardena. Sydney: Angus and Robertson.

Hogbin, H. I.
1934. Native Culture of the Wogeos. *Oceania* 5:308–337.

Horney, K.
1926. Flight from Womanhood. *International Journal of Psycho-Analysis* 7:324–339.

Horowitz, M. J.
1965. The Body Buffer Zone: An Aspect of the Body Image. Paper presented at the Western Divisional Meeting of the American Psychiatric Association, Honolulu.

Hoskin, J. O.
1969*a*. Community Psychiatry in the Islands Region of New Guinea: I. Epidemiology. *The Australian and New Zealand Journal of Psychiatry* 3 (4):376–382.
1969*b*. Community Psychiatry in the Islands Region of New Guinea: II. A Design. *The Australian and New Zealand Journal of Psychiatry* 3 (4):383–389.

Hoskin, J. O., Friedman, M. I., and Cawte, J. E.
1969. A High Incidence of Suicide in a Preliterate-Primitive Society. *Psychiatry, Journal for the Study of Interpersonal Processes* 32 (2):200–210.

Hoskin, J. O., Kiloh, L. G., and Cawte, J. E.
1969. Epilepsy and *Guria:* The Shaking Syndromes of New Guinea. *Social Science and Medicine* 3: 39–48.

Idriess, I. L.
1931. *Lasseter's Last Ride.* Sydney: Angus and Robertson.

Jung, C. G.
1953. *Collected Works.* New York: Pantheon Books.

Kaberry, P.
1939. *Aboriginal Woman, Sacred and Profane.* London: Routledge.

Kardiner, A.
1945. The Concept of Basic Personality Structure as an Operational Tool in the Social Sciences. In *The Science of Man in the World*

Crisis, edited by R. Linton. New York: Columbia University Press.

Kessler, C. S.
1971.   Is "Totem" Taboo? *Mankind* 8:31–36.

Kidson, M. A.
1967.   Psychiatric Disorders in the Walbiri, Central Australia. *Australian and New Zealand Journal of Psychiatry* 1:14–22.

Kiev, A.,
1964.   Editor. *Magic, Faith and Healing*. New York: The Free Press.
1968.   *Curanderismo. Mexican-American Folk Psychiatry*. New York: The Free Press.

Kim, K.
1970.   The Psychological Function of Shaman's Dreams during Initiation Process. *Journal of Korean Neuropsychiatric Association* 9 (1): 47–56.

Klopfer, P. H.
1969.   *Habitats and Territories: A Study of the Use of Space by Animals*. New York: Basic Books.

Kluckhohn, C.
1939.   Theoretical Bases for an Empirical Method of Studying the Acquisition of Culture by Individuals. *Man*, 39:98–104.
1944.   *Navaho Witchcraft*. Papers of the Peabody Museum of Archaeology and Ethnology 22, no. 2. Cambridge: Harvard University.
1962.   Universal Categories of Culture. In *Anthropology Today*, edited by Sol Tax. Chicago: University of Chicago Press.

Laughlin, H. P.
1956.   *The Neuroses in Clinical Practice*. Philadelphia: Saunders.

Langfeldt, G.
1959.   The Significance of a Dichotomy in Psychiatric Classification. *The American Journal of Psychiatry* 116: 537–539.

Lawson, H.
1896.   *While the Billy Boils*. Sydney: Angus and Robertson.

Lebra, W. P.
1969.   *Culture and Mental Health in Asia and the Pacific Newsletter*: December, no. 3. Honolulu: University of Hawaii.

Leighton, A. H.
1959.   *My Name is Legion: Foundation for a Theory of Man in Relation to Culture*, vol. 1. New York: Basic Books.
1971.   The Other Side of the Coin. *The American Journal of Psychiatry* 127 (11):123–125.

Leonhard, K.
1961.   Cycloid Psychoses: Endogenous Psychoses Which are Neither Schizophrenic nor Manic-Depressive. *Journal of Mental Science* 107:633–648.

Levi-Strauss, C.
   1963.   *Totemism*. Translated by R. Needham. London: Beacon Press. Our copy published 1969. Middlesex, England, Pelican Books.
Lewin, B. D.
   1959.   Some Psychoanalytic Ideas Applied to Elation and Depression. *American Journal of Psychiatry* 116:38–43.
Lewis, O.
   1959.   *Five Families*. New York: Basic Books.
Lommel, A.
   1951.   Modern Culture Influences on Australian Aborigines. *Oceania* 21:14–24.
McElwain, D. W., and Kearney, G. E.
   1969.   *The Queensland Test*. To measure general cognitive capacity under conditions of reduced communication. Melbourne: Australian Council for Education Research.
Macintosh, N. W. G.
   1965.   The Physical Aspect of Man in Australia. In *Aboriginal Man in Australia*, edited by R. M. Berndt and C. H. Berndt. Sydney: Angus and Robertson.
Malinowski, B.
   1922.   *Argonauts of the Western Pacific*. London: Routledge.
Margetts, E. L.
   1960a.   The Future for Psychiatry in East Africa. *East Africa Medical Journal* 37:449–456.
   1960b.   Subincision of the Urethra in the Samburu of Kenya. *East Africa Medical Journal* 37:105–108.
Marwick, M. G.
   1966.   *Sorcery in its Social Setting: A Study of the Northern Rhodesian Cerva*. Melbourne: Melbourne University Press.
Mead, M.
   1945.   Research on Primitive Children. In *Manual of Child Psychology*, 2nd ed., edited by L. Carmichael. New York: John Wiley and Sons.
   1967.   Interaction of Social and Cultural Factors in Mental Health: Adult Roles. In *Transcultural Psychiatry*, edited by A.V.S. De Reuck and Ruth Porter. London: Churchill.
Meggitt, M. J.
   1955.   *Tjanba* among the Walbiri. *Anthropos* 50:375–403.
   1962.   *Desert People*. Sydney: Angus and Robertson.
Milliken, E. P.
   1963.   Population Data of the Northern Territory. Paper presented to ANZUS Conference, Adelaide.
   1969.   *Research Sponsored or Conducted by the Welfare Branch*. Missions Administration Conference Report. Darwin: Welfare Branch, Northern Territory Administration.

Mitchell, I. S.
    1968.   Epilogue to a Referendum. *Australian Journal of Social Issues* 3:9–12.

Money, J., Cawte, J. E., Bianchi, G. N., and Nurcombe, B.
    1970.   Sex Training and Traditions in Arnhem Land. *The British Journal of Medical Psychology* 43:383–399.

Montagu, M. F. A.
    1937*a*.   The Origin of Subincision in Australia. *Oceania* 8:193–207.
    1937*b*.   *Coming into Being among the Australian Aborigines.* London: Routledge.

Mulvaney, D. J.
    1966.   Fact, Fancy and Aboriginal Australian Ethnic Origins. *Mankind* 6 (7):299–305.

Munn, N. D.
    1964.   Totemic Design and Group Continuity in Walbiri Cosmology. In *Aborigines Now*, edited by Marie Reay. Sydney: Angus and Robertson.

Northern Territory Administration
    1955.   Pastoral map of the Northern Territory. Darwin: Survey Office of the Northern Territory Administration.

Nurcombe, B.
    1970.   Deprivation: A Study in Definition with Special Consideration of the Australian Aboriginal. *Medical Journal of Australia* 2: 87–92.

Owen, R.
    1839.   Marsupalia. In *Todd's Cyclopaedia of Anatomy and Physiology*, 1839–1847. Vol. 3, pp. 257–330.

Packer, A. D.
    1961.   The Health of Australian Aborigines. *Oceania* 32:61–70.

Paterson, A.
    1895.   *The Man from Snowy River.* Sydney: Angus and Robertson.

Perez, E.
    1958.   *Kalumburu (formerly Drysdale River) Mission, North Western Australia. New Norcia*, Western Australia: Abbey Press.

Pitney, W. R.
    1962.   Serum Vitamin B12 Concentrations in the Western Australian Aborigine. *Australian Journal of Experimental Biology and Medical Science* 40:73–80.

Poidevin, L. O. S.
    1957.   Some Childbirth Customs among the Ngalia Tribe, Central Australia. *Medical Journal of Australia* 1:543–546.

Porteus, S. D.
    1955.   *Give Them the Tools.* A series of five articles reprinted from the *Honolulu Advertiser*. Honolulu: Hawaii State Library.

Pulsford, R. L., and Cawte, J.
1972. *Health in a Developing Country: Principles of Medical Anthropology in Melanesia*. Brisbane: Jacaranda Press.

Radcliffe-Brown, A. R.
1952. Historical Note on British Social Anthropology. *American Anthropologist* 54:275–277.

Richter, C. P.
1957. On the Phenomenon of Sudden Death in Animals and Man. *Psychosomatic Medicine* 19:191–198.

Riss, E.
1959. Are Hallucinations Illusions? An Experimental Study of Non-veridical Perception. *Journal of Psychology* 48:367–373.

Rivers, W. H. R.
1924. *Medicine, Magic and Religion*. London: Kegan Paul, French and Trubner.
1926. *Psychology and Ethnology*. London: Kegan Paul, French and Trubner.

Rogers, S. L.
1944. Disease Concepts in North America. *American Anthropologist* 46:559–564.

Robinson, M. V.
1968. Imprisonment of Aborigines and Part-Aborigines in Western Australia. In *Thinking about Australian Aboriginal Welfare*, edited by R. M. Berndt. Perth: University of Western Australia Press.

Roheim, G.
1945. *The Eternal Ones of the Dream*. New York: International Universities Press.
1949. The Symbolism of Subincision. *The American Imago* 6:321–328.

Rose, R.
1957. *Living Magic*. London: Chatto and Windus.

Rouse, I.
1962. The Strategy of Culture History. In *Anthropology Today*, edited by Sol Tax. Chicago: The University of Chicago Press.

Rowley, C. D.
1970. *The Destruction of Aboriginal Society: Aboriginal Policy and Practice—Volume I*. Canberra: Australian National University Press.

Salvado, R.
1864. *Information Respecting the Habits and Customs of the Aboriginal of Western Australia*. Report to the Colonial Secretary, Perth. (Copy seen at Kalumburu Mission, 1963.)

Sapir, E.
1921. *Language, an Introduction to the Study of Speech*. New York: Harcourt.

Schilder, P.
    1950.   *The Image and Appearance of the Human Body*. New York: International Universities Press.

Schouten, J.
    1967.   *The Rod and Serpent of Asklepios: Symbol of Medicine*. Amsterdam: Elsevier Publishing Co.

Searles, H. E.
    1960.   *The Nonhuman Environment*. New York: International Universities Press.

Singer, P., and DeSole, D.
    1967.   The Australian Subincision Ceremony Reconsidered: Vaginal Envy or Kangaroo Bifid Penis Envy. *American Anthropologist* 69:355–358.

Spencer, B.
    1914.   *Native Tribes of the Northern Territory of Australia*. London: Macmillan and Co.

Stainbrook, E.
    1954.   A Cross-Cultural Evaluation of Depressive Reactions. In *Depression*, edited by P. Hoch and J. Zubin. New York: Grune and Stratton.

Stanner, W. E. H.
    1956.   *The Dreaming*. The Bobbs-Merrill Reprint Series in the Social Sciences. Indianapolis: Bobbs-Merrill.
    1968.   *After the Dreaming*. Boyer Lectures. Sydney: Australian Broadcasting Commission.

Strehlow, T. G. H.
    1947.   *Aranda Traditions*. Melbourne: Cheshire.
    1963.   Men Without Leaders. A Review of *Desert People* by M. J. Meggitt. In *Nation*, January 12th, 1963, pp. 22–23.
    1964.   The Art of Circle, Line and Square. In *Aboriginal Australian Art*, edited by R. M. Berndt. Sydney: Ure Smith.

Strzelecki, P. E.
    1845.   *Physical Description of New South Wales and Van Dieman's Land*. London. Quoted in Mulvaney, D. J. (1966). See entry this Bibliography.

Szasz, T.
    1964.   *The Myth of Mental Illness*. New York: Harper and Row.

Tatz, C. M.
    1970.   The Health Status of Australian Aborigines: The Need for an Interdisciplinary Approach. *The Medical Journal of Australia* 2:191–196.

Thompson, C.
    1943.   Penis Envy in Women. *Psychiatry:* 6:123–131.

Tindale, N. B.
  1963.   Tribal Distribution and Population. In *Australian Aboriginal Studies*. Edited by H. Shiels. London: Oxford University Press.
Todd, R. B.
  1836–1859.
            Cyclopaedia of Anatomy and Physiology. 5 volumes. London: Sherwood, Gilbert and Piper.
Tseng, Wen-Shing.
  1972.   A Psychiatric Study of Shamanism in Taiwan. *Archives of General Psychiatry* 26:561–565.
Turner, V. W.
  1964.   A Ndembu Doctor in Practice. In *Magic, Faith and Healing*, edited by A. Kiev. New York: The Free Press.
Tyhurst, J. S.
  1951.   Individual Reactions to Community Disasters. *The American Journal of Psychiatry* 107:764–768.
Veness, H., and Hoskin, J. O.
  1968.   Psychiatry in New Britain: The Effect of Language on Association Process. *Social Science and Medicine* 1:419–424.
Warner, W. L.
  1937.   *A Black Civilization: A Social Study of an Australian Tribe*. New York: Harper and Bros.
Weinstein, E. A.
  1962.   *Cultural Aspects of a Delusion*. New York: The Free Press.
Weiss, R. J., and Payson, H. E.
  1967.   Gross Stress Reaction. In *The Comprehensive Textbook of Psychiatry*, edited by A. Freedman, and H. Kaplan, Baltimore: Williams and Wilkins.
White, I.
  1970.   Aboriginal Women's Status: A Paradox Resolved. In *Women's Role in Aboriginal Society*, edited by Fay Gale. Canberra: The Australian Institute of Aboriginal Studies.
Whiting, B.
  1950.   *Paiute Sorcery*. Viking Fund Publications in Anthropology, no. 15. New York: The Viking Press.
Whiting, J. W., and Child, I. L.
  1953.   *Child Training and Personality: A Cross-Cultural Study*. New Haven: Yale University Press.
Whorf, B. L.
  1956.   *Language, Thought and Reality*. New York: John Wiley and Sons.
Winton, R. R.
  1969.   Asklepios and the Rod-and-Serpent Emblem. *The Medical Journal of Australia* 1:237–238.

Wittkower, E. D.
  1969.   Perspectives of Transcultural Psychiatry. *International Journal of Psychiatry* 8 (5):811–824.
Wolf, S.
  1971.   Psychosocial Forces in Myocardial Infarction and Sudden Death. In *Society, Stress and Disease*, edited by L. Levi. London: Oxford University Press.
World Health Organization
  1960.   *Epidemiology of Mental Disorders.* World Health Organization Technical Report Series, no. 185. Geneva: World Health Organization.
Yallop, C.
  1969.   The Aljawara and their Territory. *Oceania* 39 (3):187–193.
Zaguirre, J. C.
  1957.   Amuck. *Journal of the Philippine Federation of Private Medical Practitioners* 6 (8):1138–1149.

Index

255

ABOUT THE AUTHOR

John Cawte is a fourth-generation Australian. He grew up in rural South Australia, and in his youth witnessed first hand the struggles of the Aborigines to cope with social change. His early acquaintance with their problems developed into an empathy and concern for a people whose entry into twentieth-century Australian life has proven so harrowing for them as individuals and as a group. For many years now, Dr. Cawte has spent much of his vacation time in remote areas of the continent using his professional training to identify and propose remedies for the ills that have slowed the acculturation process.

Dr. Cawte, M.D., Ph.D., is a fellow of the Australian and New Zealand College of Psychiatrists, a fellow of the Royal College of Psychiatrists, and a distinguished fellow of the American Psychiatric Association. He is presently coordinator of Community Medicine at The University of New South Wales and an associate professor in the School of Psychiatry at that university.

He is coauthor of *Health in a Developing Country: Principles of Medical Anthropology in Melanesia,* and author of *Cruel, Poor and Brutal Nations: The Assessment of Mental Health in an Australian Aboriginal Community by Short-Stay Psychiatric Field Team Methods,* as well as of numerous articles.

Anna Holpern : p. 183